New Collected Poems

IAIN CRICHTON SMITH was born in Glasgow in 1928. The youngest of three brothers, he was raised on the island of Lewis in the Outer Hebrides. Crichton Smith had a bilingual childhood and while he spoke Gaelic at home his education was through the medium of English. He did not leave the island until the age of eighteen, when he attended Aberdeen University and took a degree in English Literature. This was followed by two years of National Service before he started work as a high school teacher, first in Clydebank (1952–5) and then in Oban (1955–77). A prolific author, Crichton Smith would publish extensively in both English and Gaelic; however his early poetry was primarily written in the former. His first collection of poems, *The Long River*, appeared in 1955 and was followed by *The White Noon* (1959), *Thistles and Roses* (1961), *Deer on the High Hills* (1962) and *The Law and the Grace* (1965). *Consider the Lilies*, the first of twelve novels (ten in English, two in Gaelic), was published in 1968. Set during the Highland Clearances, the book would go on to become one of the high points of post-war Scottish fiction and a set text in many schools. For most of this period Crichton Smith lived with his mother in Oban, until her death in 1972. In 1977 he took early retirement from teaching to concentrate on writing full time. The same year he married Donalda Logan and in 1982 the couple moved to Taynuilt, a small village near Oban. He received an OBE in 1980 and continued to write and publish for two decades. Iain Crichton Smith died on 15 October 1998.

MATTHEW MCGUIRE is a lecturer in the Department of Scottish Literature at the University of Glasgow. He has published widely on various aspects of Scottish and Irish literature. He is the author of *Contemporary Scottish Literature* (2008) and has co-edited, along with Colin Nicholson, *The Edinburgh Companion to Contemporary Scottish Poetry* (2009).

Iain Crichton Smith

New Collected Poems

Edited by Matthew McGuire

CARCANET

Collected Poems first published in Great Britain in 1992 by
Carcanet Press Limited

This revised and enlarged edition first published in Great Britain in 2011 by

Carcanet Press Limited
Alliance House
Cross Street
Manchester M2 7AQ

A CIP catalogue record for this book is available from the British Library

ISBN 978 1 85754 960 7

The publisher acknowledges financial assistance from Arts Council England

Typeset by XL Publishing Services, Tiverton
Printed and bound in England by SRP Ltd, Exeter

To Donalda
with love

ACKNOWLEDGEMENTS

The poems in this volume are taken from the following publications: *The Long River* (Edinburgh: Macdonalds); *The White Noon* (from *New Poems*, edited by Edwin Muir, London: Eyre and Spottiswoode); *Thistles and Roses* (London: London: Eyre and Spottiswoode); *Deer on the High Hills* (Edinburgh: Giles Gordon); *The Law and the Grace* (London: Eyre and Spottiswoode); *Three Regional Voices* (London: Poet and Printer); *From Bourgeois Land* (London: Victor Gollancz); *Ben Dorain* (Preston: Akros Publications, reprinted Newcastle upon Tyne: Northern House); *Lines Review* (special edition of the author's work, Edinburgh: Macdonalds); *Poems to Eimhir* (London: Victor Gollancz); *Love Poems and Elegies* (London: Victor Gollancz); *Penguin Modern Poets 21* (Harmondsworth: Penguin); *Orpheus and Other Poems* (Preston: Akros Publications); *Poems for Donalda* (Belfast: Ulsterman Publications); *The Permanent Island* (Edinburgh: Macdonalds); *The Notebooks of Robinson Crusoe and Other Poems* (London: Victor Gollancz); *In the Middle* (London: Victor Gollancz); *The Emigrants* (Glasgow: University of Glasgow); *The Exiles* (Manchester: Carcanet); *A Life* (Manchester: Carcanet); *The Village and Other Poems* (Manchester: Carcanet); *Ends and Beginnings* (Manchester: Carcanet); *The Human Face* (Manchester: Carcanet); *The Leaf and the Marble* (Manchester: Carcanet); *A Country for Old Men and My Canadian Uncle* (Manchester: Carcanet).

CONTENTS

INTRODUCTION

Iain Crichton Smith was a prolific writer. During his career he produced twenty-seven volumes of poetry, fourteen novels, twelve short story collections and a number of plays for both radio and stage. Friend and fellow poet Norman MacCaig once joked that he was worried about Iain: 'He hasn't published a new book for… days.' Such creative abundance presents obvious challenges to the editor of Crichton Smith's work. The present volume is a fully revised and updated version of Carcanet's original *Collected Poems* (1992) which was both a Poetry Book Society Special Recommendation and a winner of the Saltire Prize. Unsurprisingly perhaps, Crichton Smith continued to write and publish throughout the 1990s, producing four additional volumes of poetry: *Ends and Beginnings* (1994), *The Human Face* (1996), *The Leaf and The Marble* (1998) and *A Country for Old Men* and *My Canadian Uncle* (2000). This new edition contains seventy additional poems, the majority of which are taken from these four volumes and, for the first time, extracts from Crichton Smith's 1971 translation of Sorley MacLean's epic *Dàin do Eimhir agus Dàin Eile* (1943), or *Poems to Eimhir*, often regarded as the founding moment of modern Gaelic poetry. The importance of this sequence, along with the sheer quality of Crichton Smith's translation, more than merits its inclusion. The *New Collected Poems* also reinstates the date and title of individual collections within the body of the text, enabling the reader to contextualise particular poems whilst listening out for the inflection of particular volumes. Of course, the preoccupations of Crichton Smith's work transcend both the volumes and periods in which they initially appeared. The current collection allows Crichton Smith's themes to emerge, including his preoccupation with island life, Calvinist religion, the role of art and the nature of exile. To this end I have included a number of poems omitted from the original 1992 *Collected Poems*: 'Moonlight over the island', 'The place without music', 'The Island', 'Poem for Auden', 'My Uncle', 'Clouds', 'The Survivors' and 'To hell with this poetry reading'. This *New Collected Poems* represents the most complete and comprehensive collection of Iain Crichton Smith's poetry to date.

* * *

Born in Glasgow in 1928, Iain Crichton Smith moved with his family to the Hebridean island of Lewis when he was two years old. His father, a sailor, died of tuberculosis when Iain was one and his family was raised by their mother in Bayble, a small village on the island's east coast. Like the rest of this generation, Crichton Smith experienced a bilingual upbringing on Lewis. Whereas Gaelic was the language of home, it was English that was the language of school: as a result, Crichton Smith's formal education was in the medium of a foreign tongue. These circumstances, the experience of living and moving between two cultures, had a profound effect on the kind of poetry he would subsequently write. If English opened up vast new worlds of experience, such gains were not without their cost. The Gaelic poet Derick Thomson, who grew up in the same village as Crichton Smith, wrote:

The heart tied to a tethering post…
And the mind free.
I bought its freedom dearly.

In 1945, at the age of seventeen, Crichton Smith left Lewis for the first time and travelled to Aberdeen for university and an honours degree in English Literature. This was followed by two years' National Service, before he began work as an English teacher, first in Clydebank (1952–5) and then in Oban (1955–77). In 1977 Crichton Smith retired from teaching and devoted his energies to writing full time. In the same year he married Donalda Logan. Having received an OBE in 1980, the poet moved with Donalda to the village of Taynuilt in Argyll. He lived here from 1982 until his death in 1998.

The people, places and events of childhood left indelible marks on Iain Crichton Smith and his vision of the world. The poet admitted that as a boy he had little feeling for Scotland as a country, except perhaps through football, and felt intuitively that he belonged to Lewis. Such assertions interrupt the nationalist assumptions that often underpin the appreciation of modern Scottish poetry and can be seen in recent anthologies such as *Dream State: The New Scottish Poets* (1994) and *Scotlands: Poets and the Nation* (2004). The nature of island life, its separation from the mainland, creates a distance, both physical and emotional, between Crichton Smith and the preoccupations of Scottish nationalism. Islands, of course, figure prominently in the work of other twentieth-century Scottish poets, most notably Edwin Muir and George Mackay Brown. However, unlike Muir and Orkney, Crichton Smith's Lewis did not represent some form of cherished territory, a mythic space that must be sought out and recovered. In an essay entitled 'Real People in a Real Place' (*Towards the Human*, 1986), the poet writes:

> To grow up on an island is to grow up in a special world. Many of the books that I have read on the Hebrides, however, make this world appear Edenic and unreal: others suggest that the islander is a child who appears lost in the 'real world', and even invent for him a language that was never spoken by anyone. It is easy to assign the islander to this misty, rather beautiful world, and leave him there.

It is this mystical otherworldliness that Crichton Smith's poetry continually attempts to unravel. At the same time he is highly alert to the sacred, otherworldly quality of everyday experience. For the literary critic George Watson the urge 'to connect the parish to the universe' is one of the most enduring notes within Crichton Smith's poetry.

Lewis, then, as both inspiration and obstacle, sanctuary and prison. One aspect of island life that was particularly important in this regard was the influence of the Free Presbyterian Church. Edwin Muir had argued that the Protestant Reformation of the sixteenth century signalled a moment of acute despair for Scottish culture. If this was the case, then the Free Presbyterian Church was arguably the most distilled form of such constrictive energies. Indelibly stained by original sin, mankind lived in a world of ubiquitous temptation. Music and dancing were sinful indulgences; storytelling a kind of vanity. A dour practicality eclipsed the pleasures of a rich imaginative life. In early poems such as 'The

Dedicated Spirits', 'Highland Sunday' and 'Love Songs of a Puritan' Crichton Smith confronts the repressive nature of this culture. And in 'Poem of Lewis' he depicts an island where:

> They have no place for the fine graces
> of poetry. The great forgiving spirit of the word
> fanning its rainbow wing, like a shot bird
> falls from the windy sky. The sea heaves
> in visionless anger over the cramped graves
> and the early daffodil, purer than a soul,
> is gathered into the terrible mouth of the gale.

On a place like Lewis, nature itself seems to conspire against such delicate flights of fancy. There is the sense of an agenda being laid out in these early poems and much of Crichton Smith's subsequent writing attempts to escape such imaginative poverty, to articulate 'the fine graces of poetry', to locate 'the great forgiving spirit of the word' amid the carefully crafted line. Despite the rejection of Calvinism, a deeply religious rhetoric ('grace', 'forgiveness') informs Crichton Smith's vocabulary. Such self-contradiction echoes the Yeatsian notion that poetry emerges out of the argument we have with ourselves. In 'Real People in a Real Place', Crichton Smith comments: 'Religion has been internalised in my personality whether I like it or not and its dilemmas will always be with me.' Embracing such contradictions also serves to rebuke the dogmatic certainties of the Free Presbyterian Church. Throughout his poetry Crichton Smith cultivates a Keatsian sensibility, a willingness to exist amidst uncertainty and doubt, without striving after fact or reason. Such impulses are revealed in the titles of various collections: *Thistles and Roses* (1961), *The Law and the Grace* (1965) and *Ends and Beginnings* (1994). Crichton Smith's is a poetry of contestation, of contingency and conditionality: 'Dogma teaches people to give superficial answers to very profound questions,' he said in a 1993 interview. 'I feel a lot of my poetry is questioning, rather than providing answers.' As a result, Lewis cannot be embraced, yet nor can it be completely abandoned. Despite its cold conservatism it remains a community, and for Crichton Smith this is not something to be forsaken lightly:

To work harmoniously within an accepting community must be as high a pleasure as is known to man [...] One of the problems of modern man is that he does not have a real home, and for the modern writer that he does not have a real audience, only individuals scattered here and there, pin-points of light answering each other from space.

Throughout Crichton Smith's work the tensions outlined above are inextricably bound up with questions of language. The infallibility of 'The Word' is contrasted with the fallibility of words, their straining to capture the quiddity of human experience. The poem is not a sacrosanct object and its truth, if it contains any at all, is elliptical and elusive. Such propositions find their fullest working out in *Deer on the High Hills* (1962), which the poet himself regarded as his greatest work. The poem deals with the essential strangeness of the world, the chasm between objective reality and our attempts to render it through language. An extended meditation on a single scene, *Deer on the High Hills* is symptomatic of the Imagist tendency within Crichton Smith's work. To this end, the cultural and spiritual nuances of Lewis are made manifest in one of the most recurring images in his poetry, the old woman. Eight poems in the *New Collected Poems* refer to the old woman in their title. She is also the main character in Crichton Smith's most successful novel, *Consider the Lilies* (1968), a story set during the Clearances about an elderly woman confronted by eviction. The image of the old woman is rooted in the poet's childhood, spent among the many widows and spinsters of the two world wars that scarred the first half of the twentieth century. It is also informed by his relationship with his own mother, who was herself a strict Free Presbyterian and someone the poet remembered as being generally unaffectionate. Many of the poems are attempts to achieve a level of intimacy that was absent from the poet's Lewis childhood. In contrast to a writer like Norman MacCaig, Crichton Smith has little interest in writing about landscape, generally preferring people as subjects for his poetry. Many poems, such as 'Encounter in a School Corridor', 'She Teaches *Lear*' and 'School Sports, at the Turnstiles', draw directly on his professional life as a teacher. His working life exerts a grounding effect within his writing, rooting abstract experiences in everyday reality. A fine example of such transfiguration of the commonplace is the elegy for a fellow school teacher, 'For Angus MacLeod':

A useful life with pupils and with poems:
sufficient honours (his humour asked no more)
he takes his place in many minds and rooms.
Without their knowing it, his patient care

instructs far hands to turn a new lever,
a voice to speak in a mild-mannered tone.
The deeds we do reverberate forever.
Inveterate justice weighs the flesh and bone.

His best editions are some men and women
who scrutinise each action like a word.
The truest work is learning to be human
definitive texts the poorest can afford.

And whilst Crichton Smith does write out of his own local experience, he is not a parochial poet, a Highlander merely writing about Highland life. His poetry evinces a voracious literary appetite; it forms an imaginative constellation whose stars include Marcus Aurelius, Shakespeare, Daniel Defoe, Samuel Johnson, and George Orwell. For Edwin Morgan this is the triumphant note of Crichton Smith's creative life, illustrating 'how someone brought up in a narrow, constricted environment can be open to the whole intellectual world if he wants to be'. It reveals an author committed to the universe in its entirety, to what the Irish poet Louis MacNeice called 'the drunkenness of things being various'.

* * *

Although most of his work is in English, Gaelic was of crucial importance to Iain Crichton Smith. Several of the volumes that make up the *New Collected Poems* are translations of work by other Gaelic poets, including *Ben Dorain* from the eighteenth-century poet Duncan Ban Macintyre and *The Birlinn* from the Gaelic of Alexander Macdonald. Also featured are poems from *The*

Permanent Island and *The Emigrants*, translations by the poet of his own Gaelic originals. As mentioned earlier, the *New Collected Poems* also contains part of the translation of Sorley MacLean's 1943 epic *Dàin do Eimhir agus Dàin Eile*, or *Poems to Eimhir*. There is a nice synchronicity here, as the young Crichton Smith was given a copy of this book as a school prize when he was a fifth year pupil at the Nicholson Institute in Stornoway. Influenced by the Spanish Civil War, the rise of Communism and the work of W.B. Yeats, MacLean's sequence marked a radical turning point in the evolution of modern Gaelic verse, signalling a decisive shift away from the oral tradition of Gaelic poetry and its familiar styles, metrics and themes.

The twentieth century was, of course, a period of considerable turbulence within Gaelic-speaking areas. It witnessed a relatively isolated, monoglot culture increasingly penetrated by the forces of modernity. In 1901 a census recorded over 200,000 Gaelic speakers living in Scotland; by 2001 that number had fallen to less than 60,000. In 'Real People in a Real Place', Crichton Smith writes: 'We are born inside a language and see everything from within its parameters: it is not we who make language, it is language that makes us [...] For Gaelic to die would be for the islands to die a more profound death than economics could bring.' Poems such as 'Shall Gaelic Die?' explore the implications of linguistic death:

He who loses his language loses his world. The Highlander
who loses his language loses his world.
The space ship that goes astray among planets loses the world.

The conflation of Gaelic and galactic imagery emphasises the scale of such a loss. It also alludes to the technological roots of such narratives. Radio, television and the computer have all had dramatic implications for the feasibility of Gaelic as a living language and in poems such as 'Speeding Up' and 'By the Sea' the poet casts a cold eye over the advances of the electronic age. This being said, Crichton Smith was never a naive dreamer, patiently waiting the heroic rehabilitation of some mythical Gaelic order. His writing is highly alert to the clichés of Gaeldom; in poems like 'The Gaelic Proverb' he takes to task the pithy phrasemaking of inherited wisdom. Elsewhere, in poems like 'Eight Songs for a New Ceilidh', it is a fully integrated, modern Gaelic culture that Crichton Smith attempts to imaginatively invoke. Most of his poetry was written in English, and the poet admitted that such a choice often felt like an act of betrayal. However, we might read such preference in light of Crichton Smith's extended introduction to the craft, both at school and university, through English-language verse. This bitter-sweet pill is one that almost all Gaelic writers had to swallow during the course of the twentieth century. If bilingualism entailed partial estrangement from one culture, though, it also opened the doors to a whole new literary universe. Like Sorley MacLean before him, Crichton Smith reaches far beyond the oral traditions of the Gaelic-speaking regions of Scotland. His early school reading was in Shelley, Kipling and D.H. Lawrence. Later, the two poets he would come to regard as the most exciting and significant influences on his work were an Englishman, W.H. Auden, and an American, the confessional poet Robert Lowell. In fact, Crichton Smith would write his own version of Lowell's groundbreaking collection *Life Studies* (1959) in 1986, under the title *A Life*. His work echoes that of his contemporary, the Glasgow poet Edwin Morgan, in terms of its willingness to transcend any discernibly local or national tradition.

If other poetry in English was crucial to Crichton Smith's vision, there are two other important influences, which might be termed the classical and the intellectual. In *A Life* the poet describes leaving Lewis for Aberdeen for the first time, clutching 'my Homer steady in my hand'. Throughout the *New Collected Poems* both *The Odyssey* and Virgil's *Aeneid* offer lenses through which Crichton Smith views life in the Highlands, not least its acute experience of exile. In 'Real People in a Real Place' he writes: 'The fact of the islands stronger than any other is that of exile: it is that which casts its guilt continually backwards like the rays of a setting sun. The islander has never had the chance of staying where he is: history has condemned him to departure, and afterwards to the choice of whether or not to return.' Homer and Virgil allow the poet to recontextualise such formative experiences within the Gaelic-speaking world. In *A Life* he quotes the Headmaster of Oban High School, who was also a classical scholar:

'Transposing Greek to Gaelic is no toil.
They had their clans, their sea terms. And the style
of the great *Odyssey* is what Gaelic knows.'

Ancient poetry enables Crichton Smith to retain a quiet poise, to locate the modern Gaelic experience as part of a deeper, more universal set of historical narratives. The use of Homer simultaneously evokes a writer like James Joyce, for whom the ambivalent nature of home also offered a well of creativity from which great art might be drawn. In poems like 'No Return' however, Crichton Smith realises that not all stories of estrangement are fulfilled by a mythic homecoming: 'you can't go back to / that island any more. The people / are growing more and more unlike you'. At the same time, poems such as 'The Departing Island' suggest the persistence of a spiritual umbilical cord, a connection that remains and can never be completely severed:

It's the island that goes away, not we who leave it.
Like an unbearable thought it sinks beyond
assiduous reasoning light and wringing hands,
or, as a flower roots deep into the ground,
it works its darkness into the gay winds
that blow about us in a later spirit.

In terms of an intellectual or philosophical context, Crichton Smith is equally cosmopolitan, drawing upon European traditions of existential thought. A scepticism of religious dogma becomes a suspicion of all abstract systems. Like the existentialist philosopher, Crichton Smith prefers subjective experience as the foundation stone for determining human behaviour. In 'The White Air of March' he writes:

I speak now of those who told the truth.
Let them be praised.
             Dostoevsky, Nietzsche, Kierkegaard,
Kafka – let them be honoured.

Out of all these thinkers it was the Danish philosopher Sören Kierkegaard who most influenced Crichton Smith's poetry, particularly through his belief in individual authenticity and the importance of self-reflection and introspection as a means of its attainment. The working out and exploration of such tensions pervade this *New Collected Poems* and their enduring relevance of such questions in the twenty-first century is merely one of many reasons why Iain Crichton Smith's poetry will continue to fascinate.

Finally, mention must be made of Crichton Smith's wife Donalda. The poet's friend Alasdair MacRae describes his marriage to Donalda as the making of Iain Crichton Smith. She domesticated and humanised him, 'encouraged him and opened up areas of life new to him, [and] taught him much about trust and love'. Some of the most exquisite touches within Crichton Smith's work occur when the poet turns his gaze on the most rewarding aspect of his life. In 1974 he published the collection *Poems for Donalda*. The *New Collected Poems* also contains *The Leaf and the Marble* (1998), a sequence inspired by a trip to Rome, where the monuments of the faded empire, for all their grandiosity, are eclipsed by the perennial rejuvenations of love.

> When everything trembles, only love holds it together.
> Rome is an act of the will, but the leaf protects us.
> Day after day, year after year, Rome with its stony walls and
> > statues is
> built above a cage of wolves.
> But love is not an act of the will.
> No legions can defend or destroy love.
> When the walls fly apart, when the horizons shimmer, only
> > love can save us.

It is only fitting that this *New Collected Poems*, like so many of Crichton Smith's previous publications, is dedicated to Donalda.

SELECTED FURTHER READING

Novels
Consider the Lilies (London: Gollancz, 1968)
The Last Summer (London: Gollancz, 1969)
My Last Duchess (London: Gollancz, 1971)
Goodbye, Mr. Dixon (London: Gollancz, 1974)
The Village (Inverness: Club Leabhar 1976)
An End to Autumn (London: Gollancz, 1978)
On the Island (London: Gollancz, 1979)
A Field Full of Folk (London: Gollancz, 1982)
The Search (London: Gollancz, 1983)
The Tenement (London: Gollancz, 1985)
In the Middle of the Wood (London: Gollancz, 1987)
The Dream (London: MacMillan, 1990)
An Honourable Death (London: MacMillan, 1992)
Listen to the Voice (Edinburgh: Canongate, 1993)

Short Fiction
The Red Door: The Complete English Stories 1949–76, ed. Kevin
  MacNeil (Edinburgh: Birlinn, 2001)
The Black Halo: The Complete English Stories 1977–98, ed. Kevin
  MacNeil (Edinburgh: Birlinn, 2001)
Murdo: The Life and Works, ed. Stewart Conn (Edinburgh: Birlinn,
  2001)

Play
Visitor, in Ricardo Galgani, Linda McLean and Iain Crichton
  Smith, *Family: Three Plays* (London: NHB, 1999)

Literary Criticism
Towards the Human: Selected Essays (Edinburgh: Macdonald
  Publishers, 1986)
Introduction to *Sangschaw and Penny Wheep: Lyric Poems by Hugh
  MacDiarmid*. Spoken word CD compiled to commemorate the
  centenary of the birth of Hugh MacDiarmid (Glasgow:
  Scotsoun, 1992, 2002)

Critical Works on Iain Crichton Smith

John Blackburn, *The Poetry of Iain Crichton Smith* (Aberdeen: Association for Scottish Literary Studies, 1992)

Gerry Cambridge, 'Interview: Iain Crichton Smith at Seventy', *The Dark Horse* 6, Spring 1998, pp. 46–55

Douglas Gifford, 'Deer on the High Hills: The Poetry of Iain Crichton Smith', in *Gaelic and Scots in Harmony* (Proceedings of the Second International Conference on the Languages of Scotland, University of Glasgow, 1988), ed. Derick S. Thomson (Glasgow: University of Glasgow, 1990)

Carol Gow, *The Mirror and the Marble: The Poetry of Iain Crichton Smith* (Edinburgh: Saltire Society, 1992)

Colin Nicholson (ed.), *Iain Crichton Smith: Critical Essays* (Edinburgh: Edinburgh University Press, 1992)

Poem, Purpose and Place (Edinburgh: Polygon, 1992)

Alasdair D.F. MacRae, 'Remembering Iain Crichton Smith', *The Dark Horse* 8, Autumn 1999, pp. 52–8

Edwin Morgan, 'The Contribution of Iain Crichton Smith', *Scotlit* 23, 2001, www.arts.gla.ac.uk/scotlit/asls/ICSmith.html

Isobel Murray (ed.), *Scottish Writers Talking, 2: Iain Banks, Bernard MacLaverty, Naomi Mitchison, Iain Crichton Smith, Alan Spence* (East Linton: Tuckwell Press, 2002)

Stan Smith, *Poetry and Displacement* (Liverpool: Liverpool University Press, 2007)

Moray J. Watson, 'Iain Crichton Smith's Perception' (Ph.D. thesis, University of Aberdeen, 2001)

Christopher Whyte, *Modern Scottish Poetry* (Edinburgh: Edinburgh University Press, 2004)

Grant F. Wilson, *A Bibliography of Iain Crichton Smith* (Aberdeen: University of Aberdeen Press, 1990)

NEW COLLECTED POEMS

from THE LONG RIVER

(1955)

The Dedicated Spirits

The dedicated spirits grow
in winters of pervasive snow
their crocus armour.
Their perpendiculars of light
flash sheerly through the polar night
with missionary fire.

The red and sombre sun surveys
the footsteps of the ancestors
in the white ghostly snow:
from pasts without a season they
inhabit the imperfect day
our grieving spirits know.

About us the horizon bends
its orphan images, and winds
howl from the vacant north.
The mapless navigator goes
in search of the unscented rose
he grows in his heart's south.

Turning on the icy wheel
of image without substance, heal
us whatever spirit lies
in polar lightning. Let the ice
break, lest our paralysis
destroy our seeing eyes.

The faceless night holds dialogue
with us by the ancient rock.
The demons we abhor
dwell in the waste of mirrors we
choose to protect us from the fury
of the destructive fire.

O chosen spirits turning now
to your large skies the sun from snow
has swept at last,
let music from your rising wings
be heard in islands where we sing
to placate a lost ghost.

'Some days were running legs'

Some days were running legs and joy
and old men telling tomorrow would be
a fine day surely: for sky was red
at setting of sun between the hills.

Some nights were parting at the gates
with day's companions: and dew falling
on heads clear of ambition except light
returning and throwing stones at sticks.

Some days were rain flooding forever the green
pasture: and horses turning to the wind
bare smooth backs. The toothed rocks rising
sharp and grey out of the ancient sea.

Some nights were shawling mirrors lest the lightning
strike with the eel's speed out of the storm.
Black the roman rocks came from the left squawking
and the evening flowed back around their wings.

Poem of Lewis

Here they have no time for the fine graces
of poetry, unless it freely grows
in deep compulsion, like water in the well,
woven into the texture of the soil
in a strong pattern. They have no rhymes
to tailor the material of thought
and snap the thread quickly on the tooth.
One would have thought that this black north
was used to lightning, crossing the sky like fish
swift in their element. One would have thought
the barren rock would give a value to
the bursting flower. The two extremes,
mourning and gaiety, meet like north and south
in the one breast, milked by knuckled time,
till dryness spreads across each ageing bone.
They have no place for the fine graces
of poetry. The great forgiving spirit of the word
fanning its rainbow wing, like a shot bird
falls from the windy sky. The sea heaves
in visionless anger over the cramped graves
and the early daffodil, purer than a soul,
is gathered into the terrible mouth of the gale.

Anchored Yachts on a Stormy Day

Nine yachts are rocking in the sullen water,
one mast to each, one mast narrow and straight,
almost (so one would think) about to break
but never breaking quite. Indeed a kind of laughter
a demon gaiety, lightens their dull weight
so that the wave and wood, moving together,
blend into one as if they yearned to make
a unity in spite of love or hate
and the dense rancour of the heaving weather.
Though a tenth lies there capsized, the others dance
their stormy demon dance as if awake
they know the chances they must always take
when seas are riding high: and that their tether
is what will save them when the waters shake.

from THE WHITE NOON
(1959)

False Summer Leans

False summer leans across the dwindling veins:
the crags are wild with flowers and dear indeed
the sails, green-leaved, that dizzy the blue waves:
and pleasant that boat's engine, gravely humming
like Sunday pots on boil. The winter's pains
hang out like ragged washing, whitely streaming.

These are fine mornings when the boats at anchor
ride, freshly-painted, on the winking waves
and seagulls, yellow beaked, sidle down piers.
The herring surge into the wide Atlantic
and those, who come with flowers to growing graves,
are caught, like bees, within them, lost to tears.

Such music stirs within the naked rocks.
Such waves remember where the dear heads range
studying water in a purer tide
that ageing mouths gulp up the air like hawks:
for now, indeed, time is no longer strange
but walks beside us calmly, groom and bride.

And this is much that, from the dizzied cliffs,
descending late, we reach the level land
where growth as free as this can take our place.
This is a season we have never planned
but meets us gravely, face to equal face,
content to die, nor seek to understand.

In Luss Churchyard

Light strikes the stone bible like a gong:
blank leaves gape open. Greenness of grass is most
what, raging round the slabs, astonishes
the casual visitor drifting like a ghost
among the inscriptions and the wishes
chiselled on stone, prayed for a dead tongue.

A bird flickers from bough to windless bough
unsettled, frenzied perhaps with heat
or violence of the breast, a pagan joy.
The stranger remarks anew his moving feet
so constantly labouring in his employ
and walking without thought as they do now:

and the very inscriptions mirror modes of death –
the early stately and the later terse
(the very early almost invisible).
Consider how this eighteenth-century verse
glides with a quiet charm through pastoral
landscapes of the wandering breath.

Here however a skull, there crossed bones
leap out with tigerish instancy, like fire
burning through paper: with a savage force
punch through electric noon where the hands perspire
and prickle with the sun. This is indeed a coarse
imagery to be carved on harmless stones.

The adjacent river rambles quietly on
with wayward music, hardly disturbing even
the image of a leaf or stone or stick
but holding all the amplitude of heaven –
the fiery blueness of a composed Atlantic –
arching an earth poised in the breathless noon

where living and dead turn on the one hinge
of a noon intensely white, intensely clear.
The eyes read dates: the hands steady and rest
on leaning stone without a twitch of fear
merely an aimless curiosity. The breast,
empty with indifference, broods in change.

Yet, should a charge populous, terrible,
burst through the feeding greenness, capsizing this
mound like a knotted table, knees would sink
into the imponderable abyss
where the one star burns with a convulsive wink
in a white sky, blown outwards like a bubble.

The silence holds. A saw nags at a tree.
The settled bird chirps briefly while a breeze
ruffles its breast. The eye confused by dates
is pleasurably excited by the trees
arching a coolness over the heavy gates.
Therefore out of the noon's implacable sea

of hammered light the feet, still steady, go.
The hands touch wood and push the gate away
from the dreaming body which casts a little shade.
Out of the hectic greenness into a day
of dusty roadways the feet, suddenly gripping, wade
gathering power, changing to swift from slow.

Highland Sunday

Striped-trousered, hard-black-hatted, sunday-sunned,
swayed to clasped hands they stand at the church door
the graced, unwasted flock: and small, half-stunned
by the bells' summering welcome, I implore
a sudden lightning out of thunderous sound.

The Sunday palms with gentleness the roar
of ghostly waves that swell this cold-railed ground.
A band of bounded black defines the shore.
The threshold glitters to the whinnying souls
hand-clasped from anguish.
                              Has this circle's core
its purple darkness?
                        In assembling heat
the pouring roses drown their glowing shoes
and riotous gods, flexing warm muscles, fuse
their summer ardours with a loved defeat.

End of the Season on a Stormy Day – Oban

In the dead park a bench sprawls drunkenly.
Buoys bob in the bay.
The ghostly waters rise in laddered spray.

Blank-faced hotels stand stiffly by the shore
in the dead silence after crockery falls.
Their sighing landscapes sink into the walls,
the visitors being gone, the season ended.

Boats lag on the waves untenanted.
There's thinner patter of walking on the winded
grey extended front. The soldier draws
into his Great War stone from loose applause.

A motor boat, stern-flagged, drives steadily through
the seething waters. Braced to a splayed poise
a yellow sailor digs his cockerel claws.

And so! And so! His harvest in his hold
he weathers another season, drives through cold
towards his roped stone quay, his dead fish fold.

School Teacher

She was always earlier than the bell at nine.
She trod the same stone street for forty years.
(The stone might show a broken-backed design
of prints that slowly slant from toe to heel
as the years told.) Boys saluted well
as, morning-mounted, light struck spinning wheels
of cycles heading schoolward. Poets' lines
shimmered within boys' cheering. Globes and faces
spun, blurred. Open atlases
shouted their naked countries, bright as paint
created for her pupils. ('Stand. Recite.')
And who stood up? John's father? John? The faint
graph of her will climbed the wavering wall.
It climbed for forty years. It made a white
snake on distemper. ('Who was the famous saint
who crossed from Ireland in a flimsy boat,
Columba or Columbus? Surely you remember?'

'Remember, answering questions you must quote.
Never forget what the poet really wrote.')

The iambic's broken by the clanging bell.
The room's destroyed by noise, by leaving feet.
What was the message she had tried to tell
for forty years? She knew she had a debt
to pay for living. It had started well.
Yes, there was something she had tried to tell.
She'd never told it, for the moment passed
into the seething waters as a cast
wavers in underwater, taking shape
from shaken river movement, from the swell.
Yes, there was something. But she could not tell.
The walls wavered into moving lines.
John? John's father? stood in a bright class
hurrying the dead metres of his race
well-brushed, well-mannered. Irony perhaps?
Was that the message – that we'll never learn?
That all our atlases have shining maps?

The classroom wavered. The four walls poured in.
Her barren gown hung in the sea's spin.
'I want that apple. Bring it here at once.'
And smilingly he came to lay it flat
on the clear desk. It hissed like a red cat:
and standing quietly by her unlearnèd breast
the boy's eyes shone with an oblique unrest.
Sighing, she locked the lid. The apple lay
in her loved desk, soon to decay.

The Widow

That's his harem on the shelves.
                                    I don't know
whether to keep them or to ask some men
to take and marry them. Would that be wrong,
a posthumous divorce? No, I think no,
they shall bed here: at least they'll have a roof
even though he's gone without a single proof
of late repentance. But 'he had a stroke' –
how could he show repentance? Being aloof
was always his best nature. I had proof.
Surely if anyone knows I ought to know.
Let me be clear – his chair is rocking now
as if he's sitting in it writing scripts
for his societies – (Lamb it was he liked
of all the writers – he had wounded wings).

He should have told me forty years ago.
The church echoed my wifehood. There is no
happiness like that, the golden rings
growing to children's curls. And then the snarl,
barren and savage, on our wedding night.
The light burned late, the bare electric light
mocked my new body. You're an ageing girl.
The two rooms shook loudly in the night.

It wasn't right. No, though you're sitting there
it wasn't right, I tell you. You were tired
or so you told me when you came from where
you taught your pupils. They at least were fired
by passions that your bookishness could share
only by proxy. You would make them write
their growing into grammar ('would' to 'might').
And then you were a child again. The stroke
twitched your left eye. I towered you lying white
each gaping morning. What it was that broke
was mended out of pity by the night.
I did not love you. I did what I would do
for any sufferer. You had gone beyond
the limits of the landscape that I knew.

I'll not be jealous of books. I can't afford
to let this anger shake me. The white sword
rusts in the bookcase. It's a thousand years
since I first met you. 'Clever lad' they said
'and diligent as well, but, more than these
a faithful son, his mother's tireless nurse.'
O, it's what I knew. Your bedroom's polished board
shakes with your pacing. It was you, not me,
whose anguish throbbed the house when like a tree
you felt your birds all leave you, without a word
hunched at your glittering window. What went free
that should have stayed? Your heart clicked like a glove.
Perhaps you loved me as you loved those boys
and girls you taught, leading to stricter joys
their halting minds? Perhaps it was a love
the spirit not the flesh might understand.
Why did you marry me? (I long to know.)
I hear you saying: 'They must learn to love
the purest light shed from the purest mind'
as, raincoated and thin, you'd strike through wind
into the endless struggle to be true
to what is most untrue, the being-bound
to loveless loving. Should I read your books
not leave them in the glass case where I found

them, neatly ordered? You can write each night
here on this table. I will rub it white.

How could you forgive me if you could
never forgive yourself? That's why you're dead.
'There's nothing to forgive,' I might have said
but that's untrue. You know it is untrue.
Could you expect from me a gratitude
I could not feel? Often in the night
I heard you tossing like a guilty child
calling his mother through the shaken wood.
You wouldn't marry till she died. I knew
or thought I knew that that was true and right.
Can I forgive you or be reconciled
when you would scourge yourself? It's past my knowing.
Are there such people whose true life is dying?
O, if there are, you certainly were one
Whose best success was failure.
                              To cease growing –
that is the worst of all. Therefore must I
hug your cold shoulders all the wintry night
and summer too? Old woman like a sky
open to rain and lightning. Am I God
so to forgive you or to leave the Why
nailed to my cross? Your chair is rocking, rocking,
as if with grief. I see you with a rod
whipping your bony body. Stop, I say.
Stop, child, you mustn't. You were all I had.

Statement by a Responsible Spinster

It was my own kindness brought me here
to an eventless room, bare of ornament.
This is the threshold charity carried me over.
I live here slowly in a permanent

but clement weather. It will do for ever.
A barren bulb creates my firmament.
A sister cries: 'I might have learned to wear
sardonic jewellery and the lineament

of a fine beauty, fateful and austere.
I might have trained my perilous armament
on the learnèd and ferocious. A lover
would have emerged uniquely from that element.'

I know that for a lie, product of fever.
This is my beginning. Justice meant
that a man or woman who succumbs to fear
should not be married to good merriment.

I inspect justice through a queer air.
Indeed he lacks significant ornament.
Nevertheless he does not laugh or suffer
though, like pity's cruelty, he too is permanent.

And since I was trapped by pity and the clever
duplicities of age, my last emolument
returns, thus late, its flat incurious stare
on my ambiguous love, my only monument.

Night Walk 1

Someone had painted a moon on the sky.
He had added chimney smoke and painted houses.
It was really the sort of night you could get for Christmas
if nights were given for gifts or if you could buy
the earth as its own painting. The roads were painted
a hollow repetitive yellow as if all the way
from station to cottage a great yellow dog had panted
its yellowness up the long road by the side of the bay.
The dog would be part of the painting, not a live dog
and its breath would also be painted. Similes flog
the huge real brutes out of their slavering day.

Whoever had painted that night had knocked corners off.
You could hardly imagine you could bear to live in a world
thus painted and flattened. You'd have to be painted yourself
that is to say
you'd have to be less than human or inhuman enough
not to get up in the night to drive that nightmare away.

Night Walk 2

The tall lamps burn their sockets late
like ambitious men who cannot sleep at night
for thinking of a crown or of a slight
endured in inward fury.
                              I walk this street
also in fury (though I don't know what
or whom to train it on). Only the light,
a sickly yellow, gathers round my feet
till they are yellow too, an incomplete
tinkle of hollow bells, neutral, not sweet.
This is the sound I make – of echoing wells
tapped by my yellow feet, as tired and late
they ring on the street's door their yellow bells.

It is this yellowness that wakes my fury
though to be furious with a colour is
matter for laughter, and one should be chary
of such an almost-madness, like the lilies
furiously spinning in a flat air.
Therefore, though I seem to swim in bare
and sickly yellowness, I must curb this rage
for rage is yellow too and makes a cage
of slovenly light around a parrot's stare.

Seagulls

These have the true cold avarice beyond
anything we can say of them or write down.
Their hunger
as they plunge
in a squabble of devils on to a ringed pond
of paper, orange peel, and all the trash
we throw down water to them (their small cash)
attracts nobility through their obscene
beggary by singleness of will
that, screeching here, like selfish children, they
demand from us to be responsible
for the gifts of food they ask, screaming their way
through panes of meaning that, invisible,
make rocks in twisting air: and their beaks are
like children's fingers scrabbling on a pane
caging the gift they think their right. It's there –
therefore it's theirs, invented for their own.

These have the true cold avarice beyond
anything of spirit you could suppose.
They are like
the ragged quick
nervous fears that make dim islands round
the circle of our gayest happiest thoughts

or like our sins that follow us in hordes
of running angular screams back to the house
we poorly guiltily inhabit. These
are screeched despairs that on our tallest mast,
beside our yellow ropes, perch high and curse
all that was best in climbing, all the most
impeccable and sated intercourse
that our illuminated beings had:
and strike with swearing voices through the bold
webs of analysis that good or bad
hang out their azure meanings on our field.

There is nothing anyone can do with these
sheer naked wills that dominate this sea.
Nearer to stone
than to a thinking man
they have no cruel look or kind. Amuse
yourself with fantasies, these will not come
out of the different air which is their home.
Your circles cannot touch. No tangent may
even lightly curve through blue to join you to
a seagull's world which at the centre is
the single-headed seagull in the blue
image you make for it, its avarice
its only passion that is really true.
You cannot admire it even. It is simply
a force that, like a bomb slim as a death,
plunges, itself, no other, through the ample
imperial images that disguise your truth.

Room for Living

You should stop here and not step
into that land of strange waters and strange
persuasive drum beats which have power to change
skin and skeleton to an earlier shape
till, like a mumbling cannibal, you set up
your own headstone on a dazzled slope.

These sights trouble your dreams. Like a toothed moon
rearing from rank forest lands you go
in silver aseptic light over the slow
entangled swamps and, as in a bright spoon,
see huge queer shapes dancing: a slant grin
splitting a face as dangerous as a lion.

Nevertheless, if you wish to keep
yourself to yourself and not become
a sort of music beaten on a drum
in a kind of shapelessness and dying sleep
you should stay quietly by this river, not rig ship
to take you down far water, bright and sharp.

If you listen calmly, you can hear music here
of rusted broken strings, an orchestra
that gathers volume like an autumn star
filling your sky with light, stranger more dear
than any light through any atmosphere
of foreign land, nourished by native fear.

A kind of courage glitters in that huge
corrupted music and heroic men
win crippled victories on a staring plain.
If you listen tranquilly you will enlarge
yourself to more than you till the white surge
will bear you also down its stream of courage.

Beautiful Shadow

Beautiful shadow, cool, fastidious,
that follows substance like a wife or child,
you push the world a stage away from us
and you are all that from the huge and wild
riotous abandon of the exodus
of colour and of shape remain for us.
I do not think you the ridiculous
follower or yesman of the old
lying phenomena that the eyes unfold:

but rather shy and quiet and moving here
in your cool tracks like a soft-stepping deer
and in your inner darkness burning all
false decoration from the actual.

Therefore remain with me, fine shadow, for
you are the ending of a metaphor
and all aesthetics gather round you till,
thus loving you, I find you at the end,
beyond the anguish of the ethical,
my best follower and my truest friend.

For the Unknown Seamen of the 1939–45 War Buried in Iona Churchyard

One would like to be able to write something for them
not for the sake of the writing but because
a man should be named in dying as well as living,
in drowning as well as on death-bed, and because
the brain being brain must try to establish laws.

Yet these events are not amenable
to any discipline that we can impose
and are not in the end even imaginable.
What happened was simply this, bad luck for those
who have lain here twelve years in a changing pose.

These things happen and there's no explaining,
and to call them 'chosen' might abuse a word.
It is better also not to assume a mourning,
moaning stance. These may have well concurred
in whatever suddenly struck them through the absurd

or maybe meaningful. One simply doesn't
know enough, or understand what came
out of the altering weather in a fashioned
descriptive phrase that was common to each name
or may have surrounded each like a dear frame.

Best not to make much of it and leave these seamen
in the equally altering acre they now have
inherited from strangers though yet human.
They fell from sea to earth from grave to grave
and, griefless now, taught others how to grieve.

The Window

We walked that night between the piled houses.
It was late and cold. Frost gleamed on the road
like the sheen of over-learning. Beaked and bowed,
the lamp-posts lectured light, dispensed discourses.

All windows were dark. As on the edge of a cliff
we warily walked, stepping on steeps of silence
except for the click-click-click of our heels, the parlance
of stones that down a well make a crooked graph.

A bus like a late planet turned a corner.
There was nothing else, we and darkness merely.
These ancient houses had never stood in an early
atmosphere or radiance of summer.

At day's end they sank heavily into slumber
as a man sleeps open-mouthed at his fire when
too much light and heat exhaust his brain.
He floats on darkness like a tired swimmer.

None but we two, walking almost as over
a world's end. Yellow light sang and sang
into our coats, our faces, skin and tongue.
We thought each other shook with a yellow fever.

Then she said: 'Look, there's a light up there'
and, slowly climbing the cliff-face, my eyes came
to a square light that shone with a blunt flame.
It was solid and dull and red in the yellow air.

And I wondered whose it was – a sleepless man
turning and turning between a window and bed
cursing his sleeplessness and the huge dread
shrill light that pecked at his bemused brain?

Or was it perhaps one studious and grave
who, grasping his pale book, would listen to
the sound it made, the authentic echo
of words returning what he thought and gave?

Or was it a mother, waking for her child,
who could not sleep because of the cold air,
and stumbled between dull bed and dull chair
in the red light imperious and wild?

At least the light was human: and we looked
into each other's eyes shyly as if
a house had suddenly sprung from a dead cliff
and it was all our searching spirits lacked.

from THISTLES AND ROSES
(1961)

Old Woman

And she, being old, fed from a mashed plate
as an old mare might droop across a fence
to the dull pastures of its ignorance.
Her husband held her upright while he prayed

to God who is all-forgiving to send down
some angel somewhere who might land perhaps
in his foreign wings among the gradual crops.
She munched, half dead, blindly searching the spoon.

Outside, the grass was raging. There I sat
imprisoned in my pity and my shame
that men and women having suffered time
should sit in such a place, in such a state

and wished to be away, yes, to be far away
with athletes, heroes, Greek or Roman men
who pushed their bitter spears into a vein
and would not spend an hour with such decay.

'Pray God,' he said, 'we ask you, God,' he said.
The bowed back was quiet. I saw the teeth
tighten their grip around a delicate death.
And nothing moved within the knotted head

but only a few poor veins as one might see
vague wishless seaweed floating on a tide
of all the salty waters where had died
too many waves to mark two more or three.

Luss Village

Such walls, like honey, and the old are happy
in morphean air like gold-fish in a bowl.
Ripe roses trail their margins down a sleepy
mediaeval treatise on the slumbering soul.

And even the water, fabulously silent,
has no salt tales to tell us, nor makes jokes
about the yokel mountains, huge and patient,
that will not court her but read shadowy books.

A world so long departed! In the churchyard
the tilted tombs still gossip, and the leaves
of stony testaments are read by Richard,
Jean and Carol, pert among the sheaves

of unscythed shadows, while the noon day hums
with bees and water and the ghosts of psalms.

A Note on Puritans

There was no curtain between them and fire.
Every moment was a moment when
a man could sink into a tranced despair
or shake his heels to vanity and turn
with frenzied gaiety from that drying air.

Therefore their urgency. That fire glowed
along their blackened senses, hour by hour.
Only the book they clutched so tightly cheered
hearts that might stop, eyes that their burning fear
could hole with flame: heads that their thoughts had charred.

Garden and gardener, book and reader glowed:
limbs crackled their sins: silks twitched in a blue flame:
a man's flesh melted in the mouth of God:
he lost his name to earn a lasting name.
A heaven flashed where all that oil flowed.

That was great courage to have watched that fire,
not placing a screen before it as we do
with pictures, poems, landscapes, a great choir
of mounting voices which can drown the raw
hissing and spitting of flame with other fire.

That was great courage to have stayed as true
to truth as man can stay. From them we learn
how certain truths can make men brutish too:
how few can watch the bared teeth slow-burn
and not be touched by the lumps of fire they chew

into contempt and barrenness. I accuse
these men of singleness and loss of grace
who stared so deeply into the fire's hues
that all was fire to them.
                              Yes, to this place
they should return. Cheeks have the fire men choose.

Schoolgirl on Speech-day in the Open Air

Here in their health and youth they're sitting down
on thick tight grass while bald official men,
heavy with sunshine, wear a moment's crown
and put it by reluctantly again.

I look at one who lies upon her side,
wearing bright yellow for the clasping light.
No ring of shadow has engaged her pride
or wolfed her, fallen, in the circling night.

Her scorn springs out like swords. A smile plays round
her unstained lips, as if a joke would spill.
She turns her shining head into that sound
which stumbles downward from low hill to hill.

And then I turn again and see how one
dangles her will from every word he spins
and think how thirty years can fence a man
by what he loses and by what he wins

into a little ground where he can see
the golden landlords, pursed with luck, stride past.
And schoolgirls flashing by are far and free
as fish he played for but new men will taste.

And the timed applause which falls from rock to rock
and then to silence is the way he came.
She gathers, like necessity, her cloak.
The schoolgirl rises – and must do the same.

Dying is not Setting Out

Dying is not setting out
in a full flower of sails.
More complex ropes are taut
across the blue pulse.

Dying is not like sailing
by the shores of Mull or
Tiree. Sheet's less willing
and twists in thick air.

It's not for Skye we make.
Not with simple hands
use south wind for luck.
We wear our islands

unconnected in spite of
intellect's glittering stride.
We sail into the grave
of the more than dead.

John Knox

That scything wind has cut the rich corn down –
the satin shades of France spin idly by
the bells are jangled in St Andrew 's town –
a thunderous God tolls from a northern sky.
He pulls the clouds like bandages awry.
See how the harlot bleeds below her crown.
This lightning stabs her in the heaving thigh –
such siege is deadly for her dallying gown.

A peasant's scythe rings churchbells from the stone.
From this harsh battle let the sweet birds fly,
surprised by fields, now barren of their corn.
(Invent, bright friends, theology or die.)
The shearing naked absolute blade has torn
through false French roses to her foreign cry.

About that Mile

'It all grew in a garden, all that sin,'
said he with his tormented face.
'You ask me for the meaning of our pain
and the thick darkness boiling with God's grace.
You ask me how a shining moral knife
cuts apples into slices like a housewife.

You ask me why Satan like a malcontent
enters our plays and always steals the show
dressed in his bitter black, most eloquent
to speak of slavery and the way we grow
aslant into the wind, like bending corn.
As if the evil lay in being born.

You ask me why a helpless child should die
in speechless agony, or a woman drag
her cancer like a creel, or how an eye
must stare unblinking on a hanging rag
to find the flesh beneath it: or the reason
for such a death as sucks us like a passion

down to the briny dregs. All these you ask.
And why two people living in a mile
of perfume and vast leisure failed their task.
And why across that innocence and smile,
a stinging whip spoke savagely from space
across the mortal and decaying face.

Yet I, like you, have heartbreaks of my own.
I die of no ideas but of men.
You think me moral like the weighted stone
engraved on graves. Yet you take your pen
and write a poem in the space you fear.
Could you do this if space were everywhere?

You ask me this. I am not God,' he said.
'I build my fence nor do I say I can
hit every nail exactly on the head
not even those nails which drove the Son of Man
deeper against the wood. I munch my way
across these pastures till the edge of day.'

'About that mile,' I said, 'about that mile
you talked of there.' 'Well,' he pursued, 'what then?'
'Do you not,' I questioned with a half-smile,
'dream of it sometimes, wish it back again?'
But he with an equal smile said then to me:
'I turn to poetry for such foolery.'

Sunday Morning Walk

Sunday of wrangling bells – and salt in the air –
I passed the tall black men and their women walking
over the tight-locked streets which were all on fire
with summer ascendant. The seas were talking and talking

as I took my way to the wood where the river ran quiet.
The grass lay windowed in sunlight, the leaves were raging
in furious dying green. The road turned right
round the upstanding castle whose stone unageing

marks how a world remains as I being now
pack of a wandering flesh take holiday strolling
far from the churches' declaiming. Health will allow
riots of naiads and nymphs, so wantonly rolling

with me in leaves in woods, thinking how once
Jove took his pleasure of Leda or – splendid embracing –
god would mate with a goddess – rapid the pounce,
fruitful the hot-thighed meeting, no need for unlacing.

And occupied thus, I came where a dead sheep lay
close to a fence, days gone. The flies were hissing and buzzing
out of the boiling eyes, wide open as day.
I stood in the sunlight beside it, watching and musing.

Three crows famished yards off. Live sheep grazed far
from the rotting carcass. The jaw, well-shaved, lay slackly
there on the warm quiet grass. The household air
was busy with buzzing like fever. How quickly, how quickly

the wool was peeled from the back. How still was the flesh.
How the visiting flies would not knock at the door of the sockets.
How the hole in the side gaped red, a well-sized gash.
How the clear young lambs grazed in the shade of the thickets.

And the sun blazed hot on my shoulder. Here was no shade.
But the sheep was quiet, so quiet. There was nothing to notice
but the grape-bunched flies and the crows. Could a world have stayed
if I'd taken a stick in my hand and beat off the flies?

They would merely return when I'd gone and busy as always
inhabit this larder again, no matter how brightly
I struck with my smart sharp stick. All I could praise –
yes, all I could praise – was the sheep lying there so quietly

not knowing not knowing. High summer was raging around.
I stood in my slack clean clothes. The stones were burning.
The flies in the wound continued their occupied sound
as I turned my back on a death of no weeping or mourning.

Love Songs of a Puritan

1

You've put salt on my bread
and black sparks in my eye.
The hole in my side
is packed with God and devilry.

Your coiled hair gleams my death.
In bare Eden there springs up
a green snake with a red mouth.
It shoots from a rocky map.

If all were honey, this an album,
and toy poems were my pride
I'd not remember the ripped scream
and the reaped zone of the full bride.

As if one should write theology
and be dumb to heresies and the cross
or turn a blind and gentle eye
to the scorching apples in your dress.

Therefore from this old see-saw
let me jerk upward to my joy
according to the brutal law:
'To every man his own boy.'

2

My eyes are heresies to the clear
and grave theology yours speak to me.
I make a Luther in your catholic air
though speechless sermons should have made me free.

God has the devil for shadow and I too
strike long diagonals at your angel's step.
All my religion would awake to you
if you would shining grant me angel sleep.

3

The day's in love with you as suns with gardens.
The dappled shade shakes thought across your brow.
If this is prison you spread out your pardons
for all dark sentences we suffer now.

You govern guilt by innocence, and dungeons
open like leaves to green and cool keys,
the twisted inmates straighten like a conscience
and by your glance all shufflers stand at ease.

And all the darkness gathers light about it
to hide its devilish shame as devils do.
If this is heresy can devils doubt it
who've made their best theology of you.

No mineral in your earth to tempt to stealing:
such tender shadows merely can provoke
the longing for a perfectness of feeling
we've almost spoken but we never spoke.

For only at rarest moments can we scent it
the garden we have lost but cannot find
and you the shining page that clearly meant it
already turn to print across the mind.

4

I know a young girl of great wit
who walks like Venus in her stylish gait
and some would say 'Conceit' but I would say:
'A sun contents us if the clouds are grey,'
and also, 'Have you seen between the stones
the water running as the water runs?'

All things that speak of surety and grace
proclaim us heretic from our proper place
though venomous devils preach against the light
which opens heavens at her precious feet.
Yet even these by sneers and laughs make known
the dear theology they now disown.

Kierkegaard

Forced theologian of the minimum place,
the Copenhagen of the hunchback soul
eclipsed yet strengthened all his natural rays.
Imagine him daily taking his cramped stroll
by sniggering windows to a North Pole
where his wit spawned its cold rainbow oil.

His father was Abraham on a high hill.
The knife cut Isaac to the head and heart.
Ingenious loneliness decorated hell
with books he fathered on a girl's spirit.
She sank her roses into his cold desert
who drove his body deeper into art.

Tragedy? or Comedy? These meet
in the written mirrors furnishing his chill
and flashing Danish room, for all the light
was self-absorbed into that crucial
omnivorous intelligence so cruel
it mocked the pain that made the bare brain howl.

Till the new category, the individual,
rose like a thorn from the one rose he knew.
The crucifixion of the actual,
by necessary acceptance brought him through
to where his father standing calm and new
cutting his head and life made one from two.

By Ferry to the Island

We crossed by ferry to the bare island
where sheep and cows stared coldly through the wind –
the sea behind us with its silver water,
the silent ferryman standing in the stern
clutching his coat about him like old iron.

We landed from the ferry and went inland
past a small church down to the winding shore
where a white seagull fallen from the failing
chill and ancient daylight lay so pure
and softly breasted that it made more dear

the lesser white around us. There we sat
sheltered by a rock beside the sea.
Someone made coffee, someone played the fool
in a high rising voice for two hours.
The sea's language was more grave and harsh.

And one sat there whose dress was white and cool.
The fool sparkled his wit that she might hear
new diamonds turning on her naked finger.
What might the sea think or the dull sheep
lifting its head through heavy Sunday sleep?

And later, going home, a moon rising
at the end of a cart-track, minimum of red,
the wind being dark, imperfect cows staring
out of their half-intelligence, and a plough
lying on its side in the cold, raw

naked twilight, there began to move
slowly, like heavy water, in the heart
the image of the gull and of that dress,
both being white and out of the darkness rising
the moon ahead of us with its rusty ring.

Culloden and After

You understand it? How they returned from Culloden
over the soggy moors aslant, each cap
at the low ebb no new full tide could pardon:
how they stood silent at the end of the rope
unwound from battle: and to the envelope
of a bedded room came home, polite and sudden.

And how, much later, bards from Tiree and Mull
would write of exile in the hard town
where mills belched English, anger of new school:
how they remembered where the sad and brown
landscapes were dear and distant as the crown
that fuddled Charles might study in his ale.

There was a sleep. Long fences leaned across
the vacant croft. The silly cows were heard
mooing their sorrow and their Gaelic loss.
The pleasing thrush would branch upon a sword.
A mind withdrew against its dreamed hoard
as whelks withdraw or crabs their delicate claws.

And nothing to be heard but songs indeed
while wandering Charles would on his olives feed
and from his Minch of sherries mumble laws.

A Young Highland Girl Studying Poetry

Poetry drives its lines into her forehead
like an angled plough across a bare field.
I've seen her kind before, of the live and dead
who bore humped creels when the beating winds were wild.

Nor did they know much poetry but were skilful
at healing children, bringing lambs to birth.
The earth they lived from did not make them soulful.
The foreign rose abated at their mouth.

Yet they were dancers too and feared the season
when 'pale Orion shook the seas with fire'.
Peculiar waters had their inner reasons
for curing wastrels of a mental star.

And she – like them – should grow along these valleys
bearing bright children, being kind to love.
Simple affection needs no complex solace
nor quieter minds abstractions of the grave.

For most must walk though some by natural flying
learn from the bitter winds a kind of praise.
These fruits are different. She will know one dying
but he by many deaths will bless her days.

For Angus MacLeod

Headmaster, and Editor of Gaelic Poems

Today they laid him in the earth's cold colour,
a man from Lewis with his seventy-five
years struck from his head. Teacher, scholar,
he had worked a true task when all alive,

building a school, elucidating texts.
The Gaelic shone quite clearly in his bones.
A casket filled with ashes had been mixed
with filtered sunlight and the small stones.

A useful life with pupils and with poems:
sufficient honours (his humour asked no more)
he takes his place in many minds and rooms.
Without their knowing it, his patient care

instructs far hands to turn a new lever,
a voice to speak in a mild-mannered tone.
The deeds we do reverberate forever.
Inveterate justice weighs the flesh and bone.

His best editions are some men and women
who scrutinise each action like a word.
The truest work is learning to be human
definitive texts the poorest can afford.

Studies in Power

1

Today at a meeting while I sat confused
by motions, counter-motions, and the vague
appalling ardour of the dialogue
I was struck by terror (being thus bemused)
that I (O certainly no albatross
of a dear unearthly climate) should be there,
somehow a stranger, at a total loss
(no, not uncommon, let me be quite clear)

till this fear struck me with a dizzy force
that this was real and the poems I make
mere cardboard coins to fill a childish purse.

And I was terrified lest my world be fake
and these blunt men who make all words opaque
should stand like giants by my dwarfish verse.

2

I thought of power and its sources while
the table trembled under a bronze thought
and men grew marble of a dreaming sort
all round me even here. Mile upon mile
the violent and the beautiful strode on
one in her deadly silks, the other in
black Roman leather with the brassy belt
and both impervious to my senseless guilt.

Till suddenly there I saw a vase in bloom
gathering light about it clearly clearly
in adult daylight not by a moon obscurely,

and its harder language filled the small room
with its bare constant self, its paradigm
of straining forces harmonised sincerely.

Home

To have to stay
in spite of scorn, hatred,
in spite of shattered
illusions also. To be unable
to break cleanly away
since this is truly home
simple imperishable
since otherwhere is chill,
dull-breasted, dumb.

Since this too is hated,
loved, willed to be perfect, willed
to a finer yield
fiercer, less barren, richer,
its harvests be completed.
Since to have seen tall men
moving in light and fire
yet human too is more
grace than can be given

this (one says) is tragic
(to be fixed on a wheel
implacable internal
as tears break. As roses,
bowed gravely down to rock,
proliferate endless versions.)
Is not tragic but cause
of fresh honours, horses
impelled by used reins.

For My Mother

She is tougher than me, harder.
Elephant body on a miniature stool
keels when rising till the drilled stick
plants it upright. Rock
fills the false room

who has more air about her.
Kneaded life like good butter.
Is at seventy not afraid
of the perished dead
who spit and rear

snarling at me, not her,
though forty years younger.
Not riches do I wish me
nor successful power.
This only I admire

to roll the seventieth sea
as if her voyage were
to truthful Lewis rising,
most loved though most bare
at the end of a rich season.

DEER ON THE HIGH HILLS
(1962)

I

A deer looks through you to the other side,
and what it is and sees is an inhuman pride.

II

Yesterday three deer stood at the roadside.
It was icy January and there they were
like debutantes on a smooth ballroom floor.

They stared at us out of that French
arrogant atmosphere, like Louis the Sixteenth
sustained in twilight on a marble plinth.

They wore the inhuman look of aristocrats
before a revolution comes, and the people
blaspheme the holy bells in the high steeple.

Before the ice breaks, and heroes in spring
come up like trees with bursting wrongs in their arms
and feed the nobles to the uniform worms.

So were these deer, balanced on delicate logic,
till suddenly they broke from us and went
outraged and sniffing into the dark wind.

Difficult to say where they go to
in the harsh weather when the mountains stand
like judging elders, tall on either hand.

Except that they know the ice is breaking now.
They take to the hills pursued by darkness and lie
beneath the starry metaphysical sky.

Sometimes in a savage winter they'll come down
and beg like fallen nobles for their bread.
They'd rather live in poverty than be dead.

Nevertheless there's something dangerous
in a deer's head. He might suddenly open your belly
with his bitter antlers to the barren sky.

Especially in winter when tormented
by loneliness they descend to this road
with great bounding leaps like the mind of God.

In summer they can be ignored. They crop so gently
among the hills that no one notices
their happy heads sunk in the feeding cresses.

But beware of them now when ice is on the ground.
A beggared noble can conceal a sword
next to his skin for the aimless and abhorred

tyrants who cannot dance but throw stones,
tyrants who can crack the finest bones:
tyrants who do not wear but break most ancient crowns.

III

One would be finished with these practical things
in order to return as deer do
to the tall mountain springs.

Nevertheless one should not so return
till soldier of the practical or doer
one wholly learns to learn

a real contempt, a fine hard-won disdain
for these possessions, marbles of unripe children,
as, again,

a deer might walk along a sweating street
stare in a cramped window and then go
back to the hills but not on ignorant feet.

IV

Forget these purple evenings and these poems
that solved all or took for myth
the pointed sail of Ulysses enigmatic.

There was Hector with his child in his arms.
Where is that other Hector
who wore the internal shield, the inner sword?

Ulysses scurries, like a rat trapped in a maze.
He wears the sharp look of a business magnate.
Late from the office he had a good excuse.

Ideas clash on the mountain tops.
By the appalled peaks the deer roar.
Simply a question of rutting, these cloudy systems

or as yesterday we saw a black cloud
become the expression of a tall mountain.
And that was death, the undertaker, present.

And all became like it for that moment,
assumption of anguish, and the hollow waters
the metaphysics of an empty country

deranged, deranged, a land of rain and stones
of stones and rain, of the huge barbarous bones,
plucked like a loutish harp their harmonies.

V

You must build from the rain and stones,
from the incurable numbers: the grasses
innumerable on the many hills.

Not to geometry or algebra,
or an inhuman music, but
in the hollow roar of the waterfall,

you must build from there and not be
circumvented by sunlight or a taste of love
or intuitions from the sky above

the deadly rock. Or even history.
Prince Charles in a gay Highland shawl,
or mystery in a black Highland coffin.

You must build from the rain and stones
till you can make
a stylish deer on the high hills,
and let its leaps be unpredictable!

VI

Duncan Ban McIntyre, the poet,
knew them intimately, was one of them.
They had waxen hides, they were delicate dancers.

They evolved their own music which became
his music: they elected him
their poet laureate.

It was a kind of Eden these days
with something Cretan in his eulogy.
Nevertheless he shot them also.

Like shooting an image or a vivid grace.
Brutality and beauty danced together
in a silver air, incorruptible.

And the clean shot did not disturb his poems.
Nor did the deer kneel in a pool of tears.
The stakes were indeed high in that game.

And the rocks did not weep with sentiment.
They were simply there: the deer were simply there.
The witty gun blazed from his knowing hand.

VII

What is the knowledge of the deer?
Is there a philosophy of the hills?
Do their heads peer into the live stars?

Do rumours of death disturb them? They do not live
by local churchyards, hotels or schools.
They inhabit wild systems.

Do they outface winds or lie down
in warm places? Winter, interrogant,
displaces spring and summer, undulant.

Their horns have lucked in blood. Yes, their horns
have gored bellies. The dainty hind
has absolute passion, similar and proud.

It is not evil makes the horns bright
but a running natural lustre. The blood
is natural wounding. Metaphoric sword

is not their weapon, but an honest thrust.
Nor does the moon affect their coupling, nor
remonstrant gods schoolmaster their woods.

Evil not intentional, but desire
disturbs to battle. The great spring is how
these savage captains tear to indigo

the fiery guts. Evil's more complex, is
a languaged metaphor, like the mists that scarf
the deadly hind and her bewildered calf.

VIII

Supposing God had a branched head like this
considering Himself in a pool.
It is not the image of the beautiful

makes it so, simply as in a mirror,
but in its fadingness, as on the ice
the deer might suddenly slip, go suddenly under,

their balance being precarious. It is this,
that makes her beautiful, she who now obscures
unconscious heavens with her conscious ray,

is concourse of bright flesh, sad, is remembering
herself so going, so implacable,
her failing voyages to the obstinate rocks:

as deer so stand, precarious, of a style,
half-here, half-there, a half-way lustre breaking
a wise dawn in a chained ocean far.

As dear, so dear, Vesuvius, rocket, you
being ice and water, winter and summer, take
the mountainous seas into your small logic.

God may not be beautiful, but you
suffer a local wound. You bleed to death
from all that's best, your active anima.

The deer and you may well be beautiful,
for through your bones as through a mathematics
concordant honouring beauty richly breaks.

IX

Deer on the high peaks, calling, calling,
you speak of love, love of the mind and body.
Your absolute heads populate the hills

like daring thoughts, half-in, half-out this world.
As a lake might open, and a god peer
into a room where failing darkness glows.

Deer on the high peaks, there have been heads
as proud as yours, destructive, ominous,
of an impetuous language, measureless.

Heads like yours, so scrutinous and still,
yet venomed too with the helpless thrust of spring,
so magisterial, violent, yet composed:

heads of a thirsty intellect, sensuous as
the thirst of bellies in a summer day
July and waspish, on a murmuring ground.

Heads like valleys where the stars fed
unknown and magical, strange and unassuaged,
the harmonies humming in a green place.

So proud these heads, original, distinct,
they made an air imperial around
their pointed scrutiny, passionate with power.

Electric instinct of the high hills
till later later peasants in the valleys
felt in their bones disquieting kingdoms break

and matrons, by small cottages, would sense
implacable navies in their native wombs,
a generation of a harder wit

and later later when the senses quickened
(the hills being bare again) in a new season
in a night honoured with a desperate star

another head appeared, fiercer than these,
disdain flashed from his horns, a strange cry
perplexed the peasants, somnolent, appeased.

X

Deer on the high peaks, the wandering senses
are all, are all: fanatic heads deceive,
like branches springing in a true desert.

Smell now the cresses and the winter root,
passage of heather, journey of rank fox
mortal and moving on the strange hills.

In spring the raven and lascivious swallow,
migrant of air, the endless circle closing,
unclosing, closing, a bewildering ring

of natural marriage, pagan, sensuous.
Return of seasons, and the fugitive
Culloden of scents, erratic, hesitant.

The snow returning, and the summer wasp
more caustic than idea, hum of bees
at their devotions to the wild honey.

The hind crowned with her wanton sex,
rage of the sap in trees, the urgent salmon
pregnant with oceans dying into streams.

And these return in spite of the idea,
the direct reasoning road, the mad Ulysses
so unperverted, so implacable,

so wearing late his dull ironic crown
among a people he has never loved
nor felt in boredom kinship ominous

but fixed on a reasoned star his obstinate gaze
who came at last to where his childhood was
an infant island in an ancient place.

XI

Deer on the high peaks, let me turn
my gaze far from you, where the river winds
its slow way like an old man's argument.

The rocks obstinate, the rains persistent,
the stones ingathered into their chastened fury,
all things themselves, a fierce diversity.

The rampant egos of the flat plains,
the thorns gentle with their sour flowers,
tongues of the sharp stones, the water's business.

Contorted selves that twist in a dark wind,
far from the mountains, from the far and clear
ordered inventions of the stars ongoing.

And here, below, the water's business
smoothing the stone, consenting to the heads
that, easy of a summer, stare and stare

and speak: 'I am, I am. Preserve me, O preserve.
Make me in mirror matchless and the earl
of such imagined kingdoms as endure.

I pray, I pray, a marchioness of this
dismembered kingdom, let my face be seen
not mortal now but of a lasting grace.'

Roar of the waters, prickly thrust of thorn,
immutable stone, sand of a brute fact,
these are the maenads of necessity.

And the deer look down, Platonic dawn breaks
on Highland hills as distant as a thought,
an excellent Athens, obstinate mirage,

while the stone rears, the venomed stone rears
its savage being, and the waters pour
illusive summers to the real seas,

while the deer stand imperious, of a style,
make vibrant music, high and rich and clear,
mean what the plain mismeans, inform a chaos.

XII

Deer on the high hills, in your halfway kingdom,
uneasy in this, uneasy in the other,
but all at ease when earth and sky together

are mixed are mixed, become a royalty
none other knows, neither the migrant birds
nor the beasts chained to their instinctive courses.

That halfway kingdom is your royalty
you on a meditative truth impaled
the epicures of feeding absolutes

you of a metaphysics still and proud
native to air native to earth both,
indigenous deer beneath a cloudburst sky:

to whom the lightning's native and the thunder,
whose sockets flash with an annunciant fire,
whose storms are vegetation's dearest friend.

Your antlers flash in light, your speed like thought
is inspiration decorous and assured
a grace not theological but of

accomplished bodies, sensuous and swift,
of summer scents enjoyers, and of winters
the permanent spirits, watchful, unappeased:

of summer hills a speaking radiance,
the body's language, excellent and pure,
discoursing love, free as the wandering wind:

of scentless winters the philosophers,
vigilant always like a tiptoe mind
on peaks of sorrow, brave and scrutinous:

on peaks of sorrow, brave and scrutinous,
on breakneck peaks, coherent and aplomb,
the image silent on the high hill.

XIII

Do colours cry? Does 'black' weep for the dead?
Is green so bridal, and is red the flag
and eloquent elegy of a martial sleep?

Are hills 'majestic' and devoted stones
plotting in inner distances our fall?
The mind a sea: and she a Helen who

in budding hours awakens to her new
enchanting empire all the summer day,
the keys of prisons dangling in her hands?

Is night a woman, and the moon a queen
or dowager of grace, and all the stars
archaic courtiers round ambiguous smiles?

Are rivers stories, and are plains their prose?
Are fountains poetry? And are rainbows the
wistful smiles upon a dying face?

And you, the deer, who walk upon the peaks,
are you a world away, a language distant?
Such symbols freeze upon my desolate lips!

XIV

There is no metaphor. The stone is stony.
The deer step out in isolated air.
We move at random on an innocent journey.

The rain is rainy and the sun is sunny.
The flower is flowery and the sea is salty.
My friend himself, himself my enemy.

The deer step out in isolated air.
Not nobles now but of a further journey.
Their flesh is distant as the air is airy.

The rivers torrents, and the grasses many.
The stars are starry, and the night nocturnal.
The fox a tenant of no other skin.

Who brings reports? There's one head to the penny.
A door is wooden, and no window grieves
for lovers turned away, for widows lonely.

The deer step out in isolated air.
The cloud is cloudy and the word is wordy.
Winter is wintry, lonely is your journey.

'You called sir did you?' 'I who was so lonely
would speak with you: would speak to this tall chair,
would fill it chock-full of my melancholy.'

So being lonely I would speak with any
stone or tree or river. Bear my journey
you endless water, dance with a human joy.

This distance deadly! God or goddess throw me
a rope to landscape, let that hill, so bare,
blossom with grapes, the wine of Italy.

The deer step out in isolated air.
Forgive the distance, let the transient journey
on delicate ice not tragical appear

for stars are starry and the rain is rainy,
the stone is stony, and the sun is sunny,
the deer step out in isolated air.

from THE LAW AND THE GRACE
(1965)

Old Woman

Your thorned back
heavily under the creel
you steadily stamped the rising daffodil.

Your set mouth
forgives no one, not even God's justice
perpetually drowning law with grace.

Your cold eyes
watched your drunken husband come
unsteadily from Sodom home.

Your grained hands
dandled full and sinful cradles.
You built for your children stone walls.

Your yellow hair
burned slowly in a scarf of grey
wildly falling like the mountain spray.

Finally you're alone
among the unforgiving brass,
the slow silences, the sinful glass.

Who never learned,
not even ageing, to forgive
our poor journey and our common grave

while the free daffodils
wave in the valleys and on the hills
the deer took down with their instinctive skills,

and the huge sea
in which your brothers drowned sings slow
over the headland and the peevish crow.

The Witches

Coveys of black witches gather
at corners, closes.
Their thin red pointed noses
are in among the mash of scandal.

Poking red fires with
intense breath, hot as the imagined
rape riding the hot mind.
The real one was more moral

and more admirable because animal.
In an empty air they convene
their red, sad, envious beaks. The clean
winter rubs them raw

in a terrible void, hissing
with tongues of winter fire.
Pity them, pity them. Dare
to ring them with your love.

Two Girls Singing

It neither was the words nor yet the tune.
Any tune would have done and any words.
Any listener or no listener at all.

As nightingales in rocks or a child crooning
in its own world of strange awakening
or larks for no reason but themselves.

So on the bus through late November running
by yellow lights tormented, darkness falling,
the two girls sang for miles and miles together

and it wasn't the words or tune. It was the singing.
It was the human sweetness in that yellow,
the unpredicted voices of our kind.

Old Highland Lady Reading Newspaper

Grasping the newspaper in kneaded hands
in her ordered bed, the tablets at the side,
she slowly reads of all her friends who've died
in the black holds of the approaching islands

where the horses and the daffodils are dead,
unfashionable skirts have swirled away
down the Dutch cornfields and the fields of hay
into the numerous caves of her bald head

bent over print and old remorseless hands
grasping these deaths, the tombstones all in white
her eyes traverse with gritty appetite
in the slow justice of her mouth's small sounds.

Lenin

In a chair of iron
sits coldly my image of Lenin,
that troubling man
'who never read a book for pleasure alone.'

The germ inside the sealed train
emerged, spread in wind and rain
into new minds in revolution
seeming more real than had been

for instance Dostoevsky. No, I can
romanticise no more that 'head of iron'
'the thought and will unalterably one'
'the world-doer', 'thunderer', 'the stone

rolling through clouds'. Simple to condemn
the unsymmetrical, simple to condone
that which oneself is not. By admiration
purge one's envy of unadult iron

when the true dialectic is to turn
in the infinitely complex, like a chain
we steadily burn through, steadily forge and burn
not to be dismissed in any poem

by admiration for the ruthless man
nor for the saint but for the moving on
into the endlessly various, real, human,
world which is no new era, shining dawn.

The Argument

Our world is not predestined. So he chose
or did not choose to argue, being him.
And I being me in an excited pose
argued for our destiny, the trim
tracks that contain us, but he all aflame

spoke of the clear nobility of the soul,
himself both proud and noble. I replied
with words imperfectly in my control
how the will drives us, we undeified
unfree even for honour. He from pride

repelled such low dishonour. I appealed
to his pure passion, in a passionate tone
as if myself were suffering from guilt
but he quite calmly answered: 'We are known
to no one else.' I answered: 'The cold stone

suffers its gravity, and why should we
assume such freedom of the phantom skies.
We are a part of sad eternity.'
But he then honestly with flashing eyes
as if by grace and not the law replied:

'We are no stones. How could we speak of this
unvaried destiny if this were true?'
I did not listen to hypothesis
but watched his face where passion through and through
showed grace more varied than his reason knew,

a coiling of the spirit working there,
a human anguish of the beating soul,
and knew at last, had I not known before,
the struggle's what we live by, not the whole
unknown completion. I could humbly kneel

to such humanity predestined too,
noble behaviour of the best we are,
restless and proud, to abstract passion true.
Some world takes notice of the best and rare
as I of him, a passion of our star.

Johnson in the Highlands

A reasoning mind travels through this country.
In these sad wastes a Londoner by choice
sees water falling, and some meagre deer.

Examines with his tough reasoning mind
lochs, deer, and people: is not seduced
by Mrs Radcliffe's green hysteria

from a musical prose we've never once achieved,
whose fences cannot reach between the words
whose arguments are broken-backed with exile.

A classical sanity considers Skye.
A huge hard light falls across shifting hills.
This mind, contemptuous of miracles

and beggarly sentiment, illuminates
a healthy moderation. But I hear
like a native dog notes beyond his range

the modulations of a queer music
twisting his huge black body in the pain
that shook him also in raw blazing London.

Face of an Old Highland Woman

This face is not the Mona Lisa's
staring from a submarine
greenness of water. There's no grace
of any Renaissance on the skin

but rocks slowly thrust through earth
a map with the wind going over stone
beyond the mercies of Nazareth.
Here is the God of fist and bone

a complex twisted Testament
two eyes like lochs staring up
from heather gnarled by a bare wind
beyond the art and dance of Europe.

The Clearances

The thistles climb the thatch. Forever
this sharp scale in our poems,
as also the waste music of the sea.

The stars shine over Sutherland
in a cold ceilidh of their own,
as, in the morning, the silver cane

cropped among corn. We will remember this.
Though hate is evil we cannot
but hope your courtier's heels in hell

are burning: that to hear
the thatch sizzling in tanged smoke
your hot ears slowly learn.

'It is the old'

It is the old
who get up in the night to build the fires for the young.
Their gods, they imagine, are disposed
in a leisurely lazy heaven and prolong
a Norman sleep against the cold
and bitter frost.

And so they set
a delicate structure of sticks, enfolded in this
fear of their power, idolatry of their poise.
Not knowing in Saxon dawns how the abyss
their precarious tilt of sticks steadily lights
is what their boys

dread in their beds,
while dreaming of lords they can serve
of brilliance courage and wit.
Roads are built on each nerve –
Roman and servile and powerful. Their needs
point to the fire in the night.

At the Firth of Lorne

In the cold orange light we stared across
to Mull and Kerrera and far Tiree.
A setting sun emblazoned your bright knee
to a brilliant gold to match your hair's gold poise.

Nothing had changed: the world was as it was
a million years ago. The slaty stone
slept in its tinged and aboriginal iron.
The sky might flower a little, and the grass

perpetuate its sheep. But from the sea
the bare bleak islands rose, beyond the few
uneasy witticisms we let pursue
their desolate silences. There was no tree

nor other witness to the looks we gave
each other there, inhuman as if tolled
by some huge bell of iron and of gold,
I no great Adam and you no bright Eve.

The Law and the Grace

It's law they ask of me and not grace.
'Conform,' they say, 'your works are not enough.
Be what we say you should be' even if
graceful hypocrisy obscures my face.

'We know no angels. If you say you do
that's blasphemy and devilry.' Yet I have
known some bright angels, of spontaneous love.
Should I deny them, be to falsehood true,

the squeeze of law which has invented torture
to bring the grace to a malignant head?
Do you want me, angels, to be wholly dead?
Do you need, black devils, steadfastly to cure

life of itself? And you to stand beside
the stone you set on me? No, I have angels. Mine
are free and perfect. They have no design
on anyone else, but only on my pride

my insufficiency, imperfect works.
They often leave me but they sometimes come
to judge me to the core, till I am dumb.
Is this not law enough, you patriarchs?

Hume

More than this I do not love you,
Hume of the reasonable mind.
There was an otter crossed the sound,
a salmon in his cold teeth.

The mist came down. Between two capes
there was no road. There was a French
salon, an adoring wench.
He picked the salmon with his teeth.

Delicate Hume who swims through all
the daring firths of broken Scotland,
there were no roads across the land.
The causes, like old fences, yawned

gravely over wit and port.
Diplomacies are what displace
the inner law, the inner grace,
the Corrievreckan of bad art.

Rythm

They dunno how it is. I smack a ball
right through the goals. But they dunno how the words
get muddled in my head, get tired somehow.
I look through the window, see. And there's a wall
I'd kick the ball against, just smack and smack.
Old Jerry he can't play, he don't know how,
not now at any rate. He's too flicking small.
See him in shorts, out in the crazy black.
Rythm, he says, and ryme. See him at back.
He don't know nuthing about Law. He'd fall
flat on his face, just like a big sack,
when you're going down the wing, the wind behind you

and crossing into the goalmouth, and they're roaring
the whole great crowd. They're up on their feet cheering.
The ball's at your feet and there it goes, just crack.
Old Jerry dives – the wrong way. And they're jearing
and I run to the centre and old Bash
jumps up and down, and I feel great, and wearing
my gold and purpel strip, fresh from the wash.

Preparation for a Death

Have I seen death conquered at last in you
dying by inches, yet with lucid sight
examining its gains? The world was new
and sparkled with a gay Renaissance wit,

but now the Reformation has set in.
A narrow Luther hedges the red blood
and bellows from his pulpit like a pain.
The blossoming angels in their painted red

are withered into devils. All the pardons
are snatched inhospitably from your open wound
and nothing's left but a creeping host of sins
which you consider with a bleak mind

on the very edge of nothingness looking out,
like Drake going off beyond all human shores
and no Elizabeth to dub you knight
but mind itself to open its black doors.

Encounter in a School Corridor

Supposing today walking along this passage
in a flicker of gown Death were to turn and look
with his white skull face, raising his eyes from his book,
and I were to stare directly into that visage

which is almost over-learned and frightened too
as if to say: 'Surely not you as well.'
In this hygienic place without sound or smell
what would I, late cold Roman, say or do

but this perhaps: 'Always there was correction.
After the Fall, the careless summer leaves
must learn strict order, for the heart deceives
by wayward and incurious affection.

And the seasons always begin. There is no end
to the iron ring of law, the field of grace
whose shadows slant before the footballers.'
He then might show some pity as he turned

to face me down the dim-lit corridor
his arms so piled with books, face grained with thought,
and his slow legs remembering that riot
of flowering shadows and that youthful force.

To Forget the Dead

To forget the dead. How to forget the dead
when they slowly sigh, walking about the rooms
where we are lying, deep in a white bed.
How to forget that with discoloured arms

they are searching drawers for their property –
a favourite ribbon, book – while we lie still
under the bedclothes lest they hear us cry,
and stuffing sheets in our round mouths, till

we are the dead, swathed in our tight linen,
and those who leave no shadow in the glass
stand at the door a moment, but refrain
from touching our white gravestones as they pass.

The Chess Player

When the badness came he was playing chess again.
'Someone most dear to you,' they said, 'has died.'
He scouted round the board and picked the queen.
(What use are bishops, knights?) 'We found,' they cried,
'your brother dead. His wounds were in the side.'

'Not in the head?' he said, not looking up.
'In the head and heart as well,' they answered. He
moved the tall queen delicately as in hope
but the king escaped again. 'Did he say of me
anything hopeful?' he asked savagely,

moving a pawn, his head carved to the wood
the king was carved from. 'No,' they said. '"Please tell
my brother this. Tell him I've understood
a very little." That's what he told us.' 'Well,
the chessboard tells me what of heaven or hell

I need to know and that's too much,' he cried,
shifting the queen. (The king escaped again.)
He smiled a little with the jaunty pride
one sometimes notices in desperate men.
'You see,' he said, 'when you came in just then

I had a vision of that very board.
They do not know, you see, none of them knows.
They're all quite evidently so far apart.
What do they know of each other? I dispose –
but each is wooden, in archaic pose.'

And then they saw (each one standing beside
the terrible trivial wrestler) with a start
that someone most dear to him indeed had died,
and stared at him grappling with his mental art,
and carefully made ready to depart.

Envoi

Remember me when you come into your kingdom.
Remember me, beggar of mirrors, when you are confirmed
in the sleep of fulfilment on the white pillow.

Remember me who knock at the window,
who hirple on my collapsing stick, and know
the quivering northern lights of nerves.

Remember me in your good autumn.
I in my plates of frost go
among the falling crockery of hills

stones, plains, all falling and falling.
In my winter of the sick glass remember
me in your autumn, in your good sleep.

from THREE REGIONAL VOICES
(1968)

The Departing Island

Strange to see it – how as we lean over
this vague rail, the island goes away
into its loved light grown suddenly foreign:
how the ship slides outward like a cold ray
from a sun turned cloudy, and rough land draws down
into an abstract sea its arranged star.

Strange how it's like a dream when two waves past,
and the engine's hum puts villages out of mind
or shakes them together in a waving fashion.
The lights stream northward down a wolfish wind.
A pacing passenger wears the air of one
whom tender arms and fleshly hands embraced.

It's the island that goes away, not we who leave it.
Like an unbearable thought it sinks beyond
assiduous reasoning light and wringing hands,
or, as a flower roots deep into the ground,
it works its darkness into the gay winds
that blow about us in a later spirit.

Old Woman

Overwhelmed with kindnesses – and you have nothing.
They bring you roses to refresh their hearts
and still the bitter voices.
They greet you sweetly, you are now their child,
they flatter you completely,
and you have nothing to present to them
objects to objects, just your used self.

Only a god I think could take such gifts
and not feel hatred. Only a god could bear
such manifold penances, and be the vase
for all these guilty roses.

You are no god and therefore should you snap
suddenly out at them between old teeth
like a fox dying in a sweet country
I should not turn from that poor twisted face
bayed in its autumn by solicitous smiles.

Money-man Only

Money-man only, yes I pity you
the sea's incredible series being closed
to all but silver, though myself it pierces
with arrow after arrow in my ring
defended as King James by Scottish fighting.

But you, on your gold rails, I pity
since never yet under the painful waves
of fire and salt have you descended
under the needles weaving hopeful blue.
I pity your mean suit, and pity you –

who in my psalms unchristian speak aloud
of the busy lilies in their yellowness
and innocent harmlessness in rough air.
Your head is of a narrowness too clear
for me in my hot cauldron to bear.

To slide your car along a riven road
towards a house of the entire silver
and a wife yapping from her glass kingdom –
this I think is treachery to our kind.
I excommunicate you from my undesigned

church of the crooked spire, the scrawled pane,
the minister wearing his clown's cloak,
the uncertain affirmations of my choir.
You own a grave I would not dare to share.
I know no crime graver than not to care.

Returning Exile

Home he came after Canada
where for many years he drank
his failure into the ground.
Westward lay Lewis. He never wrote.
The snow needs a gay pen.
However at the age of fifty-five
he put on his hat, his painted tie,
and packed his trunk (being just alive).
Quietly he sailed over waters
which made him cry secretly by rails
through which he saw his home all green
and salmon leaping between deer's horns.
Arrived home he attended church
(the watch chain snaking his waistcoat).
None was as black or stiff as he.
He cast his bottles into outer darkness

where someone gnashed his teeth
each evening by the quay
watching the great ship sail out
with the girls laughing
the crew in white
and the bar mazy with mirrors.

Some called her SS Remorse
others the bad ship Envy.

She Teaches Lear

Much to have given up? Martyr, one says?
And to read *Lear* to these condemning ones
in their striped scarves and ties but, in the heart,
tall, cool and definite. Naval, in this art.
'Brought it on himself. He ran away,
then strained to keep his pomp and circumstance.'

Of course it's true. Much to be said for Regan,
Goneril too. Cordelia just a tune,
and also beautiful as I am not.
'Life must be lived. Life is beyond thought.
These two were living.' Who says that? It's Brown.
The smallest one (with glasses) in the room.

So I go home towards his bitterness,
achieved selfishness, clinging so with claws
to chair and pipe, a dreadful bitter man.
He hates all life, yet lives. Helpless in pain,
trains pain on others. 'Pray', at night he says,
'undo this button', and yet hates, for this,

me out of helplessness. And yet I stay.
'Regan and Goneril had some place to go.'
('Some*where*.' Correct this young American.)
Which side is right? For there is young pale Jean –
she might be one. Responsibility
is weighty, living, in the to-and-fro

of these cool deadly judgments. So she listens
the true Cordelia, library-white face,
thin-boned and spectacled, speechlessly unhappy
and ready for all art, especially poetry.
'They had some place to go and pure passions.
The rest's hypocrisy.' Purity of the race?

No, not as far as that. Simply a lie,
to live and feed with one so selfish grown,
as age is always selfish. The proud two
spur their tall horses into the bright blue
in search of lust, are willing so to die,
the absolute hunters, Goneril and Regan,

beautiful too with their own spare beauty
when one forgets the haunted piteous fox
(there's always a fox whenever such ride by).
Does Jean, as I do, sniff it? Memory
of dear addictive fences, of the high
tall splendid brutes, past little dreaming flocks.

And yet… More simply: They are what they are,
I am what I am? The sensitive eye
broods by packed windows of interior pain
fastened to writhings, knowing rages mean
often unhappiness, that old men wear
their stubborn angers out of dignity

the failing vigour – eyes, arms, knees.
Gravity pulls them down into the ground.
Last angers blossom on its final lip.
'Lear is a child', I hear. Is this the deep
Greek brilliant irony? I find my peace
in this dictator because I have no kind

child to nourish? No, it's not quite that.
'We'll come to this', I cry. 'No', Moira says,
quite definite and calm. 'If I should come
to such a state, let all drive me from home.'
Easy enough, I think, (but hold the thought)
to speak such words when interested praise

makes your face happy at the Saturday
school-club dance, in yellow, and a hand
glides down your bare arm, it seems forever.
Why should I speak this loud, my own fever?
And then I know it's right as far's mind may
(without sly falsity) hope to understand.

'It's just in case', I say, 'In case, malformed'
(how vulnerable ties and scarves, how pure!)
'by living we are made. It's just in case' –
the need, the need! – Polite and curious
they know of no such need (but Jean). Not armed
nor yet disarmed they sit. Sure or unsure

it hasn't touched them yet, the fear of age.
Regan and Goneril seem more natural.
From our own weakness only are we kind.
Admire such ones but know in your own mind
how they would bring upon us innocent carnage,
the end of Lear, and *Lear,* their own worse will.

from FROM BOURGEOIS LAND
(1969)

Entering Your House

Entering your house, I sniff again
the Free Church air, the pictures on the wall
of ministers in collars, all these dull
acres of brown paint, the chairs half seen
in dim sad corners by the sacred hall

under the spread antlers of that head
mildly gazing above leathern tomes.
So many draperies in so many rooms.
So many coverlets on each heavy bed.
A stagnant green perpetuates these glooms.

And then the stairs. The ancient lamps and the
scent of old prayers, texts of 'God is Love'.
Did any children grow through all this grief?
The ceilings seem to sigh, the floor to be
carpeted by a threadbare dim belief.

Such pressures on the head. And then I see
in an oval frame an eighteen-year-old girl
like Emily Brontë staring from the peril
of commandments breaking round her. And I pray
that she was happy, curl on winding curl,

even though I see the stains around her face,
the ancient tints of brown that eat at brow
and hair and nose, and make me see her now
as almost rusted in this world of grace.
How little beauty conscious sins allow!

I enter the great garden with its red
and dripping roses, laburnums and the tall
tulips and the columbines, the small
and holy Rose of Sharon. All the dead
are lost in colour as the dewdrops fall.

I watch a bee nuzzling from tower to tower
of brilliant yellow, each with soundless bell,
its hairy body busy in the smell
and light of evening. From flower to flower
it flies and sucks, quivers, then is still,

so gross and purposeful I can forget
the tall and simple flowers it feeds on here
in this bright garden of a freer air.
pray that she, some gross and fruitful night,
under less heavy coverlets as bare

as these tall flowers, allowed new life to start
from her body's honey, turning to the wall
that portrait of her father, stern and tall.
And that the Rose of Sharon at her heart
quivered and quietened in her radiant fall.

Hamlet

Sick of the place, he turned him towards night.
The mirrors flashed distorted images
of himself in court dress, with big bulbous eyes,
and curtains swaying in a greenish light.

Save me from these, he cried, I could not kill.
I did not have the true and pure belief
even to marry, reproduce myself
in finite mirrors, tall and visible.

Bad jokes and speeches, I endured them all,
so therefore let my death be a bad joke.
I see in the warped mirrors rapiers shake
their subtle poisons perfuming the hall

reflecting accidents, a circus merely,
a place of mirrors, an absurd conclusion.
Images bounce madly against reason
as, in a spoon, wide pictures, fat and jolly.

I could not kill, but let them have their deaths
imprisoned in this air in which they perish
where only lies and ponderous jokes can flourish

Remove the mirror, for there is no breath.

Epitaph

This is the Law. What you love best you get.
Position on the Council if you wish it.
Enough money never to be in debt
and to attract if not repay a visit.
Because your honour is most firmly set
in every action no one will dismiss it,
and lastly, when you die, they'll not forget
to buy a hasty wreath for your deposit.

If you had wanted greatness you'd have got it.
At least I suppose you would for some still do,
(especially the ones who most have sought it).
And when one thinks of you, so gross, untrue,
and then of failures from real greatness parted,
why then they wished it less than smallness you.

'It was the heavy jokes'

It was the heavy jokes, the dreadful jokes,
the pewter-coloured jokes that drove you mad.

It was these jokes, the ornaments of zero,
the squat sad china made you die of shame.

It was the jokes that know no airiness,
immune to seasons, drove you to your knees.

It was the spoon-faced jokes, the Hall of Mirrors,
the circus air that made your speech opaque.

It was the flat-faced men with silver borders
of gold and silver made you live in fire.

It was their speeches robbed you of your speech
and caused pure silence to reflect your love.

The guns with crooked sights brought no reward
but pewter plates and a dishonoured word,

a doll shaped like Ophelia and a vase
vulgar as kings, as Claudius obese.

In Youth

In youth to have mocked the pompous and shot down
these busy cruisers from an infinite sky
was such a sport as good as wittily
to shoot bon-mots at films. It seemed the moon
and the raw air justified utterly

all brilliance, all scorn of fat proud men,
pursing their names from newspapers, on stages
trapped by the fierceness of our tingling rages,
for after all they could not know of pain
but lived on vanity and subterfuges.

To think that, pelted by our quick depth charges,
zigzagging and crisscrossing in that sea,
they should survive, should cruise eternally
was not within our thought, for all the ages
had taught us surely that the boring die

and that the salon is the lasting room.
But that it isn't so our mirrors tell,
preparing early an inscrutable
face to outface the daytime and our shame,
and thinking too we'd have been capable

of the wittiest deeds if these had not before us
walked with the same grave pace as we do now
in self-protection from the gangs who prowl
mindlessly our actions in slow chorus,
foes of those burdened by 'the true and real'.

The Wind Roars

The wind roars. Thousands of miles it came
from Biafra or Vietnam. I lift my spoon
and see in it faces without hope or name.

I lift my spoon and lay it down again.
The mouth works forward. The high wind's a drum
lashing my body into fog and rain.

It is a dream, I cry, it is a dream.
The mouth breaks on the spoon with frenzied gum.

Young Girl Singing Psalm

Just for a moment then as you raised your book –
it must have been the way your glasses looked

above the round red cheeks – as you poured out
the psalm's grim music from a pulsing throat,

that moment, as I say, I saw you stand
thirty years hence, the hymn book in your hand,

a fleshy matron who are now sixteen.
The skin is coarser, you are less serene.

What now is fervour is pure habit then.
To bridge devoted and to thought immune,

a connoisseur of flowers and sales of work,
you cycle through round noons where no sins lurk,

your large pink hat a garden round your head,
the cosy wheel of comfort and of God.

And, as I see you, matron of that day,
I wonder, girl, which is the better way –

in innocent fervour tackling antique verse,
or pink Persephone, innocently coarse.

At the Sale

Old beds, old chairs, old mattresses, old books,
old pictures of coiffed women, hatted men,
ministers with clamped lips and flowing beards,
a Duke in his Highland den,
and, scattered among these, old copper fire-guards,
stone water-bottles, stoves and shepherds' crooks.

How much goes out of fashion and how soon!
The double-columned leather-covered tomes
recall those praying Covenanters still
adamant against Rome's
adamant empire. Every article
is soaked in time and dust and sweat and rust. What tune

warbled from that phonograph? Who played
that gap-toothed dumb piano? Who once moved
with that white chamber pot through an ancient room?
And who was it that loved
to see her own reflection in the gloom
of that webbed mirror? And who was it that prayed

holding that Bible in her fading hands?
The auctioneer's quick eyes swoop on a glance,
a half-seen movement. In the inner ring
a boy in serious stance
holds up a fan, a piece of curtaining,
an hour-glass with its trickle of old sand.

We walk around and find an old machine.
On one side pump, on another turn a wheel.
But nothing happens. What's this object for?
Imagine how we will
endlessly pump and turn for forty years
and then receive a pension, smart and clean,

climbing a dais to such loud applause
as shakes the hall for toiling without fail
at this strange nameless gadget, pumping, turning,
each day oiling the wheel
with zeal and eagerness and freshness burning
in a happy country of anonymous laws,

while the ghostly hands are clapping and the chairs
grow older as we look, the pictures fade,
the stone is changed to rubber, and the wheel
elaborates its rayed
brilliance and complexity and we feel
the spade become a scoop, cropping the grass,

and the flesh itself becomes unnecessary.
O hold me, love, in this appalling place.
Let your hand stay me by this mattress here
and this tall ruined glass,
by this dismembered radio, this queer
machine that waits and has no history.

'More than twenty years ago'

More than twenty years ago you heard it
in a far desert tantalisingly floated

towards your tanks and tents that drifted white
in that voluminous gritty skin of light –

'Lili Marlene' in German. By a gate
standing in whorish raincoat, cigarette

dangling eternally from the schoolgirl lips
she waits in lamplight while the guard half sleeps

leaning on his rifle. Now she snores
beside you in your terrace house. There roars

a car accelerating and on the ceiling
its lights converge and cross, a searchlight feeling

for some invisible enemy. In its cot
your swathed child sleeps, so vulnerably white,

the moonlight on its skull, a small thin dome.
A helmeted Junker thunders round your home.

The umbrella collapses on pearl-headed sticks
and blooms at morning to a tent. What tricks

that belly dancer had! How cool mess tins
in these barbaric Mediterranean dawns!

And, late at night, that taunting German voice.
Oh, how you miss it, tense with tenderness

among the bowler hats, the frozen *Times*,
Lili Marlene the schoolgirl of sweet rhymes

standing forever in her raincoat near
the fading lamps of martial leather gear

now rotting as you watch another dawn
reveal your wife camped in her flesh and bone

and, faintly past the lawn so flat and green,
a mocking voice that sings 'Auf Wiedersehen'.

'I take it from you'

I take it from you — small token of esteem —
this ponderous watch that holds a soundless scream

and give you back — a gift that haunts your sky —
the howling faces of eternity.

'To hell with this poetry reading'

To hell with this poetry reading, he cried —
your faces that are clocks within my side —

It's you my works supposed to be attacking
so why in God's name don't you cease your clapping?

'What's your Success?'

What's your Success to me who read the great dead,
whose marble faces, consistent overhead,

outstare my verse? What are your chains to me,
your baubles and your rings? That scrutiny

turns on me always. Over terraced houses
these satellites rotate and in deep spaces

the hammered poetry of Dante turns
light as a wristwatch, bright as a thousand suns.

'Children, follow the dwarfs'

Children, follow the dwarfs and the giants and the wolves,
into the Wood of Unknowing, into the leaves

where the terrible granny perches and sings to herself
past the tumultuous seasons high on her shelf.

Do not go with the Man with the Smiling Face,
nor yet with the Lady with the Flowery Dress.

Avoid the Crystal, run where the waters go
and follow them past the Icebergs and the Snow.

Avoid the Man with the Book, the Speech Machine,
and the Rinsoed Boy who is forever clean.

Keep clear of the Scholar and the domestic Dog
and, rather than Sunny Smoothness, choose the Fog.

Follow your love, the butterfly, where it spins
over the wall, the hedge, the road, the fence,

and love the Disordered Man who sings like a river
whose form is Love, whose country is Forever.

BEN DORAIN

(1969)

Translated from the Gaelic of Duncan Ban Macintyre

The movement of the poem is based on pibroch: 'Urlar', 'Siubhal' and 'Crunluath'
represent different speeds or tempi or variations.

1

URLAR

Honour past all bens
to Ben Dorain.
Of all beneath the sun
I adore her.

Mountain ranges clear,
Storehouse of the deer,
the radiance of the moor
I've observed there.

Leafy branchy groves,
woods where the grass grows,
inquisitive the does
that are roaming there.

Herds with white rumps race –
hunters in the chase.
O I love the grace
of these noble ones.

Spirited and delicate
and shy,
in fashionable coat
he goes by

in mantle well arrayed,
suit that will not fade,
dress of waxen-red
that he's wearing now.

Weapon that brings death,
bullet that stops breath,
expert studied youth
with his rifle there.

Flint that's notched and true,
on its head a screw,
a cock that would strike to
the hammers, it.

Eight sided, without flaw,
gun-stock would lay low
the great stag in the flow
of his own blood there.
One whose craft was dear –
Mozart of them –
would kill them with a pure
trick and stratagem.

One would find such men –
Patrick in the glen –
boys and dogs at one,
and he'd order them.

Bullets left and right,
fires creating light,
the hind on mountain height
gets its wound from them.

2

SIUBHAL

The hind that's sharp-headed
is fierce in its speeding:
how delicate, rapid,
its nostrils, wind-reading!
Light-hooved and quick limbèd,
she runs on the summit,

from that uppermost limit
no gun will remove her.
You'll not see her winded,
that elegant mover.

Her forebears were healthy.
When she stopped to take breath then,
how I loved the pure wraith-like

sound of her calling,
she seeking her sweetheart
in the lust of the morning.

It's the stag, the proud roarer,
white-rumped and ferocious,
branch-antlered and noble,
would walk in the shaded
retreats of Ben Dorain,
so haughtily-headed.

O they are in Ben Dorain,
so numerous, various,
the stags that go roaring
so tall and imperious.

Hind, nimble and slender,
with her calves strung behind her
lightly ascending
the cool mountain passes
through Harper's Dell winding
on their elegant courses.

Accelerant, speedy,
when she moves her slim body
earth knows nought of this lady
but the tips of her nails.
Even light would be tardy
to the flash of her pulse.

Dynamic, erratic,
by greenery spinning,
this troupe never static,
their minds free from sinning.

Coquettes of the body,
slim-leggèd and ready,
no age makes them tardy,
no grief nor disease.

Their coats get their shimmer –
fat flesh of their glamour –
from their local rich summer
in the store of the moor.

With pleasure abiding
in the pasture providing
– like milk for our children –
fresh grass from the heath.

Calves speckled and spotted,
unchilled by the showers,
are nursed by the rooted
gay, various grass.

Brindled, bright-hoovèd,
white-belted and vivid
as cinders quick-moving,
with the health of spring waters,
uncomplaining, belovèd –
these elegant daughters!

Though the snow should bewilder
they'll be seeking no shelter
except in the Corrie –
other dwelling disdaining.

Among banks and steep columns
and hollows mysterious
they'd bed by the solemn
Haunt of the Fairies.

3

URLAR

Pleasant to me rising
at morning
to see them the horizon
adorning.

Seeing them so clear,
my simple-headed deer
modestly appear
in their joyousness.

They freely exercise
their sweet and level cries.
From bodies trim and terse,
hear their bellowing.

A badger of a hind
wallows in a pond.
Her capricious mind
has such vagaries!

How they fill the parish
with their chorus
sweeter than fine Irish
tunes glorious.

More tuneful than all art
the music of the hart
eloquent, alert,
on Ben Dorain.

The stag with his own call
struck from his breast wall –
you'll hear him mile on mile
at his scale-making.

The sweet harmonious hind –
with her calf behind –
elaborates the wind
with her music.

Palpitant bright eye
without squint in it.
Lash below the brow,
guide and regulant.

Walker, quick and grave,
so elegant to move
ahead of that great drove
when accelerant.

There's no flaw in your step,
there's all law in your leap,
there's no rust or sleep
in your motion there.

Lengthening your stride,
intent on what's ahead,
who of live or dead
could outrace you?

The hind is on the heath
where she ought to be.
Her delicate sweet mouth
feeding tenderly.

Stool-bent and sweet grass
the finest food there is
that puts fat and grease
on her flanks and sides.

Transparent springs that nurse
the modest water cress –
no foreign wines surpass
these as drink for her.

Sorrel grass and sedge
that grow on heath and ridge,
these are what you judge
as hors d'oeuvres for you.

Luxuries for does
between grasses,
St John's wort, the primrose,
and daisies.

The spotted water-cress
with forked and spiky gloss;
water where it grows
so abundantly.

This is the good food
that animates their blood
and circulates as bread
in hard famine-time.

That would fatten their
bodies to a clear
shimmer, rich and rare,
without clumsiness.

That was the neat herd
in the twilight
suave and trim, unblurred
in that violet!

However long the night
you would be safe and right
snug at the hill's foot
till the morning came.

The herds of the neat deer
are where they always were
on the wide kind moor
and the heathland.

When colour changed their skins
my love was most intense.
They came not by mischance
to Ben Dorain.

4

SIUBHAL

Luxuriant mountain
sprouting and knolled
more healthy and cloudless
than all hills in the world.

How long my obsession!
My song and my passion!
She's the first in the nation
for grace and for beauty.

Her gifts are so many,
her fruits are so bonny,
and rarer than any
her bushes and leafage

in flawless green raiment
as bright as the diamond
your blooms in agreement
like elegant music.

The cock with his vital
and rapid recital,
colourful, brutal,
among the small birds.

The buck small and nimble
quick on the green
neat as a thimble –
a clever machine!

Bright-hooved in the weather,
as light as a feather,
among moorland and heather
exploring the corrie
he saunters forever
through bracken and story

along by each river
on the height of each hillock
playful and vivid
eel-like, elusive.

When he's startled to motion
he's as swift as your vision
with speed and precision
he speeds through each forest
without seeming exertion
he's nearest, then furthest!

In the autumn-hued landscape
he skips in his gallop
each second brown hillock
as he's greeting his sweetheart.

His small doe is dwelling
with the fawns in a corrie:
sullen and snarling
she guards them with fury:
sharp ear cocked for hearing,
quick eye ever peering,
she relies on the veering
quick tricks of her motion.

Though Caoilt and Cuchulain
are expert and nimble
and every battalion
King George can assemble

if the flash and the bullet
would leave her unsullied
no man on this planet
would catch her or find her:
just like the minute
and brilliant cinder.

White-tailed and lightning-like
though hunting dogs can frighten her –
steep though the height to her
you'll not see her blunder.
Haughty and spritely she's
a head-tossing wonder!

Sharp-eyed, disdainful,
restless and wary,
her home is the corrie
along with her neighbours.

5

URLAR

Volatile the hind
among saplings,
cropping the young plants,
the slim stripling.

Tender leaves or heather
are her caviare,
delicacies rare
without flaw in them.

Manners mild and light,
gay and clear and bright,
O my lovely idiot,
so carefree!

Elegant of style
modestly to dwell
in the greenest dell
most luxuriant.

Often she will frolic
by Creag Mòr.
Week-days are idyllic –
Sundays too.

There she would sleep sound
the bushes all around
breaking the north wind
and protecting her.

In the Doire Chrò
sheltered by the Nose
among caves and hollows
and the spring blossom.

Transparent water's brew
plentiful and new
is tastier to you
than beer is.

Mountain springs refine
her agility –
she learns from this green glen
no debility.

By stratagem and trick
elegant and quick
she'd elude the pack
that was hunting her.

In yellow and in red
the flickering bright bride
so variously bred
of good character.

Indifferent to chill:
in speed incomparable
in Europe who can tell
of an equal to her?

6

SIUBHAL

That troupe was beloved
assembling in order –
ascending, bright-hooved,
each cliff that's in nature.

Between the Poor Pasture
and the Corrie of Fastness –
not buying repast there
but eating it freely.

Beside Corrie Rannoch
by the flank of the Bealach
by the Field of the Calder
and round by the Dog Mead –
on the shanks of the headland
the roguish brigade there.

By the Feinne's location
they'd take their position
in the Crag of the Willows
untroubled secure.

Their love and their pleasure
to parade on the level
being sportive and civil
like frolicsome soldiers.

In mud-bogs and marshes
playfully fussing
in happy caressing
and daft exultation.

Their tongues without dryness –
From Annat Burn's clearness
sweeter than honey's
that delicate water.

White honey of nature –
it flows to the future –
than cinnamon sweeter
and common to all.

Eternal bright blessing
from the earth it's uprising –
it doesn't need pricing,
you can drink it quite freely!

This luminous water –
which provides her with nurture –
is found in the quarter
which finds me in Europe,

so clear and so active
so pure and creative
with innocent motive –
not suited to tavern,

with delicate eddies
in the gloom of the cresses
ringed by cold mosses
of species so various.

Elegant civil
(as it winds through the gravel)
in its sinuous travel
down the back of Ben Dorain.

One side of the landslope's
bright and delightful
and the Deer-forest's landscape
causes eyes to be grateful.

Precipitous, hilly,
with hollow and valley,
ruffled and knolly,
mountainous, hairy:
Clustered and furry
tufted and curly.

Paths daunting and rugged
with shaggy grass jaggèd
I could easily brag of
the pleasure I taste there.
Belled, budded, bright twiggèd,
not haggard, that pasture.

With the rosy clean darnel
and the grass of rich kernel
the wood has a vernal
and suited behaviour.

7

URLAR

The wide and empty moor
with its hollows.
The Corrie of the Heather
gives me solace.

That's the gentle soil
of a laughing style.
Calves and stags beguile
with their sauntering.

Warm against the sun
sheltered and immune
the pretty hind remains
here with willingness.

Consort of the tall
stag of haughty style.
Their union is not legal –
unclerical!

Her body's whole and clean,
she's modest in her mien,
she's not a brazen queen
but is maidenly.

The corrie has entranced
every boy whom
nature ever chanced
to employ there.

Whistling to the hounds
the hunters wake the winds
gathering for hunts
in their companies

On the rising braes
where the deer would graze –
in a bright red blaze
they'd assemble there.

Full of finest food
abundant as the dew
wild raspberries exude
and wet rose-blossoms.

The fish are never sparse
in her streams –
stalking them with flares
as in dreams!

A narrow fishing spear.
Yew-made is the gear
that the fishers bear
in their hunting.

Merry was the leap
of trout in torrent steep
sniffing at the trap
of the surface flies.

There's no sea or wood
has more plenitude
of various good food
than your boundaries.

8

AN CRUNLUATH

When the hind is in this solitude
O ignorant the stalker
who (untrained, unpractised) would
seek to find or take her.

Cautiously and stealthily
prudently and perfectly
wisely, with such delicacy –
else she will evade him!

Every pit and shallow he
must deploy to follow her
every stone and hollow and
cloud-shade to aid him.

Gently he will creep and edge
Using every subterfuge
till he traps her in her lodge
by excelling cunning

with judgment and carefulness
he'll bring his gun to bear on her
she's fixed in that gold radiance
in her aloof hauteur.

His finger on the trigger
he watches her fixed figure –
exactitude and rigour
are what his training's taught him.

A gun flint – and he's tightened it –
hammers that would strike to it –
the powder always will ignite
for the experienced stalker.

The powder dry and virulent
behind the rags of tow or lint
would soon create a violent
hailstone of small fire.

O what more zealous messenger?
What Mercury more fatal?
How lightning-like this passenger
that pierces to the vital!

Bleeding from that armament
the deer of finest lineament
whose bodies are an ornament
to the health-giving moorland.

The army of the Willow Crag
(so arrogant in monologue)
will not for man or gun or dog
be driven from their homeland.

Unless subdued and mastered there
by dogs that fill the pasture there
with the barks that bring disaster and
grief and death in chorus.

The music then diminishing
as the dogs close to finish her
– she frenzied 'mong these sinister
assassins of the morning.

A pleasure for professionals
ingenious in stalking
to be about the passes when
sport was for the taking.

When the deer were bellowing
and the men were following
and the light was yellow and
red in its explosion.

With dog that's quick, discriminate
– his tail alert and animate –
tonguing, whining, dynamite
vigorous and joyful.

Assassin, fierce and serious,
courageous and imperious
single (and not various)
in the art that is his own.

His hackles rising, bristling,
sandy, shag-browed, vicious,
he quivers like a species
of animated Murder.

Erratic was the veering then
and rapid in its motion
when they would go sheering on
short cuts with exertion.

Tumultuous the baying and
echo of the crying as
the hairy-coated violent
dogs would show their paces.

Driving them from summits to
lakes that are unplumbable
bleeding dying swimming and
floundering in water.

Hounds hanging to their quarries while
they sway and toss and rock and kill –
their jaws will never let them feel
their haughty style again.

The little that I've sung of them
is not enough to tell of them
O you'd need a tongue for them
of a most complex kind.

from LINES REVIEW
(1969)

Old Woman with Flowers

These are your flowers. They were given to you
so nurse them carefully and tenderly.
Though flowers grow freely elsewhere, here in this room
there's not much space, so therefore like a child
let no one else go near them.
                           O dear God
wherever you are, I am almost driven wild
by your frightening flowers whose blossoms are turned to bone
for an old woman to look at, in a small room alone.

Glasgow

City, cauldron of a shapeless fire,
bubbling with brash Irish and a future

that stares from fifteen stories towards the Clyde.
The cotton and tobacco plants have died,

Plantation St is withered. You love your ships,
hate your police, in whisky-coloured sleeps

adore your footballers. Victoria's not amused
at Celtic Park or Ibrox where the horsed

dice-capped policemen, seared by pure flame,
trot in white gauntlets round your serious game

and the roaring furnaces bank your last pride.
They shed the rotting tenements flying goalward.

The House We Lived In

The house we lived in for five years
in slummy Dumbarton
was almost falling down.
Everything had a padlock and chain.

Above us were fights each night.
Chairs broken like matches
and the wife sporting a black eye.
'I slipped' – defiantly.

Every Friday night
her husband would doll himself
by the one rayed mirror
in his suit sharp as a razor.

Every Friday night
he'd be beaten up
by swarming Catholics
for cursing the good Pope

robed in his Vatican
under the Italian blue
and far from the hubbub
of that fierce provincial pub.

Every Saturday morning
her blacked eye would shine
like a new sin
in her unvanquished face.

Scrubbing the marble cinema steps…
her husband strolling by
unemployed and spry
wearing his blue suit

with the blood scrubbed away.
Nothing green, I remember,
but for the innocent eyes
calm and murderous.

Return to the Council House

Box on box, on ledge after ledge rising
I used at midnight to come home
to your uniform sparkle on a bare hill,
my Rome of the clamped mussels.

O Rome, city of the wolves,
in what office did a man sit
among diminished clarities
designing you with a rigid appetite?

Under crown after crown of neon light
I approached you, the Yale in my hand,
as to an alien island
whirling in the blue sky of TV

and the wife hoarding her plot
her little handkerchief of green,
where the mower lay on its side
and she had her day for the washing.

From the scarred bus shelter I climbed
to my Rome of fixed lines.
The pad of the wolves is tense
among the chequered shadows,

the drift of figures in the blue caves,
the writing on the wall,
the stone steps in their spiral,
from room to room the same.

School Sports, at the Turnstiles

This is impossible. Though I know
(and have been told) the world's absurdity
(a dewdrop poised on nothing,
a zero
containing continually our comic seething)

and though all day wearily I've watched the flags
droop a little lower and heard money
clink at the long strides of young runners
negotiating curves in the uninteresting
way sports have, of having no ceasing,

yet suddenly I cheered as in the twilight
over the soaking ground the last came running
stretching for a prize they might not have
for more than a moment, as if somehow coming home
could be like this, a proud and hopeful yearning.

Mr M.

O how Mr M.'s Latin gown
frothed after him like a boat in water.

Raised on grammar, he flushed from these woods
not pheasants but Aeneas and the rest

dressed in the supine and infinitive
ghosts of words, ghosts of innocence, language
beautiful, tough, persistent.

Caesar and the ablative absolute together
harrying barbarous tribes.
The Roman roads undeviating as
an arrow or a sword.

And the wooden desks cut with knives.
Names of children deep in knotted fields
buried like Roman legions.

These fought their own battles
in the lavatories of weeping stone.
Under the taps, inverted heads
sucked at their cold fountains.

And today the holiday planes
ferry them to Italy
on cheap excursions to effeminate
wine and flowering music.

O that school where we were young,
the order's broken. We visit its old stones,
dishonoured consuls visiting Hades
(green field and ponderous doors)

but there are only ghosts there now.
We clutch your ghostly gown like Orpheus
clutching at Eurydice while Pluto
giggles on iron coins.

In the Classics Room

In summer how lovely the girls are
     here where Virgil is king of the walk,

where the hooded owl eyes have brooded all winter
on a text, a lacuna, a gap in a line
where the power is undischarged

and the dusty bulbs swung metrically in a draught
blowing in from the Western Sea.

How easy it was to forget them, the girls,
how easy to believe they were only dresses,
satchels, hollow heads to be filled with poetry.

Now it is they themselves who fill with poetry
brimming each day with more and more of their wine.

O Dido, in your pillar of fire
excessively burning in Carthage,
who is this Aeneas whose wood has grown subtle

who is this Roman whose glasses reflect your fire
whose legs twitch uncontrollably like an infant's
whose book shakes like a leaf?

Hear us, O Lord

Hear us, O Lord. Aggression is part of us.
You polish your jewellery in the salons of heaven.
Everything about you glitters, your wristwatch, the diamond
at your invisible breast, below your invisible beard.

We are such ferocious animals, Lord, we're irrational.
The long journey of the lizard was propelled by this
to the green jaguar standing in the driveway.
As you polish your nails, we begin to hate you.

All those who tell us the truth we hate.
All those who were strong – like Hitler and Stalin – we loved.
We are obsessed by the table with the green light on it.
We practise with knives in the boudoir and the church.

Ah, if it were only a game. But all things happen.
Because we have spoken too much, a heaven has fallen.
Because we have loved too much, a door has been slammed.
We stare at the light of Envy, green in the night.

What should we do to be saved? The screen slowly brightens.
You watch us with interest, a glass of pale wine in your hand.

'The things that they do, the plays that my actors perform.'

We keep you alive in the silence, in an absence of angels.

Homage to George Orwell

1

You knew well in advance
of the rest of us what's true –
that you can't look at a rose
without seeing a Fascist
with his closed red fist.
That the hazy hills
around us every day
are the hills of Spain
where the dry olives
patter into graves.
That 'concentration' means,
among other things,
concentration camps.
And that over the leaves
of your loose notebook
not the light of the lamp
only, but the two
yellow eyes of the sick
Deutschland, the paranoic
warmly-feathered gauleiter,
burning brighter and brighter
nightly on your cottage
implacably perpend.

2

In my little house
on a distant island
I used to scribble poems
on an oil-skinned table.
But I didn't know
what I've learnt to know –
what inhuman pressures
keep a line of verse

on its own course.
How a cult of slaves
kept in their fixed place
the elaborated lines
of a Greek vase.

3

Lorca falls
with the poem in front of his face
riddled with holes.
Cloaks like playing cards
turn away
across Spain,
a green piece
in a jigsaw.
He falls
deep in the scarred earth,
a lift plunging.
Now he rises
Inside the golden box
he plays his proud guitar.

4

The pack surround him,
Jacks, kings and queens.
Spades dig in the green
earth. Clubs
fall out of the air.
Hearts turn small, fear
makes the bright diamonds shrink.
The pack falls
on a green table
under green hands.
His face, part shade, part light,
holds its hauteur

carving the future
like a prow.
Outside,
the gipsy music invigorates his mask.
Rectangular cloaks retain
pistols and holsters.
Under a yellow moon
bodies put off their gear,
are fish in the silver pools,
are silver reeds,
are gipsies
telling his fortune.

5

Lorca goes marching underground
with his phosphorescent guitar.
He strolls into a bar
and the peasants gather round.

His breast is full of holes
and all that music
sets his white shirt dancing
just like so many souls

all divided, all united,
by the bullet holes.

from *Transparencies*
A Sequence

1

Does the Renaissance
mean red pictures?
Or a brute snake
casting its skin?
Or a child in
perfect amazement blowing
purple bubbles
and trying
to clutch them?

2

In the evening
the sea seems to come home:
after its great adventures
it speaks quietly
with a spare force.

3

I would love
to write
a 'great' poem,
big as the Cuillins.
Instead,

I sniff a yellow rose,
a great yellow
bourgeois
garden
rose.

And I stick a
carnation in my
buttonhole.
Deep red inside,
pink outside.

I thrust my cuffs out.
They are like the blur
of autumn
at the edge of a
leaf.

4

My name
is
Miss Twiss.

I like
biographies.

I speak
in a loud
tremulous
voice.

I admire
fierceness.

I want
to be neat
with a rose
at my throat.

Today
I walked down the road
with my dog on his lead.

Someone was burning
rubbish
in a garden.
There was a nasty tang
from the smoke.

They should stop that.

They should stop that
at once.

Shall Gaelic Die?

1

A picture has no grammar. It has neither evil nor good. It has only
colour, say orange or mauve.
Can Picasso change a minister? Did he make a sermon to a bull?
Did heaven rise from his brush? Who saw a church that is orange?
In a world like a picture, a world without language, would your mind
go astray, lost among objects?

2

Advertisements in neon, lighting and going out, 'Shall it…
shall it… Shall Gaelic… shall it… shall Gaelic… die?'

3

Words rise out of the country. They are around us. In every month in
the year we are surrounded by words.
Spring has its own dictionary, its leaves are turning in the sharp wind
of March, which opens the shops.
Autumn has its own dictionary, the brown words lying on the bottom

of the loch, asleep for a season.

Winter has its own dictionary, the words are a blizzard building a tower of Babel. Its grammar is like snow.

Between the words the wild-cat looks sharply across a No-Man's-Land, artillery of the Imagination.

4

They built a house with stones. They put windows in the house, and doors. They filled the room with furniture and the beards of thistles.

They looked out of the house on a Highland world, the flowers, the glens, distant Glasgow on fire.

They built a barometer of history.

Inch after inch, they suffered the stings of suffering.

Strangers entered the house, and they left.

But now, who is looking out with an altered gaze? What does he see? What has he got in his hand? A string of words.

5

He who loses his language loses his world. The Highlander who loses his language loses his world.

The space ship that goes astray among planets loses the world.

In an orange world how would you know orange? In a world without evil how would you know good?

Wittgenstein is in the middle of his world. He is like a spider.

The flies come to him. 'Cuan' and 'coill' rising.

When Wittgenstein dies, his world dies.

The thistle bends to the earth. The earth is tired of it.

6

I came with a 'sobhrach' in my mouth. He came with a 'primrose.'

'A primrose by the river's brim.' Between the two languages, the word

Cuan means 'sea' and *coill* means 'wood'.

'sobhrach' turned to 'primrose.'
Behind the two words, a Roman said 'prima rosa'.
The 'sobhrach' or the 'primrose' was in our hands. Its reasons
belonged to us.

7

'That thing about which you cannot speak, be silent about it.'
Was there a pianist before a piano? Did Plato have a melodeon?
Melodeon in the heavens? Feet dancing in the heavens? Red lips and
black hair? Was there a melodeon in the heavens? A skeleton of notes.

8

'Shall Gaelic die?' A hundred years from now who will say these
words?
Who will say, 'Co their? Who? The voice of the owl.

9

If I say 'an orange church' will I build an orange church?
If I say 'a mauve minister' will I create him?
The tartan is in its own country.
The tartan is a language.
A Campbell is different from a Macdonald (this is what a tartan
teaches).
The tartans fight each other. Is that why they had to put a colourless
church between them?

10

Said Alexander Macdonald, 'It was Gaelic that Adam and Eve spoke
in that garden.' Did God speak Gaelic as well, when he told them

Co their? – 'Who will say?'

about the apple? And when they left that garden, were they like exiles sailing to… Canada?

11

Shall Gaelic die? What that means is: shall we die?

12

An orange church with green walls. A picture on a wall showing ships like triangles. On another wall, a picture of a café with men made of paint. 'Gloria Deo' in the language of paintings, an orange bell, a yellow halo around the pulpit where there are red dancers.

13

Were you ever in a maze? Its language fits your language. Its roads fit the roads of your head. If you cannot get out of the language you cannot get out of the maze. Its roads reflect your language.
O for a higher language, like a hawk in the sky, that can see the roads, that can see their end, like God who built the roads, our General Wade. The roads of the Highlands fit the roads of our language.

14

When the ape descended from the trees he changed his language.
He put away the green leaves. He made small sharp words, words made of stones.

15

The dove returned to Noah with a word in his mouth.

16

The scholar is sitting with a candle in front of him. He is construing words. He is building a dictionary. Little by little, inch by inch, he is building a dictionary. Outside the window the children are shouting, a ball is rising to the sky, a girl and a boy are walking without language to bed. What will he do when the ball enters the quiet room, breaking the window, stopping him at B, and Z so distant.

17

Whom have you got in the net? Who is rising with green eyes, with a helmet, who is in the net?
Cuchulain is in the net, he is rising from the sea, ropes of moonlight at his heels, ropes of language.

18

'When you turn your back on the door, does the door exist?' said Berkeley, the Irishman who was alive in the soul.
When the Highlands loses its language, will there be a Highlands, said I, with my two coats, losing, perhaps, the two.

19

A million colours are better than one colour, if they are different.
A million men are better than one man if they are different. Keep out of the factory, O man, you are not a robot. It wasn't a factory that made your language – it made you.

20

Like a rainbow, like crayons, spectrum of beautiful languages.
The one-language descended like a church – like a blanket, like mist.

21

God is outside language, standing on a perch. He crows now and again. Who hears him? If there is a God let him emanate from the language, a perfume emanating from the dew of the morning, from the various-coloured flowers.

22

Death is outside the language. The end of language is beyond language.
Wittgenstein didn't speak after his death. What language would he speak? In what language would you say, 'Fhuair a' Ghaidhlig bas?'

23

When the name 'Adam' was called, he turned his back on the hills. He saw his shadow at his feet – he drew his breath.

24

You cannot say, 'Not-Adam'. You cannot say 'Not-Eve'. The apple has a name as well. It is in the story.

25

The gold is new. It will not rust. 'Immutable universal,' as the Frenchman said. But the pennies, the pounds, the half-crowns, these coins that are old and dirty, the notes that are wrinkled like old faces, they are coping with time,
to these I give my allegiance, to these I owe honour, with sweetness.
'Immutable, perfect,' Midas with his coat of gold and of death.

Fhuair a' Ghaidhlig bas – 'Gaelic is dead.'

Translated from the Gaelic of Sorley MacLean

I

Girl of the gold-yellow hair,
Indifferent, to you, is my desire:
Girl of the gold-yellow hair,
Indifferent, to you, this patient fire.

Tonight on the floods of Ratharsair,
My distant hand rests on the tiller.
Not languid is the wind that shakes the sails.
Languid my heart because your music fails.
Becalmed my sea where no large wind prevails.

Round dark Dùn Cana soundless mists are creeping.
Angry the grasses on the mountains sloping.
The western wind across the sea unsleeping.
This is the death of dreaming and of hoping.

Around the masts the barren winds are shrieking.
Before the boat the whitening waves are breaking.
But let the wind be fierce and masts be creaking,
What do I care for battles of their making?

Girl of the gold-yellow hair,
Indifferent, to you, is my desire:
Girl of the gold-yellow hair,
Indifferent, to you, this patient fire.

II

And if our language says that love
And reason are the same
She's lying.

When first your beauty struck my eyes
They did not learn to be wise,,
They weren't scholars of such terms.

When first I heard your voice, my clay
Was not sundered in this way,
Not the first time.

The assault was more indirect
Against my heart and intellect.
Later, the storm grew strong.

With all I had of prudence
I fought in my defence.
I used sagacious eloquence.

And from my ancient wisdom I
Spoke from the chaos of my sky:
'I do not want you here nor yet away.'

My love was on the inside,
My wisdom remained outside,
That thin partition was destroyed.

And reason spoke to my love thus:
'How foolish is this doubleness.
Love is the reason we possess.'

III

Never was I so tormented
or troubled in my clay
by Christ's wanderings on the earth,
or the millions of the sky:

and I gave no heed to that silly dream –
the woods of a far air –
as my stiff heart melted in the power
of her laughter and golden hair.

And her beauty laid a shadow on
poverty and our bitter birth,
on Lenin's intellectual world,
his patience and his wrath.

IV

Girl of the yellow, heavy-yellow, gold-yellow hair,
the tune of your lips and Europe's pain together.
Lustrous, ringletted, joyful, beautiful lass,
our time's shame would not infect your kiss.

Can the music of your beauty hide from me
the ominous discord in this harmony?
The rampant thief and brute at Europe's head,
the ancient songs, your lips so proud and red.

Can a body's whiteness and a forehead's sun
conceal that impudent treachery from my brain –
spite of the bourgeoisie, poison of its creed,
a dismal Scotland, feeble and weak-kneed?

Can beauty and the mendacity of verse
deceive the patient with its transient cures
or hide the Spanish miner from his doom,
his soul going down without delirium?

What is your kiss, electrical and proud,
when valued by each drop of precious blood
that fell on the frozen mountain-sides of Spain
when men were dying in their bitter pain?

What is each ringlet of your golden hair
when weighed against that poverty and fear
which Europe's people bear and still must bear
from the first slave-ship to slavery entire?

VIII

*The innocent and the beautiful
have no enemy but time.*

W.B. Yeats

I thought I understood from you
that these lines were exact and true,
nor did I think that I would find
their falsehood bitter in my mind.

But that plausible epigram
proved itself another dream
when on that Monday I saw with dread
the steel helmet on your golden head.

XI

Often walking quite alone
Edinburgh's grey sunless stone
it would flash with your sudden rays
white-starred, uniquely precious.

XIV

Poet struggling under strain,
corruption of gifts and the cheap chain
which has enticed so many men:
surely not I, not I, would cry:
Surrender gives relief from pain.

But I have said (this isn't new)
that I would sell my soul for you
(not false to love though to the rest untrue.)
Yet that was blasphemy, I see it now,
that was a heresy love led me to.

Forgive me therefore for that sordid thought
that you, my dear, could possibly accept
a wretch dishonoured and dispirited:
that you could watch, indifferent, the sale
for even your love of honesty and wit.

And therefore I will say it yet again:
I'd sell my soul for you, my heart's queen
not once but twice: the first time for your keen
beauty: and the second time because
you would not take a soul so small and mean.

XVII

Tumultuous plenty in the heavens,
gold-sieve of a million stars,
cold, distant, blazing, splendid,
silent and callous in their course.

Fullness of knowledge in their going,
an empty, chartless, ignorant plain.
A universe in soundless motion.
A brooding intellect alone.

It was not they who woke my thinking
It was not the miracle of their grave
fearful procession, but your face,
a naked universe of love.

XVIII

Now that the ivory towers are down
and my desire is but a thin
shade of a tale that's dead and gone,
there is only: Let me strengthen
my own spirit against pain.

For I have watched while Spain, struck dead,
salted the eyes within my head
and slowed my wheels of pride and blood,
with thoughts of nothingness and death
and heroes who have lost their breath.

And now we see on every side
heart-break and the death of pride,
the nothingness that will deride
every generous thought we nursed
to satisfy the spirit's thirst.

Cornford in his heroic day
prayed that his love would not betray
Spain and her cross of agony –
Cornford afraid his love was near,
Cornford afraid of his fear.

What of *my* fear? Can I sustain
the torments that will pierce my brain
now that I've heard the storms begin?
They say that nightmares now annoy
and deadly famine strangles joy,

that hunger walks about the earth
with solemn ghosts of thirst and dearth
cropping our tender lives at birth
and forcing to the low grave
all our arrogance and love.

And do you think that I will pray
against the terrors of my way?
(Stopping of heart and blinded eye)
That you, my love, be wrenched and torn
from the bitter roots where you were born?

That thus I might be purified
from the infirmity in my side.
Or should I pray for a soul arrayed
in blood and battle, proudly dressed
like Dimitrov, Connolly and the rest?

Today I clearly understand
the gulf that cracks across the mind,
strife on behalf of human-kind,
the choice that catches at our breath,
immortal dying or a living death.

Mine is a hopeless death alive
because I did not force my love
out of my splendid private grove,
because when History strode by
I loved a woman in my secret sky.

I saw blood beating like a pulse,
the spirit's lightning on the hills,
the poor world shedding all its ills,
I understood with a heart impure
the language of the wounded deer.

He whose heart is cleansed and pure
will walk unswerving through the fire,
will climb huge hills and never tire,
but mine is not the hero's part,
who lives with a corrupted heart.

And this, the prayer you hear me pray,
is vain and blasphemous and dry,
corrupt and crooked and awry,
a prayer to pray and nothing more,
the shadow of a false fire.

I've heard about the death which comes
to terrify deceit and dreams
with thirst and famine in its arms.
How can I face their cruel charge
with a heart I could not learn to purge?

For when the heart is purged and clean
it can confront most bitter pain
and will not faint or suffer stain.
But who will say my white love
suffers the laughter of the grave?

There's no need for a catechist
to tell my prayer is but a ghost,
a shadowy figure in the mist,
to show me that my spirit is not
as hard and lucid as my thought.

And since the gods cannot be blamed –
being but wishes we have dreamed,
and Christ a man who walked unarmed –
I cannot worship or extol
Nature which made my intellect whole,
the single mind and the divided soul.

XIX

I gave you eternity
and what did you give me?
Only the bitter arrows
of your hurting beauty.
You pierced me with hard onset,
you made my days sorry
with vinegar of the spirit,
the sore gleam of glory.

Yet the eternity I gave you
was born from you and to you belongs,
you taught my five senses
to put their brilliance in my songs:
and though you almost ruined me
for our hard historical campaign
I'd still receive, if I could have,
more of your weakening gifts again.

If I could see you standing now
on the calm plains of the Land of Youth,
I in forgetfulness of ruin,
you in your white glittering cloth,
I'd wish these days to return
when my spirit struggled (though in vain)
and, rather than defeated peace,
the battle to begin again.

O most beautiful white girl,
you tore my intellect apart,
you made my journey crooked
and drew me from my single art.
Yet should I ever reach that wood
where poems burn along each leaf
you were the author of my songs
you made a bard of me with grief.

I've built you a tall monument
on the crumpling mountains of our time,
yet this is a memorial
that men will speak of when you're dumb
and though I lose you, and another
enjoy you to his every wish
you'll blaze and glitter in my songs
after the setting of your flesh.

On a Summer's Day

Thus it is.
There is much loneliness
and the cigarette coupons will not save us.

I have studied your face across the draughtsboard.
It is freckled and young.
Death and summer have such fine breasts.

Tanned, they return from the sea.
The colour of sand, their blouses the colour of waves,
they walk in the large screen of my window.

Bacon, whose Pope screams in the regalia
of chairs and glass, dwarf of all the ages,
an hour-glass of ancient Latin,

you have fixed us where we are, cacti able to talk,
twitched by unintelligible tornadoes,
snakes of collapsing sand.

They trail home from the seaside in their loose blouses.
The idiot bounces his ball as they pass.
He tests his senile smile.

Dead for a Rat

What snarls
in the corner?
It wants to live
It bares its teeth at you.

It wants to live
more than you do
Its whole body
trembles
with its want to live.

The fur arches from its body
Its green eyes spark
Its lips are drawn back from the teeth
It hates you.

It hates you
more than you hate it.
Hamlet
lie down
in the sound of the trumpet

It quests you, Hamlet
Will you go
behind the arras
behind the tapestry
will you go
Hamlet
with all the weight
of your bright thought
upon you?

Will you go Hamlet
in your shuttling armour
in your whirr
of literature
with your French rapier
sparkling, veering?

Dear Hamlet

Dear Hamlet, you were pushed beyond your strength
you had a white face and black clothes,
you stood at corners listening.

Surrounded by the voices and wondering what you should do.
The old father whom you admired so much
but who had driven you to Wittenberg
lay murdered.

To avenge him when you did not even like him
(though you admired him) wasn't easy.
He had won so many battles but you,
you had won none.

Poor schoolboy, longing to be like your father,
learning to fence when he had used an axe,
learning philosophy because he hadn't done so.
Words are not enough.

Rushing about from one commandment to another
you were finally focussed as a target
by Claudius, the small and simple man,
yes, he was simple.

So little sufficed him, just a queen, a kingdom,
salutes from guards, dinners with dinner-jackets,
bow-ties and crowns, the glitter of cut-glass,
the colour of poison.

But you, you needed more. That more was death.
You chewed it, fed on it, watched for it in mirrors,
hunted the castle for it, loved it the best
of anything you had known.

How silly Fortinbras was, not to see it
standing behind him just as he took the crown.
That was the moment he began to die
and you began to live.

How often I feel like you

Ah, you Russians, how often I feel like you
full of ennui, hearing the cry of wolves
on frontiers of green glass.
In the evening
one dreams of white birches and of bears.
There are picnics in bright glades and someone talking
endlessly of verse as if mowing grass,
endlessly of philosophy round and round
like a red fair with figures of red soldiers
spinning forever at their 'Present Arms'.
How long it takes for a letter to arrive.
Postmen slog heavily over the steppes
and drop their dynamite through the letter-box
For something is happening everywhere but here.
Here there are Hamlets and old generals.
Everyone sighs and says 'Ekh' and in the stream
a girl is swimming naked among gnats.
This space is far too much for us like time.
Even the clocks have asthma. There is honey,
herring and ham and an old samovar.
Help us, let something happen, even death.
God has forgotten us. We are like fishers
with leather leggings dreaming in a stream.

Russian Poem

I

I am too old for you.
Nevertheless
in summer under a crown of leaves…
I am in debt,
a kind of Hamlet.
Nevertheless,
Sonia, you are beautiful.
I've left my Jewish wife
mooning from piano to vodka.
She coughs all night.
You do not know the guilt…
Here in the sunshine it is fine,
you in your white dress…
People, such people.
Generals
with false red faces
booming like snipes.
Old uncles, aunts,
surplus to requirements
Sonia,
there was a time
when I had ideals
Now my back is broken.
I feel nothing, Sonia,
even should you put
lightly your hand in mine,
even should you kiss
I'd not awaken.
Sonia, I'm afraid
of this old skin.

II

Ennui covers the land.
Broken fences.
Russia is full of broken fences.
Pigs root in the muck.
Grandfathers roast themselves on stoves.
Ash on their waistcoats.

Something is bound to happen.
They click their heels like toys,
kiss over olives
fine, and cared-for, hands.
There's something I'm hearing.

Great cannon in small ears.
The stone heads tremble.
The wolves trouble our wit.
They are seething like water.

III

Hear us, Philosophy will not save us.
In our salons we have talked the 'soul' to death.

Our cigar smoke snakes from the orchard
where the apples ripen and the small hands

shine.

Our glasses reflect the sunset. Our monocles
have a raw glare. The uncles

twinkle like robins.

We have talked the 'soul' to death. Now as the sun goes down
we shiver and go in.

IV

Gogol, how your troika sparkled down our leaf-fringed lanes.
You stopped at the most absurd houses
where everyone was himself and dullness sparkled like genius.

Moral bachelor, what has happened to you? You have run to history
for protection. You have abandoned your people.
You have run your little troika into the wilderness.

V

In the siding the red light veins his beard.
The rails run elsewhere, hard and narrowing.
Our land breathed through you. Now you are breathless.
Your soul is blown sideways by the steam.

I look down the track at the raw torches
wandering hither and thither. What do I see?
Is it the mad city face of Dostoevsky?

VI

'We shall soon go to Moscow,' say the sisters
watching the great bear at the edge of the forest
bumbling along, so neat and strong.

There is the taste of autumn in the air,
the taste of aisles and pillars and of lemon,
the taste of tall clear glasses on the lawn.

The bear trots amiably among the steeples
They watch him through their telescopes so mild,
so cuddly and ingenuous. He stares

back through the telescope. And the trees shake.
The glasses shake, the ringless pale hands,
and Moscow in their silk sways without sound.

VII

Sometimes I think of the Cossacks wolfing their hunks of flesh
and the Poles equably turning
with soundless screams over their evening fires.

They would piss into the open mouths of the dead
but they polished their ikons.

How terrified we would be if in our salons
a sabre should be reflected
and a happy face smiling above the moustache,
a murderous childlike face.

I imagine our glass walls cracking before them,
our women being raped among smelling salts,
and two heels drumming on the fine silk.

Ah, our Hamlet, where are you? How your soul trembles
like a tiny drop of dew on a gibbet

as these riders scratch their raw necks,
as they spit bountifully on to the marble,
as they unhitch their belts and belch comfortably
munching legs of chicken, gazing at the wrenched limbs.

VIII

The idiot stands on the pavement
with a rainbow-coloured ball in his hands,
a large ball which he kneads continually.
He has a large Teutonic head,
his hair is crew-cut
and he has big thick lips.
Hour after hour he stands
legs spread apart
in a dull masterful strut.
He's squat, short, a boy,

but his hair is grey in the light
He is old, this idiot
far older than his toy.

IX

I hear that he came in a sealed train.
Yesterday I heard him
His head is like the round stone balls you see on gateposts.

When his arm jabs the air, you hear cannon.
The swirling snow settles on the ground.

His head is a bell tolling for theses,
articles, students, appendices and 'questions'.

He has simplified the world like an assassin.
Where his barrel points is where evil is.

X

Sonia, my fine ghost,
I see you among the rifles.
You were saying 'What need of a psychiatrist?
He would only stare at my wrist.'

Sonia, you were a sign of the times
a young girl vibrating out of phase.
I see you wearing white slacks,
legs spread apart,
reading old leaves.

Sonia, you were a generator
bouncing on a piece of waste ground.

Sonia, it has come at last.
The newspapers have gone mad.
They are punching out Reality.

If I do not die now I shall die.

Sonia, I stretch out my hand to you.
I am afraid but I stretch out my hand to you.
Sonia, let us follow the wind.

Party

Cigarette ends mounting slowly in the ashtray,
so many Hamlets speaking all at once.
'Polonius is a fool to have such power.'
I leaf through Bacon's paintings in the corner,
a butcher's shop of graduated screams.

Now they are dancing on the charred carpet.
You can tell the lost ones from their stiff arms.

The others sway to the music just like snakes.
'He's nice to me but never says he loves me.
He strokes his car's flanks over and over.'
She waggles her bum, a green suburban mermaid,
flicking her fingers, Venus of the record player
half hidden by the fog, the swirling grey.

Dipping Your Spoon

Dipping your spoon in the mash of TV
palls. Everything palls. Spy and detective stories,

watching your cold small face on its seventh gin,
hearing the ringing jokes from bell-like faces,

writing great novels on white tablecloths.
What is given is not enough to make us swing
happily on branches or to climb
these long stone stairs, watches bobbing on chains.
We want the Commandments from the gritty deserts

and shadowy ghosts in their post-Renaissance frames,
our underwater programmes. We want your Commandments
suited to a pastoral land in green,
the extinct shepherds with their pilgrim staffs,
their clouds of white sheep and visiting angels
perching on branches with their fathomless eyes.

Shane

He comes out of some place where he has invented justice.
What is good has to be protected by guns
and that is why he's so sombre. Why his silence
grows on the bustling housewife who asks about fashions.
He has learned a style from evil, he has honed it on
conflict. He knows that books will not save
the innocent man. He stands by the fence
undazzled yet alert, expecting evil
as natural as sunlight. Yet with what grief he goes
to find his guns again, to relearn his quickness.

Chaplin

Everything seems pasted on,
the baggy trousers, the moustache.
The teeth shine over a smashed dish.
The silence helps him. Watch his pose,
the V-shaped broken boots. The doors
swing shut to hide him. He fights
the moving elevators,
cycling upstream.
His cane is thin as a stem.
One could not lean on it. He pulls
thick cultures down. He trudges on
to a thriving emptiness.

End of Schooldays

Captains, this is your last day in school.
You won't wear these helmets any more.
Do you not hear the whisper in the triumph,
like a suspect heart? Do you not see
how Mr Scott, though kind, is harried
by voices inaudibly calling from his house.

Look out on the fields. Never again will you see
such a sweet greenness, as of colours leaving
a place where they've been happy for a while.
The harness is turning now to other horses.
Laughter comes up the road and mounts the brae.
The names on the doors are rewriting themselves.

Never mind, the music will not leave you
or not completely. Sometimes in a betrayal,
in the middle of a deal just turning rancid,
after the fifth gin, the fifth fat hand,
the cloudy globes, set on the cloth, you'll hear it,

the music of your Ideal, quietly humming
in locker-rooms that smell of sweat and rain.
You'll be coming home in a warm and eerie light,
legs tall and willowy, in your hand the cup,
shaking a little, in your flabby hand
the trembling cup, in your old grasping hand.

For Keats

Genius is so strange,
you were in so many ways ordinary
in so many ways wounded like us.

But the vase beckons –
continually the vase beckons –
the imperfect bird sings
in the brown mortal leaves.

Poor Tom dies in the white linen.
Sore throats! Do nightingales have sore throats?
In the nightingale's pure notes
What eloquent disease?

Happily to seek the classic –
that land without fatigue –
that which stands like the rocks of Staffa
black remarkable architecture of the sea
solider than weeping Skye.

Than the grass of summer,
devotees of England's spas,
the irritabilities of the second rate,
the helmet bruised and vain.

Fighting the scree, to arrive at autumn,
innocent impersonal accepted
where the trees do not weep like gods
but are at last themselves.

Bristly autumn, posthumous and still,
the crowning fine frost on the hill
the perfect picture blue and open-eyed
with the lakes as fixed as your brother's eyes,
autumn that will return

and will return and will return, however
the different delicate vase revolves
in the brown mortal foliage, in the woods
of egos white as flowers.

For John Maclean, Headmaster, and Classical and Gaelic Scholar

I

The coloured roses fade along the wall.
How shall we live? How perfectly they fall,
the October leaves in yellow, how exact
the woods appear, so married to the fact
of their own unwilled and accurate funeral
without interrogation. In this tract

the dazzling hearse has led us to, we stand,
hats in our hands. The serious piper plays
'The Lament for the Children' and we hear the bound
and ribboned bouquets thudding. Then we take our ways
to the waiting cars across unechoing ground

or over crackling gravel. It remains,
the body in the casket, and begins
its simple mineral weathering. We return
to our complex human burning. What we mourn
changes as we mourn it, and routines
wed and enring us as we move and burn.

II

For you it was the case that Homer lived
in our fluorescence, that Ulysses homed
through our stained and plaguey light, that Hector grieved
in his puncturable armour, that engraved
even in Skye was marble which consumed
the bodies of live Greeks who shaped and carved

contemporary sculpture. Under leaves
which dappled your warm garden (as the groves
of autumnal classic Greece) you turned a page
or made an emendation in a passage.
Exactitude's a virtue, so believes
the inveterate scholar. Happy who can judge

evil as a hiatus or a false
quantity in harmony, who knows
that what protects us from the animals
is language healthy as a healthy pulse
and that our moral being can like prose
be manifestly tested where it fails.

III

I know that it is waning, that clear light
that shone on all our books and made them white
with unanswerable grammar. That the slaves
sustained our libraries and that the wolves
and watchful eagles nourished an elite
and that the elegant and forceful proofs

of their geometers will not suffice.
I know that Athene is wandering now,
dishevelled in the shrubbery, and the nurse
beckons at evening to her. Gods rehearse
their ruined postures and the ruined brow
reflects from mirrors not of fire but ice

and that our brute Achilles drives his wheels
across the gesturing shadows: and that kneels
to cheering legions Aphrodite: packs
are watching Ajax hacking with his axe
inanely the pale sheep: and shady deals
illuminate Odysseus's tracks.

IV

You were a teacher also: what we've learned
is also what we teach: and what we are
cannot be hidden, though we walk black-gowned
along the radiant corridors, profound
in serious scholarship and that precious star
proposed by art or conscience. Where you burned

exactitude prevailed, the rule of Rome,
the gravitas of Brutus and his calm,
his stoic tenderness, his love of books,
his principles and practice. For the Dux
stands in his place, the overwhelming psalm
enchants him wholly among clean-limbed Greeks,

and if you touch him he gives out true coin.
Echo on echo, pupils make a world
which is their bronze and yours, and they will join
link on bright link to make the legions shine
with ethics and with elegance. The absurd
becomes a simple weather, clear and fine.

V

The October leaves are falling. None condemns
their seasonal abdication. What consumes
their crowns and robes is natural, a law
that's common to the weasel and the crow.
They hear no music of the funeral drums
and no cortèges shade the way they go,

no mountains brood, nor does the sharp wind mourn
nor tragic clouds move slowly. For the ice
steadily thickens over lake and corn.
In this pure azure there's no paradise
nor the hell nor purgatory that we devise
lest in the world we shiver and we burn

without the falcon's unhistorical aim,
its brutal beak, the momentary tomb
of its spontaneous moments. Or the sheep
that grazes in its own forgetful sleep
or the barbarians that struck at Rome,
its pompous destiny and shadowed hope.

VI

Though it is finished now, that scholarship,
though vases crack and hourly we may graze
on superficial quanta: though we sleep
abandoned to disorder, and the days
are flashes of small light: and what we praise
is transient and odd, we yet may keep

pictures of autumn, graver, more restrained,
with a finer balance of the weighty mind,
a wind from Rome and Greece which held our course
steady to a harbour where salt oars
received their justice and to scales assigned
the soul would shiver with a stronger force

which now in neon vibrates. But in light
(let it be legend) accompanied the leaves
to their natural assignations and the fruit
bowed to a holy earth. The swan that moves
in reedy waters bows its neck. The waves
receive it, flesh and shadow, day and night.

VII

So with your battered helmet let you be
immersed in golden autumn as each tree
accepts its destiny and will put by
its outworn crown, its varying finery,
and let the humming of the latest bee
bear its last honey home. Beneath this sky

the hexagonal coffin crowned with flowers restores
your body to the earth from which we came
to build our shaking ladders. What was yours
was no phantasmal order, and your name
planted in this place held to its aim
from wider deeper origins. If there were pyres

then a pyre you should have had, and lictors too.
And phantom legions. In this perfect blue
imagine therefore flame that's amber, yellow,
leaves of good flame, volumes that burn and glow,
the foliage of your autumn, where you grew
and where you are buried in the earth you know.

Gaelic Songs

I listen to these songs
from a city studio.
They belong to a different country,
to a barer sky,
to a district of heather and stone.
They belong to the sailors
who kept their course
through nostalgia and moonlight.
They belong to the maidens
who carried the milk in pails
home in the twilight.

They belong to the barking of dogs,
to the midnight of stars,
to the sea's terrible force,
exile past the equator.
They belong to the sparse grass,
to the wrinkled faces,
to the houses sunk in the valleys,
to the mirrors
brought home from the fishing.

Now they are made of crystal
taking just a moment
between two programmes
elbowing them fiercely
between two darknesses.

Not to Islands

Not to islands ever returning now
with much of hope or comfort. Not to you,
asleep in the blue sky of TV,
Lewis or Uist, Harris or Tiree.
Shadows assemble from America
where once the moors were silent, where once
the sea's monotony was experience.
Where once we drowsed on the hot flowers in summer
staring across the ocean to where lay
America invisible, unknown,
in ignorant mirrors hanging upside-down
invincibly at peace, the bell-like day.

For Ann in America in the Autumn

When the wind dies in New Jersey
and it is the Fall
and the horses canter home to their stables
over the late grass, the late leaves,
remember how it is here in this small
place without air far from New England's Lowell.

Gently the leaves spiral as they fall.
The logfire sparkles red as a new apple.
O hills of the Far Country you're so blue
and dead and quiet. The old clouds drift through
the old mind. The weighted earth prevails.
We're hauled towards gravity by the worn heels.

Something regrets us. Something we regret.
I smell your woodsmoke, it is pure and tart.
Here by this shore the sea turns round again.
My head swings dully in its leaves of pain.
What horses leave me in this frosty Fall –
the girls ride westwards on their rising wheel.

In the Chinese Restaurant

Because we'd never go there, it was good,
those years together. We'd never need to go
though we could talk of it and so we were
happy together in a place we'd made
so small and airless that we couldn't leave.
But we could think of it and say, 'Perhaps
we'll go there someday.' But we could not go
for as we lived so we'd lost all the maps.
It grew more perfect as the slow years passed
as if we were there already. One fine day
we'd find it all around us if we looked.
We would be in it, even old and grey.

So that, one night, in that late restaurant
with Chinese waiters round us we picked up
the menu in Chinese and understood
every single word of it. It was
a revelation when the waiters smiled.
They looked so clear as the glasses slowly filled.

The Small Snags

The small snags tug at us. The flag will not unfold
glorious in the weather of our triumph.
It is the small snags that won't let go.
For if the flag unfolds and leaves the earth
and is pure spirit, a wide heavenly cloth,
then earth will not remember us but fade
with its arrangement of small serious weasels,
its rats with clear green eyes, its stoats and foxes,
the thickets that entangle as we move.

Let not the flag unfold too widely, let not
the hero in his brilliance, let not
the silk unwind its soul's advertisements,
but be like clothes snarled in the summer hedges
where the birds sing clearly from their dying mouths
and the owl snaps through its folds.

Children in Winter

In the dark mornings
the orange coloured children
test the black streets
hand in hand.

The darkness pours down.
The moon is leaning backwards
like an exhausted woman.

They fade into their future,
like small orange sails
breasting the darkness.

Lear and Carroll

Those child-loving nonsense-writing Victorian uncles,
how they sadden us with their large heads and mild eyes,
with their imaginary bestiaries set in the tall avenues
of the shadows which destroyed them, the long skirts of windless
days.

Give Me Your Hand

Give me your hand.
Do you not feel it,
the first chill of autumn?
The azure is razor sharp
the brown nostalgic.

There is no noise.
The light is single
under the uncrowned trees
It is beaten like steel
interrupted by litter

Ah, the queens are all gone
with their brocade and silken
garments of the summer.
Without their fripperies
they are naked like us

We are at zero.
There is no babbling
of water over stones.
The stones are bearded
with unshaken moss.

The trees are thermometers
almost transparent.
There is no sap
or it's descended
to an absent country.

Give me your hand,
we are two orphans
with large blue eyes
in a story of Andersen's
on an autumnal journey.

Christmas, 1971

There's no snow this Christmas… there was snow
when we received the small horses and small cart,
brothers together all those years ago.
There were small watches made of liquorice
surrealist as time hung over chairs.
I think perhaps that when we left the door
of the white cottage with its fraudulent icing
we were quite fixed as to our different ways.
Someone is waving with black liquorice hands
at the squashed windows as the soundless bells
and the soundless whips lash our dwarf horses forward.
We diverge at the road-end in the whirling snow
never to meet but singing, pulling gloves
over and over our disappearing hands.

The Letter

Here is my letter out of the mirror
God who created us.

Why did you put the rabbit in the belly of the fox?
Why did you put man in the box of his days?
Why did you build us of frail bones?

Why did you give us hearts
to suffer hubbub and sorrow,
why aren't they like watches
small, circular, golden?

Why did you leave the eagle alone
in a nest of clouds
suspended on rays,
hammered with nails?

Why did you not make angels or beasts of us
with cold wings, with barbaric heads?
Why did you praise the sea in front of us
with a wide meaningless face?

In the mirror
a boxer's face,
in the mirror
a rusty helmet.

In the mirror is your book with a steel band,
with an edge sharp as a razor.

In the mirror there is one rose,
our hope growing,
red, shaken by the winds,
in a circle of dew.

In the Time of the Useless Pity

In the time of the useless pity I turned away
from your luminous clock-face in the hopeless dark,
appealing to me greenly, appealing whitely.
Nothing I could do, I had tried everything,
lain flat on the rug, fluttered my spaniel paws,
offered you my house like an unlocked crystal –
and so it came, the time of the useless pity
when the roots had had enough of you, when they slept,
elaborating themselves by themselves
when they shifted over from yours, seeking a place
different from yours to burst through and to pierce
with a royal purple, straight and delicate: sails
of the suave petals unfurling at the mast.

Finis not Tragedy

All is just. The mouth you feed turns on you
if not truly fed, the machine clicks
accurately in a new house.

The will that you abolished stands slackly
when you need it most, the vanquished
muscles will not answer.

The machine, powered by history, clicks
shut like a filing cabinet and on it
you read Finis not Tragedy.

Nothing is there that wasn't there.
No memos that you haven't read
over and over again

when your skull-faced secretary stood smiling
as you tore papers into little pieces
and hummed through your clenched teeth

and turning you said to him 'Remember honour.
Tell the story as it really was.'
But he is silent, smiling.

Everything Is Silent

Everything is silent now
before the storm.
The transparent walls tremble.
You can hear the very slightest hum
of a stream miles away.

The silence educates your ear.
The threat is palpable.
You can hear the boots beyond the mountains.
You can hear the breathings of feathers.
You can hear the well of your heart.

You know what it is that permits the walls,
that allows the ceiling,
that lets the skin cling to your body,
that mounts the spiral
of your beholden bones.

That sorrow is a great sorrow
and leaves you radiant
when the tempest has passed
and your vases are still standing
and your bones are stalks in the water.

from LOVE POEMS AND ELEGIES
(1972)

'You lived in Glasgow'

You lived in Glasgow many years ago.
I do not find your breath in the air.
It was, I think, in the long-skirted thirties
when idle men stood at every corner
chewing their fag-ends of a failed culture.
Now I sit here in George Square
where the War Memorial's yellow sword glows bright
and the white stone lions mouth at bus and car.
A maxi-skirted girl strolls by.
I turn and look. It might be you. But no.
Around me there's a 1970 sky.

Everywhere there are statues. Stone remains.
The mottled flesh is transient. On those trams,
invisible now but to the mind, you bore
your groceries home to the 1930 slums.
'There was such warmth,' you said. The gaslight hums
and large caped shadows tremble on the stair.
Now everything is brighter. Pale ghosts walk
among the spindly chairs, the birchen trees.
In lights of fiercer voltage you are less
visible than when in winter you
walked, a black figure, through the gaslit blue.

The past's an experience that we cannot share.
Flat-capped Glaswegians and the Music Hall.
Apples and oranges on an open stall.
A day in the country. And the sparkling Clyde
splashing its local sewage at the wall.
This April day shakes memories in a shade
opening and shutting like a parasol.
There is no site for the unshifting dead.
You're buried elsewhere though your flickering soul
is a constant tenant of my tenement.

You were happier here than anywhere, you said.
Such fine neighbours helping when your child
almost died of croup. Those pleasant Wildes
removed with the fallen rubble have now gone
in the building programme which renews each stone.
I stand in a cleaner city, better fed,
in my diced coat, brown hat, my paler hands
leafing a copy of the latest book.
Dear ghosts, I love you, haunting sunlit winds,
dear happy dented ghosts, dear prodigal folk.

I left you, Glasgow, at the age of two
and so you are my birthplace just the same.
Divided city of the green and blue
I look for her in you, my constant aim
to find a ghost within a close who speaks
in Highland Gaelic.
                    The bulldozer breaks
raw bricks to powder. Boyish workmen hang
like sailors in tall rigging. Buildings sail
into the future. The old songs you sang
fade in their pop songs, scale on dizzying scale.

'You told me once'

You told me once how your younger brother died.
It was by drowning. In the tar-black sea
he sang a psalm to bring his rescuers near.
That did not save him though. One cannot hide,
you would have said, from destiny. So here
there are two meanings working side by side.

You died of lack of oxygen. I tried
to fit the mask against your restless face
in the bumpy ambulance in which you lay.
I thought that moment of the psalm as guide
beyond our vain technology, the grey
and scarlet blankets that you tossed aside.

'My sailor father'

My sailor father died in hospital
of a consumption, forcing you to burn
all your furniture and begin again.
Chair and table blossomed in a hail

of memories which set him in the cordage
of a white schooner setting out to sea,
its sheets unfolding, moving carefully,
the trousseau and red roses of your marriage.

'That island formed you'

That island formed you, its black hatted men
and stony bibles. How your father's beard
streamed like a cataract. And the heart's devoured
by the black rays of a descending sun.
Always they're making fences, making barred
gates to keep the wind out, their slow pace
deliberate and punctual. Who has heard
of the terrible cyclones that infect deep space?
The daffodils are yellow on the wind
but in these souls where is the love, my dear,
to dally in fine leisure as the clear
smoke rises from the houses, and the cock
shrills redly from the waste abundant air?

The Space-ship

I think of you and then I think of this
picture of an astronaut lacking air,
dying of lack of it in the depths of space,

his face kneading and working under glass,
lolling inside his helmet. Then I see
a foreign space-ship steadily from space

swimming implacably, a black helmet
rearing out of the limitless azure and
a sun exploding with tremendous light.

The black mediaeval helmet fits his face
and the glass breaks without a single sound
and becomes the crystals of unnumbered stars.

On Looking at the Dead

This is a coming to reality.
This is the stubborn place. No metaphors swarm

around that fact, around that strangest thing,
that being that was and now no longer is.

This is a coming to a rock in space
worse than a rock (or less), diminished thing

worse and more empty than an empty vase.

The devious mind elaborates its rays.
This is the stubborn thing. It will not move.

It will not travel from our stony gaze.

But it must stay and that's the worst of it
till changed by processes. Otherwise it stays.

To beat against it and no waves of grace
ever to ascend or sovereign price

to be held above it! This is no hero. This
is an ordinary death. If there is grace

theology is distant. Sanctify
(or so they say) whatever really is

and this is real, nothing more real than this.
It beats you down to it, will not permit

the play of imagery, the peacock dance,
the bridal energy or mushrooming crown

or any blossom. It only is itself.
It isn't you. It only is itself.

It is the stubbornness of a real thing

mentionable as such and only such,
the eyes returning nothing. Compromise

is not a meaning of this universe.
And that is good. To face it where it is,

to stand against it in no middle way
but in the very centre where things are

and having it as centre, for you take
directions from it not as from a book

but from this star, black and fixed and here,
a brutal thing where no chimeras are

nor purple colours nor a gleam of silk
nor any embroideries eastern or the rest

but unavoidable beyond your choice
and therefore central and of major price.

'Of the uncomplicated dairy girl'

Of the uncomplicated dairy girl
in gown that's striped in blue and red
feeding the hens in a windy spring
by the green wooden shed
where shade after quick shade
endlessly shuttles let me speak
and speak unsorrowing.

As in the weather of a Lewis loom
a pastoral picture, striped against the blue,
against the stone, against the green,
against the cottage with its daisies
taking the place of roses
casting the meal from a young hand
still without its ring.

The long dress billows in the breeze
mixed like the confectionery
you'd bring home from the fishing
in the large yellow chest with hats,
silken things and coats,
just before your straight-backed brother
marched off to save the King.

Just stay there therefore for a moment,
uncomplicated dairy girl,
in your chequered screen of red and blue
holding the pail in your hand
before the sky is red and mooned
and feathered by (beyond the dance)
the beat of metal wings.

'Tinily a star goes down'

Tinily a star goes down
behind a black cloud.

Odd that your wristwatch still should lie
on the shiny dressing table

its tick so faint I cannot hear
the universe at its centre.

Contrasts

Against your black I set the dainty deer
stepping in mosses and in water where
there are miles of moorland under miles of air.

Against your psalms I set the various seas
slopping against the mussels fixed in place,
slums on the ancient rocks in salty rows.

Against your bible I set the plateau
from which I see the people down below
in their random kingdoms moving to and fro.

Against your will I set the changing tones
of water swarming over lucid stones
and salmon bubbling in repeated suns.

Against your death I let the tide come in
with its weight of water and its lack of sin,
the opulent millions of a rising moon.

Moonlight over the island

Moonlight over the island, our people gathered
into their black order, into their white,
into the Sundays of the folded hills.

The fishermen walked in Palestine and here
they also walk and in the blue air
black hats like buoys bob churchwards. Also here

the shepherds herd their sheep, and dogs will bark
under such moons explicit as once shone
over the orange groves, the pale sad face

lolling on its cross, while deep below
the crofters slept, and the stones received the moon
in their black mirrors, Palestine or Skye.

'The chair in which you've sat'

The chair in which you've sat's not just a chair
nor the table at which you've eaten just a table
nor the window that you've looked from just a window.
All these have now a patina of your
body and mind, a kind of ghostly glow
which haloes them a little, though invisible.

There is, said Plato, an ideal place
with immortal windows, tables and pure chairs,
archetypes of these, as yet unstained.
In such a world one might look out to space
and see pure roses yet untouched by hand,
the perfect patterns of a universe

of which our furniture is but editions
bred from a printing press which has no end.
The perfect Bible will remain unread
and what we have's a series of translations
which scholars make, each nodding aching head
bowed over texts they never can transcend,

and yet more lovely because truly human,
as tables, chairs and windows in our world
are ours and loved because they taste of us.
Being who we are we must adore the common
copies of perfection, for the grace
of perfect things and angels is too cold.

So in this room I take the luminous
as being the halo of our sweat and love
which makes a chair more than a simple chair,
a table more than a table, dress than dress,
and startlingly striking out of the air
the tigerish access of a crumpled glove.

Argument

He said: We argue and we come to this,
Dostoevsky saying everything is allowed
if there is no continuance after death.
If all the answers have material faces
and no one sees the fine spiritual graces
descending from the heavens in luminous dress
then there's the terror of pure nothingness.

The laws of God engraved on tables were
pure as the morning, for their authorship
was that which made the morning, after all.
The azure and the stone both came together
in a perfected and benignant weather.
The tablets were originals of the air
and made it mean exactly what we are.

If behind the morning there are no
immortal birds parading, if behind
the stubborn stone there isn't more than stone
how shall we find direction? As the hum
of bees in summer harmonises plum
and grape and apple so that these are notes
inside the music which so dominates

the else unmeaning scenery: as in art
the poet knows when he's concluded, for
there's an exactitude that he's aiming at.
He knows it by a sense beyond the poem,
he knows it as he knows a coming home,
perfection to which nothing can be added,
nor by the mind can wholly be decoded.

from LOVE POEMS AND ELEGIES (1972)   165

As even translating from one language to
another one, a residue remains,
there is a gap electricity can't leap.
So words remain ungathered (harvests too)
if that is all that words or harvests do,
that is, just mean themselves, and do not point
to a certain place where both of them are joined.

Everything is allowable, said the Russian,
if death is all there is, if we should stay
fixed to that body, empty as a vase,
which once held life but now is wholly clay,
an object without meaning in our day
of living fish and dogs. That rats should have
their sly quick purpose, their malignant grave

radiance and expression, and you none!
It cannot be that this phenomenon
should disappear as water from a jar.
The world is so impregnated with mind
there must exist a mode at which we find
conversions occurring, like the caterpillars
transformed to moths of an angelic colour.

The Greeks believed the circle was the perfect
figure. Therefore the heavens must conform.
There had to be a way to make ellipses
respectable and so explain the orbit
of planets moving gravely through the light.
It just required a little movement of
a human mind, a justice as of love.

So from a certain stance (as if backstage)
I see the transformation, how the dull
loggish stability becomes the quick
and brilliant foil which lights a whole stage up,
how from a dreary ordinary sleep
lights flash in all directions from pure faces
which are as diamonds in their clear excesses.

Or as in spring an acre becomes blue
and there are bluebells shining mile on mile,
vivid creation of the dullest earth.
Or as in genius ordinary words appear
angelic, peasant becomes peer,
brown wears the purple, and from hedges flower
whole detonations of remarkable power.

O there are moments when a certain star
rising over the waters is a song,
a glove, a perfume, a remembrancer,
a soul steadily rising, or a 'star',
a spiritual Garbo near and far,
a private public being whom the earth
cannot wholly hide though it gave her birth.

I sense a vast connection, spiritual things
bodying forth material, material too
bodying forth the spiritual, so I know
that death is just a place that we have looked
too deeply at, not into, as at a book
held that short space too close. For we must hold
back from a painting so as to see it whole.

And what was blurred becomes quite ordered then.
Out of the chaos marches a whole street
with a church, an inn and houses, people too,
and the light curves all around them with the shape
of a woman in her vulnerable hope
bent over a cradle, tucking sheet and shawl
into an order which is loved and real.

'The world's a minefield'

The world's a minefield when I think of you.
I must walk carefully in case I touch
some irretrievable and secret switch
that blows the old world back into the new.

How careless I once was about this ground
with the negligence of ignorance. Now I take
the smallest delicate steps and now I look
about me and about me without end.

The place without music

Look steadily at the place without music
for you will come to it, some day you will come.
To clench the teeth is only one device.
Another is to leaf through early days
with patience before large busy windows.
There are some others but the best of all
is to remember it is natural,
to outstare it steadily as a child does
neither with shame nor yet with penitence.

At the Scott Exhibition, Edinburgh Festival

I

He will outlast us, churning out his books,
advocate and historian, his prose
earning him Abbotsford with its borrowed gates,
its cheap mementos from the land he made.
Walking the room together in this merciless
galaxy of manuscripts and notes
I am exhausted by such energy.
I hold your hand for guidance. Over your brow
the green light falls from tall and narrow windows.
His style is ignorant of this tenderness,
the vulnerable angle of your body
below the Raeburn with its steady gaze.

II

It was all in his life, not in his books
'Oh I am dying, take me home to Scotland
where I can breathe though that breath were my last.'
He limped through an Edinburgh being made anew.
He worked his way through debts, past a dead wife.
My dear, we love each other in our weakness
as he with white grave face diminishing through
stroke after stroke down to the unpaid room.
We know what we are but know not what we will be.
I tremble in this factory of books.
What love he must have lost to write so much.

from PENGUIN MODERN POETS 21
(1972)

By the Sea

1

Sitting here by the foreshore day after day
on the Bed and Breakfast routine

I cower in green shelters, watch the sea
bubble in brown sea-pools, watch the sea

climb to the horizon and fall back
rich with its silver coins, its glittering.

Warmly scarfed, I almost remember how
beggars were, and in the thirties men

jumped from the wheel. I lock my will
on the National Health Service, will not fall

too deep for rescue but for the mind, the mind.
Two clouds loom together and are joined

as are two lovers in their nylon wings,
a yellow flutter on cramped bench. Thick rings

of routine save us, rings like marriage rings.
The yachts seem free in their majestic goings

and the great ships at rest. Helmeted girls
emerge from salons with their golden curls.

2

At Helensburgh the tide is out again –
Famous for no one but John Logie Baird
who stares with hollow vision from his soured
bust in the Gardens, given over to bowls
and large fat flowers, as vulgar as the girls
who holiday on pop and fish-and-chips.
The faded gentry turn their telescopes
on the grey Empire ships. The *Advertiser*
genteely mourns the century of the razor
and evenings on the benches tête-à-tête
the officer-like ladies with their net
handbags illuminated by the Fair's coarse lights
and cheap rotating toy world chew the sights
over and over as the mile from Rhu
shades to a ghastly colour, TV blue.

3

These hundred-year-olds preserved in glazed
skin like late apples. Where the yacht's guns blaze
they're startled in their shelters. Past MacNair –
Celtic's pre First War full-back – they can share
tales of long-shirted footballers, rotate
on a fabulous bitten park. O the huge weight
of time's dead failures. (What would you say my age…
What would you say my age was?) Pipers wage
a mimic war. Eight and two drummers seem
a hired-out autumn at the minimum
cost to the town. These centenarians know
each blade of grass, each veer of yacht, each slow
seepage of the tide. God's ancient spies
and vultures of the spirit they surprise
by the teeth's grip on meat, persistent fangs
which have outanchored wives, their busy goings.

4

IN THE CAFÉ

The leaf-fringed fountain
with the grey Scots cherub
arches water
over the waterlogged pennies.

Mouths and moustaches move.
The sad-eyed waitress
hides her unringed hand.
Umbrellas stand at ease.

Outside, rain drips
soupily, 'the soup of the day'.
The sauce bottles are filled with old blood
above the off-white linen.

('Not that I didn't have
suitors,' said the Edinburgh lady
seated in the shelter like a queen,
gloved hands on her worn sceptre.)

But the waitress meltingly watches
that white-haired three-year-old,
a huge bubble with wicked teeth
combing his hair with his knife.

5

Milk jugs, cups,
pastries with pink ice,
menus rotating through one meal.
Most of what we do is refuel,
then head for stations, lost in driving rain.

Waitresses with frilly aprons,
I can tell you

how the teeth rot under the pink ice,
and the sky-blue ashtrays contain
a little fire with lipstick, a little fire.

So few are beautiful,
so few outwear the rainy
sag of a dull air, so few ride
naturally as in woodland, the dream
of the eternally cantering proud horses.

Everything drips, drips, drips,
the water, blood, adulterated milk.
The stalls advertise 'Condensed Books'.
All week I have fed on cheap paper
turning like logged swing doors.

6

DUMBARTON

They're pulling down the Bingo hall today.
Crash! Through the glass the pole breaks to the walls
of the converted picture house. The stalls
and ornate balcony (once so outré
with its cheap cherubs of the Music Halls,
Victorian children, plump and neatly gay)
crack in white plaster on white overalls.

Where it once stood, a new smooth road will curve
to a late-night bar, pink with its lights and gin.
There will be leather seats, corners for love,
and the newly-learned cuisine
for the European progeny of those grave
unshaven unemployables who spun
one butt-end out, a river-side conclave

spitting in dirty water: who could get
their Marxist heaven from the plush back-row
watching the jerky stars in scratchy light,

who then would in soft twilight rise and go
half-swimming to the park and there would sit
eating their oily chips, the to-and-fro
of hard tall collars cutting at their throats.

7

Out of the grey the white waves mouth at the shore.
This is their day as yesterday it was mine.
Waves, you would drown me. I know it well. The shine
of your naked grins is dangerous, from what core

of unimaginable cold and dark it flashes
pure power from impure salt, the bodies broken
into a frightening Mass, where no words are spoken
but energy turns on its transformer, gnashes

at the very light and stones. I put it down
this primer on Nuclear Weapons-Science Series –
complete with diagrams, and watch the furious
toppling of the grooved and waste-filled dustbin

with the fused bulb, the soggy *Glasgow Herald*,
the ice-cream carton, empty golden pack
of Benson and Hedges, and the silver track
as of a fish swimming in that drowned field.

8
AFTER THE GALE

The stunned world stops on its axis.
Slowly the clouds venture out.
The hills steady.

O Rome, duty was not enough –
the fixed spear, the savage mask for farmers,
the sentry in his place.

The upright eaten by the circular
spin of the stormy world, Hades uprooted
by a bright removal van,

the gods turned to pictures on the carnival
rotating with its fixed masks, its wolves
still upright in their chairs.

9

YOUNG GIRL

Nothing more impermanent, it appears,
in your bare nylons twittering. The harsh

waves will not overwhelm you as you rock
on tottering heels towards the yellow clock

high on the windy pier. You toughly peck
at your oiled bag of chips, as seagulls break

herring heads like egg-shells, with bulb eyes.
I watch you in your sheer indomitableness

click the late street past yellow café light,
an H.M.S. that's joining the grey fleet.

10

DUNOON AND THE HOLY LOCH

The huge sea widens from us, mile on mile.
Kenneth McKellar sings from the domed pier.
A tinker piper plays a ragged tune
on ragged pipes. He tramps under a moon
which rises like the dollar. Think how here

missiles like sugar rocks are all incised
with Alabaman Homer. These defend

the clattering tills, the taxis, thin pale girls
who wear at evening their Woolworth pearls
and from dewed railings gaze at the world's end.

11

TOURIST DRIVER

He tells us there's a cow and there's a cow.
He names a hill for us and there it is.
I dream a little, rocking towards Hades
on my third spy story, and imagine how,
gloved and helmeted among the lilies,

he might be telling us of Achilles next
and pointing out his cairn with the bruised heel
or Orpheus perhaps becoming real:
and from that quay how well he knows his text –
old Charon pulling west each half-crown soul.

12

IN THE PARK

Over the shoes in pebbles I sit here.
Behind me, the silent bells of those red flowers.
Under that winged structure Greeks might wander,
retired Achilles in the varying shade

drifted from the Home, telling of wars,
and Helen's mouth open like that soft bloom
which turns to the sun softly in the dew
and busy orbit of the striped wasp.

On the smooth lawn a cat pursues a bird,
great Disney fool. The bird looks at him, flies,
lands and flies and this time doesn't stop.
The cat slouches back among the trees.

A lot of marble, messages in flowers –
this is Barnardo's Year – the door is open
to orphans ejected from our Welfare State,
that cosy bubble with few images.

The marble and carnations of Elysium.
Columns of lilies drink at the warm water.
All day the furious sun scans the lawns
and fat loud Ajax's waddling up to bowl.

13

Days when the world seems like an old French film
or like the old French General Alors
who waves his soldiers into the Foreign Legion.

Days when everyone has a false moustache
and like a clown one kicks the buildings down
in cycles of raw sparks.

Days when it's hard to follow what is said,
fragments of verbs, verbs in a high wind,
French thick-voiced cannonade.

Days when the rain drums steadily on the attic
where once we turned the green leaves of books
under the farmhouse rafters.

Days, days, days… O the French General
standing in the truck with his drum-shaped soldier's hat
waving us towards nothing.

14
AT THE SILENT FILMS

O Chaplin with your little black moustache,
your twitching lip, your dead-white dummy's face,
your pliant bourgeois cane.

And Valentino – sheikh of the lovely dead –
jerking through the screen's minute sand
on your crumbling marvellous horse.

And all these visual comics, collapsed chairs,
candid pie-filled faces, fluid houses,
and trains without their rails.

And the jerky dead in jerky chariots
with the blunt bucking swords and thorny helmets,
the overquick salute.

All have crumbled into the screen's sands,
Under the piano's bouncing music
they drown and drown and drown,

twittering like the early birds of spring
testing their wings. By the rackety machine
in flash-light they're devoured.

So many dead. So many stars sunk
in the absurd cloud of their furs
in their busy struts and strides.

O happy visual simplicities
elastic huge moustaches, snaky stairs,
hosepipes of comic water.

You still survive, though dead, in all your white.
The sand has not devoured you, lovely teeth.

I see your blizzard smiles.

Jean Brodie's Children

Jean Brodie's children in your small green caps,
I hear you twitter down the avenues.

The great round bells ring out, the Mademoiselle
despairs of English. In the rustling dorms
you giggle under sheets.

'Dear Edinburgh, how I remember you,
your winter cakes and tea, your bright red fire,
your swirling cloaks and clouds.

Your grammar and your Greek, the hush of leaves,
No Orchids for Miss Blandish with a torch
beneath the tweedy blanket.

Ah, those beautiful days, all green and shady,
our black and pleated skirts, our woollen stockings,
our ties of a calm mauve.

Mistresses, iron in their certainty,
their language unambiguous but their lives
trembling on grey boughs.'

If You Are About to Die Now

If you are about to die now
there is nothing I can write for you.
History is silent about this.
Even Napoleon, face huge as a plate,
disguised the advance guard and said:
'Why they sent for my brother is because
he, and not I, is in trouble.'

The screens come down. The nurses disappear
like the tails of fishes. The clouds
are white as cotton wool and also
Dettol outlives the perfume.
The unshaven man in the next ward
is given shaving lotion for Christmas.
Sorrow stands like a stork on one leg,
brooding.

The coloured windows give way to plain.
The horsemen crossing the moor are comrades
going the other way into the country
of the undisciplined and the free.
Here there is the Land of the Straight Lines
with a banner black and silent,
a black mirror
with the image of an old rose.

History does not warn us of this.
Napoleon's face expands to a window.
The manic thoughts fly outwards, beating.
'The documents did not tell me.
There was no announcement in the salon.
Why is it that the chairs are getting crooked?
Why is it that my army does not bear me?
They are eating, laughing by the stream.

I shout to them, 'Put on your armour.'
But they do not listen.
They do not know me, they are relapsing
into the marsh of their idleness.
They are schoolboys escaped from Latin.
O how afraid they are of Excellence.
They admire their faces in the water.
They splash in the new bubbles.'

The White Air of March

1

This is the land God gave to Andy Stewart –
    we have our inheritance.
There shall be no ardour, there shall be indifference.
There shall not be excellence, there shall be the average.
We shall be the intrepid hunters of golf balls.

Have you not known, have you not heard, has it not been reported
that Mrs Macdonald has given an hour-long lecture on Islay
and at the conclusion was presented with a bouquet of flowers
by Marjory, aged five?
                Have you not noted
the photograph of the whist drive, skeleton hands,
rings on skeleton fingers?
                Have you not seen
the glossy weddings in the glossy pages,
champagne and a 'shared joke'.
                Do you not see
the Music Hall's still alive here in the North? and on the stage
the yellow gorse is growing.
                'Tragedy,' said Walpole, 'for those who
                                feel.
For those who think, it's comic.'
                Pity then those who feel
and, as for the Scottish Soldier, off to the wars!
The Cuillins stand and will forever stand.
Their streams scream in the moonlight.

2

The Cuillins tower
clear and white.
In the crevices the Gaelic bluebells flower.

(Eastward
Culloden
where the sun shone
on the feeding raven.
Let it be forgotten!)

The Cuillins tower
scale on scale.
The music of the imagination must be restored
upward.

(The little Highland dancer
in white shirt green kilt
regards her toe
arms akimbo.
Avoids the swords.)

To avoid the sword
is death.
          To walk the ward
of Dettol, loss of will,
where old men watch the wall,
eyes in a black wheel,
and the nurse in a starched dress
changes the air.

The Cuillins tower
tall and white.
March breeds white sails.

The eagle soars.
On the highest peaks
The sharpest axe.

3

Scottish dance music.
                    Wagner.
'The Hen's March to the Midden'.

Sudden,
        the freshening,
the blue wave that will not be drowned.
The green knife from a café.

The four-walled pibroch is too solid.
Quickness! Fish-leap! Incompleteness!

The flash
        that is seen
                and gone!

Rain-flash
        almost.

(Scottish dance music.
                Used as torture
to make them confess,
                the prisoners.)

Outside the adobe,
                the Hen's March to the Midden.

And all shall be well,
                unbidden,
the dancers go under the hill.

4

She came one night
               and she said:
'I've written a small book
on the viola
             to be printed in London
not at my own expense
           I hasten to tell you.

And little songs
           I've also written
for a competition
              in Eurovision.
I tried to get an introduction
but he was too busy
           surrounded by the flowers
             – the lion
smiling among the glasses.

Thirty copies have been sold.
       Do you have any contacts
for such texts?
       To break into the light's centre
where the real people are is not easy,
such fakes surround them.
                  To enter,
to enter the light.'

Her hands crossed on her lap,
dazzled.
       Her eyes sparkling.

There will always be hope.

5

March, and the sails fly seaward
                  whiter, whiter.
He bends in the garden, digs his green lawn.
The soil is broken by a busy convocation
of worms, airless undulation.
At midnight they dance on the lawn,
a vivid exercise, a tortuous process.
                The hedge buds,
puts out white flowers.
                The sails fly seaward,
the rocks attend the keel.
                He bends in his garden
under the council house's wide panes
which show this pastoral scene, another house,
and the blue sky of TV.
The exiles have departed,
                carrying with them
on a green dollar
                'a country of the heart'.

At midnight the worms dance on the lawn
transforming recreating
                altering.
The endless process of the roses brings
summer to wandering tourists.

                The sails
        fly
            seaward.

6

Sundays.
        The great bells toll.
'Let us meet. Let us draw sustenance from each other.'
Let us put aside the *Observer,* let us remember
        the invocations of the *Sunday Post.*
Let our dirty jokes be told in secret
to a small circle of friends.
                But otherwise
let us make a stand.

The polished tombstones are like mirrors.
Granite. There let us see our reflections.
And, in the silence, listen to the dead growing,
pink hymn books in their hands.

Otherwise let us make a stand
        against permissiveness. If we are quoted
Say 'The Country' say 'Society'
        but
in smoking rooms let not our jokes be counted against us.

Distant, the white sails.

7

(I speak now of those who told the truth.
Let them be praised.
        Dostoevsky. Nietzsche, Kierkegaard,
Kafka – let them be honoured.
For them there shall be a cross pointing both ways.
Vertical horizontal.
The Idiot waits for the Cossacks in crystal and iron.
The hunchback squeezes the last ounce out of the wine.

Someone climbs to a castle which doesn't exist.
All shall be on trial to a deaf sheriff
and the police stand in their diced caps, so youthful,
the radiance of our law,
Over the steppes the drumming thunder of legions.
They beat on the Cross, the Either Or of his passion
                    the ring falls from his finger.
The drums beat. Who shall welcome the drummers?
At a table of crystal and linen, glitter and water,
the minister blesses their steel.)

                    8
The exiles have departed,
                    leaving old houses.
The Wind wanders like an old man who has lost his mind.
'What do you want?' asks the wind. 'Why are you crying?
Are those your tears or the rain?'
I do not know. I touch my cheek. It is wet.
I think it must be the rain.

It is bitter
to be an exile in one's own land.
It is bitter
to walk among strangers
when the strangers are in one's own land.
It is bitter
to dip a pen in continuous water
to write poems of exile
in a verse without honour or style.

9

There have been so many
exiles.
       Jews
turn on their limited space
like cows.
       So many
faces blank as watches
telling
       nothing but time.

How can you drink a cup of wine
without tasting the vinegar
without feeling the thorn?

On the high far
Cuillins
I see them climb.

10

What, out of this place,
rises
out of this
scarred ground
fought over and over
endlessly confined,
refined?

Beautiful ghost,
do you put on body,
do you cry?
It is good if you can,
if from your eyes,
bulbs, there should rise
dew,
out of that face

beaten over and over
water,
tears,
refreshment out of your eyes.

11

They died
            in a tight ring
                        around their king.

The ravens squawk over the fresh bodies
peck through the chain mail
                        as through small windows.

To the end in a hard place among stones
in the cold twilight they parried.

There shall be no withdrawal.
                        For honour, for something, they fought.
For the silks of the ladies
                        for the honour of their own arms.

Silver and gold. There was cold silver.
He lies there eaten by the ravens
who peck in the dark, nodding
their heads like small machines.

In the north there is much wailing.
There is fresh dew on the ballads.
In the morning the wells of their eyes are dry.

Remains this –
            the honour.

12

The tall buses pass by.
        The cottages trail their roses.

Look at the witch at the waterfall.
        She does Bed and Breakfast.

'Ah, Freedom is a noble thing.'

        Around the Cuillins
the clouds drift like green dollars.

13

I speak (with a little water) of the family of the MacMurrows.
They are a sept of the MacMorris and had good bards enough.
They were the repositories of much harp music
of history, of genealogy.
Much lore did they preserve, much more than we deserve.
Their ruminations are contained in the 'Book of the MacMurrows',
'The Annals of the MacMurrows' and much matter significant for
                                   scholarship
including the first use of the ablative absolute in a categorical mode
with animadversions upon the umlaut, the Dawn of the Present
                                   Participle
though in one or two places the record is unfortunately blank.
(With a drink of water) I am prepared to discourse to you
on their relationship to the *Mabinogion*.
I am willing to unearth their periphrases, to clarify their apostrophes
to investigate their commas and propose their periods
but enough I think has been said to show their importance
to the quality of our civilisation, our language, and the perpetuation
of our culture, our literature and, if I may say so, our Cause.

14

McGonagall
             why do I see you as a sign?
Why does your drama perplex me?
Endlessly you toil towards Balmoral
to the old lady knitting her slow empire.

Baffled, beaten, buffeted, scorned, despised,
You played 'Macbeth' to a theatre of villains.
You swung your sly cloak through gaslight
a devotee of Art.

All that you wrote is bad, let us agree.
Who would say that Athens is Dundee?
Or the Tay Bridge our Scots Thermopylae?

(At the 'hot gates'
a wreath for heroes.)

And yet how many more have written worse.
Why such a hatred for your bad verse
when every day we see our literature
weakened by loss of passion, loss of power?

Why should you suffer the anonymous
theses and poor parodies of those
whose competence is just as small as yours —
when they unlike you don't even love verse!

Except that they see mirrored in you their own
impenetrable dullness.
                        On her throne
Victoria sits, a 'poetess' indeed
able to beat a poet on the head

who for endeavour should at least receive
an Order more deserved than some who live
in such hypocrisy as will not be
honoured by Athens, and let's hope, Dundee.

13

The Cuillins tower high in the air –
                              Excellence.
We climb from pain to perfume:
the body opens out; gullies,
crevices, reveal the orchis.
The soul flies skyward,
impregnated with scent.
On the right hand
    the sun will tenant
Skye.
        The mist dissipates.
Gold grows at our feet.

16

            Excellence!
'costing not less than everything'
Illusion after illusion dies.
After the gay green, the blackness.
Snatches
'and I mysel in crammasie'.
Rainbows
out of the darkness.
Green,
green moments
or out of the waterfall
a sudden face –
so dearly known and killed.
Minotaur of guilt
coiled at the centre, vivid.
Flashes.
Blades.
Rotors of Glasgow knives.
Irises
held over tenements
intent, inventing,

Periphrases,
white deer stepping by Loch Lomond side.
The dead bury their dead.
The machines finished
underground.

In the white air of March
a new mind.

from ORPHEUS AND OTHER POEMS
(1974)

The Island

'And as for that island,' so he said,
'we shall remember it always however we change,
the sun on the lochs on a clear day.
We shall not comb our hair without remembering
the windy grass on the moor.'

In the Dark

Feeling across a field in the dark
one shields one's eyes against the wire fences.
The body tenses and the eye winces,
the feet feeling for ditches draw back.

And we remember that all our art
is dependent first on light and then on skill,
for how could any poet go to school
in a black field with such a checked stride?

Inching sometimes over unsteady stone
and by a black stream waiting, hearing its noise
and guessing from its small or major voice
how deep it is, how shallow, how serene,

aching intently for magnanimous light
which is the page and the reason for the page
the space which tempts us out to voyage
beyond the field, beyond its fenced limit.

Orpheus

1

And he said, I am come in search of her
bringing my single bitter gift. I have
nothing more precious to offer
than this salt venom seeming to you as love.
It is true I cannot live without her
since I am now shade who was once fire.
See, mineral spirit, how I now suffer
by the slow heavy motion of my lyre.

And the god then replying, let her stay
for by her absence your music is more clear
barer and purer. Always in the air
her distance will perfect her as Idea.
Better the far sun of an April day
than fleshly thunder in the atmosphere.

2

And he said, That is great condemnation,
to live profoundly and yet much alone.
To see deeply by a barren passion.
It was forgetfully I moved the stone
which now submits to my examination.
She was my sense; around her flowing gown
my poems gathered in their proper season.
They were her harvest yet they were my own.

And the god then replying, What you say
is what her absence taught you. Our return
is not permissible to an earlier way.
If it were possible you would learn to mourn
even more deeply. Do you never burn
poems whose language was becoming grey?

3

And he to the god, If you should let her go
I'd know my music had its former power
to melt you too as once it melted snow
to alter you as once it altered her
so that in music we both learned to grow.
It was a dance of earth and of the air.
But up above it's easier. Here below –
The shade then smiled and said, Behold her there,

and he beheld her whitely where she stood
in that deep shade. She seemed not to have changed
nor he to have changed either as he played.
And yet her apparition was so strange.
She didn't fit the music that he made.
The notes and she were mutually disarranged.

4

And the god to him, Now I must tell you clear
what you refuse to see, since it is hard
to accuse ourselves of cruelty and fear.
You wished that she should die. And what you heard
was not my voice but yours condemning her.
If you will learn to love you must go forward.
For that is how it is in the upper air.
All that you have shared you have now shared.

And Orpheus took his lyre and left that place
and moved where the shadows moved and the clouds flowed
and all that lived had its own changing grace.
As on an April day there was sun and shade
but nothing vicious or virtuous
haunted the various music that he played.

5

And he to the god, Tell me about the shades.
Are they more real above or here below?
Or is it as with trees that stand by lakes
for looking downward you will see them grow
away from you in water. I would know
whether my lyre is real or whether it fades
as my hand fades or whether on my brow
a ghostly laurel as in water shakes.

And the god to him, They vibrate both together,
your lyre and such reality as there is,
each making each as in a misty weather.
The berries that grow richly on the trees
should be sufficient for you, whether these
are just themselves or shadows of each other.

And, for your lyre, though you might feel as shade
what I might feel as solid that is no
disturbance of the harmony you have made.
If I should rise to where you come and go
the stones and trees to me would be as shade
and the white water would in blackness flow
and my black lyre would shift and change and fade
as in the twilight hills of indigo.

And he to the god, But you have never climbed
to plead with me to have your love returned
from the shades of upper air in which she moves.
Now therefore I consider that I've burned
with a more real pain and that our loves
are dearer and more near for that attempt.

But the god was silent as in Orpheus' hand
the lyre expanded and contracted like
a shadow that's projected on a wall.
Slowly he extended through the black
atmosphere his arm and took the lyre

and played such music as the zodiac
if made of solid heavy massive chains might make
which yet were banked with elegies and fire

and Orpheus almost swooned against that force
as if the very blackness spoke in joy
with its own elegance, intense and sparse.
The motion was a boulder's yet the cry
so piercing and so pure that if he died
he knew his eyes would stream with sparkling tears.

6

And he to the god, I have descended from
the city of vibrations where I see
the beggar seated in alternate gloom
and negligent neon and continually
the concentrated faces in a dream
of their own separate force are passing by
as if in passion or delirium
since each of us is crying, 'I am I'

for life must generate its vanity
and from each window waves the personal soul
singing, if necessary let others die
but as for me I have the right and will
to my own measure of the present day,
however transient and however small.

And so I think I wish to stay with you
and lay aside my lyre and sleep at last
in a monotonous place where nothing new
troubles the spirit and with face aghast
I need not always stand against the tempest
making an adamant music, being true
to a lost captain and a mutinous crew
in an ugly and adulterated waste.

And the god to him, There is no way to stay
as if you were an engine which has drawn
its final string of carriages and in May
is found among the rails where marigolds burn
in rustic sidings miles and miles away
from the main headlong tracks of sparkling iron.

For I may tell you that it ends in rust
however in the summer it appears
pleasant and archaic and exposed
to the quaint gents who hunt for souvenirs
and potter in the sunshine of the past
for precious evidence of affectionate powers
which though tremendous weren't harshly used.

In any case your destiny hasn't ruled
that you remain below. You must return
as a good driver to the upper field
without a destination. You must learn
to read the flags more closely and compelled
by an ardour of the spirit always burn
forward on tracks continually rebuilt.

7

And Orpheus walked among the broken slums
whose windows had been smashed or cracked or boarded
and saw the children play among discarded
mattresses and boxes and the scum
of moist and dirty cardboard. There were poems
chalked on the flaking walls, misspelt, ill-worded,
and in the closes women with red arms
stood talking fiercely with their aprons girded

and his lyre was clouded as with greenish slime
and all the brilliant strings appeared corroded
by it and the monotony of time
and he might have ceased to play but that the sordid
stout valiant women so unkempt, sublime,
laughed gaily in the morning without hatred.

So that beyond the shade he saw the human
invincible spirit playing, as one goes
through utter darkness and sees water gleaming
and all the way one walks through resonant meadows
or as from a fast train by tenements racing
one has a glimpse of a white-vested man
plunging his vigorous head into a basin
beyond a sudden sparkling window pane

or children blowing bubbles by a shore
where dogs retrieve thrown sticks and someone writes
with unaccustomed pen, Wish you were here,
and girls stretched out on deck-chairs dream of nights
with Elvis Presley while their mothers share
with Valentino fading appetites.

And so his lyre had a graver heavier tone
as if containing all the possible grains
that can be found in marble or in stone.
What he had lost was the sweet and random strains
which leaped obliquely from the vast unknown
concordances and mirrors but the gains,
though seeming sparser, were more dearly won

as less in mobile warfare than in trench
one sees the faces closer as they loom
in their thorny helmets whether German, French,
or some quite other nation; and they seem
so like his own – the cheeks, the teeth, the chins –
that he must love them not as in a dream
but on this smoky field of green and orange.

Breughel

A bony horse with a bird on it droops its head.
With a cart of skulls like potatoes Death drives onward.

There's a storm of monsters snouted and obscene
and on another page a neat snow scene.

Large peasants dance under a leaden sky
and ships are sinking in a black-framed sea.

The blind raise tortured faces. In Cockayne
they eat and drink and sleep and at the moon

a peasant pisses. Proverbs multiply.
Children with adult faces gravely play

while aprons break the storm, red plates and jugs,
Death in a hood and lands pulled back like rugs.

And over the countryside the black birds go
with far below them hunters in the snow.

Poem for Auden

When you died
it wasn't really like a dying,
you had done it so easily.

As your poetry is so easy
that one doesn't realise the many
zigzags you've contrived
to find your way through,

emerging like a magician with phrases
you seem to have picked up on hedges
on days luckily voracious
from the briary thorns of Old English
and the crooked spells of witches.

The sailor sets out in ice,
his harp sharp and shaggy.
He knows the hirpling monsters,
halls where the light falls,
and the doomed tippling lord
brooding on chessboard.

He learns Mozart,
the sea-knowledge of Freud,
has a face like an old map,
a dissolute pirate.

He tosses phrases like coins
while the moon blazes above him,
quizzical, humorous,
stunningly cold and bold,
absurd lovely Diana.

He turns away at the end
from all the tempests,
habituate to housework,
with a housemaid, an old dog,
and a radiant bathroom
where the body convicts the soul.

'The heel on the finishing blade of grass.'
Abruptly he enters the silence.
The sorcerer is laid in the wood
which will play forever.

The Glass of Water

My hand is blazing on the cold tumbler.
My eye looks through it to the other side.
If it were what is real, if it were heaven
how I corrupt it with my worn flesh.
How its neutrality is aggrandised
by fever and by empire. I constrain
and grasp this parish which is pastoral.

To be pure is not difficult, it's impossible.
How could the saint work to this poverty,
this unassumingness, this transparency?
How could his levels be so wholly calm?
The fact of water is unteachable.
It's less and more than honour standing up
invulnerable in its vulnerable glass.

from POEMS FOR DONALDA
(1974)

Helplessly

Helplessly I wait for you.
I think I am nothing without you.
I am like a grey street on which the sun rises
and suddenly there is a noise of cars
the cries of flower sellers
the shaking out of antique pictured rugs.

The Present

I brought you a green belt
out of green Ireland
and a Galway shawl
which is black and holed

and when you put them on
you seemed both old and young
as Ireland itself is
in its right and wrong

with its proud body,
and its ancient head,
a fierce witty lady
subdued by the dead.

The Shadows

'I think,' she said, 'we shall not see again
each other as we did.' The light is fading
that was once sunny in the April rain.
Across the picture there appears a shading
we didn't notice, but was in the grain.

The picture shows two people happily smiling
with their arms around each other, by the sea.
Whatever they are looking at is beguiling
themselves to themselves. There is a tree
with orange blossoms and an elegant styling

but they are lost quite clearly in each other.
They do not see the landscape, do not hear
the stream that tinkles through the azure weather.
It's as if really the clear atmosphere
were a creation of two souls together.

But at the back there steadily grow two shadows
one for each lover that they can't evade.
They emerge threateningly from the coloured meadows
as if they were a track the two had made
and they were ignorant of, their changeless natures.

And as they move the shades intently follow
growing steadily darker, spreading as they go
as the wings' shades pursue the flying swallow.
My dearest love, if these should make us slow –
remember late the first undying halo.

Tonight

Tonight you are a hundred miles away
and I could read perhaps, or watch TV –
that serial of water, screen of fog.
I think I'd rather hold a dialogue
after the fading routine of the day
in the midnight's darkness, in the midnight's mercy.

O what is love? philosophers have asked
and more than these, the poets, What is love?
Gather your roses while the weather's good.
Love is perhaps a similar attitude
struck by two people. Love is a gay mask.
Love is constructed from a coat or glove.

Love is a mirror lined by sweet bouquets.
It is the purest vanity we know.
It is a loss of self, as saints have taught.
Love is an article that can't be bought
in shop or supermarket. Love has days
that melt to rain after a trembling rainbow.

Love can move the sun and the other stars,
absolves the golden serpent. Is the true
colour of being. Is the finest chain.
Love's the most piercing and inventive pain.
For love we suffer profound ignorant scars.
For love we soldier, and love honour too.

… The night is quiet. There's light upon the ice.
I hear your step a hundred miles away.
Accidents can happen to the soul.
Wherever we are our hearts are both at school
and suffer and enjoy not once but twice
in the blue constant weather, in the grey.

If you are Taurus and I Capricorn
astrologers and horoscopes commend
each to the other in a thrifty marriage
by the sharp rays of prudence and of courage
and by each present we can truly earn –
to us the stars don't prodigally bend.

Love is incessant climbing to far peaks,
ambitious haunting. That is why I hear
your steps so clearly, miles and miles away
as if they moved in jealousy or envy –
you hack steps out with an uncertain axe
in a harsh vast and breathless atmosphere

where all is lost that isn't gained each hour.
I think, quiet Midnight, that the sun will rise
but do not know it. Therefore let my sight
not fade tonight but seem to bring the light –
and her – to my warm house, for your black air
is part of morning's and her shaking guise.

from THE PERMANENT ISLAND

(1975)

Translated from the author's own Gaelic

Young Girl

Young girl who goes with a straight back on the street, there are baskets of flowers in my breast, my table is furnished with your laughter.

A woman will say to me, 'There is pride in her walk.' But I will answer as is fitting, 'Is there pride in the sun in the sky? Is there jealousy between the stone and the gold?'

And when a storm goes past in its own world of rain and wind will you say, 'Pride and arrogance' to it, as it turns forests upside down?

Will you speak disparagingly of the diamond because of its glitter or the sea because of its radiance? There is a white ship among the boats and among the black hats there is a crown.

You are at the bottom of my mind

Without my knowing it you are at the bottom of my mind, like one who visits the bottom of the sea with his helmet and his two great eyes: and I do not know properly your expression or your manner after five years of the showers of time pouring between you and me.

Nameless mountains of water pouring between me, hauling you on board, and your expression and manners in my weak hands. You went astray among the mysterious foliage of the sea-bottom in the green half-light without love.

And you will never rise to the surface of the sea, even though my hands should be ceaselessly hauling, and I do not know your way at all, you in the half-light of your sleep, haunting the bottom of the sea without ceasing, and I hauling and hauling on the surface of the ocean.

Going Home

Tomorrow I will go home to my island, trying to put a world into forgetfulness. I will lift a fistful of its earth in my hands or I will sit on a hillock of the mind, watching 'the shepherd with his sheep'.

There will ascend (I presume) a thrush. A dawn or two will rise. A boat will be lying in the glitter of the western sun: and water will be running through the world of the similes of my intelligence.

But I will be thinking (in spite of that) of the great fire that is behind our thoughts, Nagasaki and Hiroshima, and I will hear in a room by myself a ghost or two constantly moving, the ghost of every error, the ghost of every guilt, the ghost of each time I walked past the wounded man on the stony road, the ghost of nothingness scrutinising my dumb room with distant face till the island is an ark rising and falling on a great sea and no one knowing whether the dove will ever return, and people talking and talking to each other, and the rainbow of forgiveness in their tears.

To an Old Woman

You are in the church listening, sitting on an uncomfortable bench to the words of one who is only half your age.

And I am sitting here writing these corrupted words, and not knowing whether it is the truth or the beautiful lie that is in my mind.

But there is one person who comes into my mind, you sitting in front of a pulpit in your simple black hat, and in your coat (black as well) and in your shoes that have walked many a long street with you.

You were not a scholar in your day. (Many a morning did you gut herring, and your hands were sore with salt, and the keen wind on the edge of your knife, and your fingers frozen with fire.)

You have never heard of Darwin or Freud or Marx or that other Jew, Einstein, with the brilliant mind: nor do you know the meaning of the dream you dreamed last night in your room in heavy sleep.

You haven't heard how the stars move away from us like calm queens through the sky. And you haven't heard how the lion with his fierce head sits at the table with us.

But you sit there in front of the pulpit and in your loneliness you say many a prayer and if the minister shakes you by the hand your mind is filled with happiness.

You remember other days, a sermon direct as a bullet, a summer pouring around a church, a gold ring and the testimony of roses opening summer like a new Bible in your memory.

And you will remember many a death and many days which went waste, a clock in the wall ticking your world to its end.

May your world prosper and you on your way home over the white streets like a man's mind, open with the edge of the knife, and boys standing in their quarrelsomeness studying nothingness: keenly they looked at you going without armour across a street burning at your feet, without armour but your harmonious spirit that never put a world in order but which will keep you, I hope, whole in your innocence like a coat.

The Old Woman

Tonight she is sitting by a window and the street like a bible below her eyes. The curtains have had many washings. There is glitter from the flowered floor.

The world was once without shape, men and women like a red fever walking about flesh and mind, nostrils tasting love and anger.

Moon and sun in the sky, hand like salmon leaping to hand, the fish of the world in a net, pain that would not leave breast tranquil.

But everything has been set in order. Table in its place, chair in its place. This room is the mirror of her thoughts, arsenal from which will arise no music of growth.

For the music that will sing it together is youth itself that will never return. Her eye is sweeping the streets. Time is crouched in the window.

At the Cemetery

I saw them yesterday at the cemetery, with black hats, and the sun
rising, a glitter of flowers about their feet, and one wearing a bitter
shirt.

Glitter of the sky, a sea singing, a pouring of grass, and a steadi-
ness of mountains, the mortal conversation of dark hats, the poetry
of summer upside down.

A wide day extending to the horizon. A bible burning in the hands
of the wind and sun, and a sea falling like an empty dress on that shore.

And he is where he is. My neighbour lying under the bee which
murmurs among sweet flowers. It was death that killed him and not
a bullet.

And a sun pouring, a sea pouring, black hats darkly sailing on a
sea of roses, as there move poor words on a tide of music.

At the Stones of Callanish

At the stones of Callanish yesterday I heard one woman saying to
another: 'This is where they burnt the children in early times.' I did
not see druids among the planets nor sun nor robe: but I saw a beau-
tiful blue ball like heaven cracking and children with skin hanging to
them like the flag in which Nagasaki was sacrificed.

What Is Wrong?

Who can tell what is wrong? I went to doctors and doctors. One of
them told me, 'It's your head,' and another one, writing small with a
pen, 'It's your heart, your heart.'

But one day I saw a black pit in green earth, a gardener kissing
flowers, an old woman squeaking in her loneliness, and a house sailing
on the water.

I don't know whether there is a language for that, or, if there is, whether I would be any better breaking my imagination into a thousand pieces: but one thing is certain, we must find the right that is wrong.

Eight Songs for a New Ceilidh

1

You asked me for a poem for yourself, thinking, I suppose, that I would put you among the stars for beauty and intelligence.

But as for me I grew up in bare Lewis without tree or branch and for that reason my mind is harder than the foolish babble of the heavens, and also at Hiroshima the kettle boiled over our music and in Belsen there was seen an example of dishonour eating love and flesh, and because of that and because of the truth and all the Evil that was done to us, and we ourselves did (among our complaints) I will never put a pen again into my fist for beauty or for intellect. Beauty is dangerous enough and as for the mind did it not spoil the glittering cities of Europe?

2

When she took the great sea on her, Lewis went away and will not return. I was not compelled to sail 'over to Australia' but around me is Hiroshima and Pasternak's book is in my hands –

I will not drink a health-giving drink from the spring of the healthy deer of May but from water full of eels which are electric and shivering on my flesh like Venus breaking through the mind and the dark-green of the clouds but it was the fine bareness of Lewis that made the work of my mind like a loom full of the music of the miracles and greatness of our time.

3

I saw myself in a camp among the Nazis and the wretched Jews. My hand was white with the innocent lamps of Guernica and my cheeks streaming with piteous tears but in one hand there was a hard gun while the gas was writhing like the mist of Lewis over cold rocks.

4

Standing at the edge of the reservoir that was dumb, menacing, with bare water, I saw the live flies hitting the dead flies on the back. The foxglove was heavy about us with summer's perfume and the sky as limpid as the music of a fiddle. In that moment you leaped and went down into the water, and I was frightened that you wouldn't rise and I shouted in spite of the skill of my intelligence but after that I became silent.

5

I will not climb these mountains for what is at the top?

The stars are holding a ceilidh but what can they say that is not in my own dark depth? I will never sail on a ship. My Pacific is in my head and my Columbus praising countries that are far below. The day of my mind is my May and my twittering of birds the quick thoughts that are black and yellow about my skies.

6

I will never go to France, my dear, my dear, though you are young. I am tied to the Highlands. That is where I learnt my wound.

And are we not tied to that as well? A door will open but where will the slavish spirit of man go? I heard the wind blowing to the Greeks at the Pillars of Hercules: our round world is more harmonious than that. O, it is not a word of manliness that I am speaking of but about the guilt that follows me from mountain and moor. My Uist is inside my head and my love like an agonising tether that is yellow and dangerous and beautiful.

'Go to London,' they said to me. 'In the great city you will compose music from the bitter hard light of your stomach.' And I was struggling with myself for many years, thinking of those streets, men with penetrating power in their faces, an illuminated glittering taxi flashing on the windows of my intelligence.

But tonight sitting at the fire and the hills between me and the sky and listening to the empty quietness and seeing the deer coming to my call I think of another one who said the truthful words: 'Look straight down through wood and wood. Look in your own heart and write.'

Will you go with me, young maiden, over to Japan where our sanity is wasting in that big bomb that fell on town and on mountain?

Not to Uist among the trees or to green Lewis among the heather nor a Farewell to Finnary burning calmly in the strait nor in the hall of Glasgow or Edinburgh and Duncan Ban walking elegantly with a bright gun among the lies that are clouds round our time.

Oban

1

The rain is penetrating Oban and the circus has gone home. The lions and wildcats have gone home through the papers and advertisements. The seats are emptying at the mouth of the shore, in front of the houses in front of the pub – rain falling through the midst of the heavy salt of the sea.

2

Shall I raise a town of paper, with coloured lions on the wall, with great fierce tigers, and the wheel of music spinning?

Shall I raise a sky of paper? Clouds of paper, white lights?

Shall I make myself into paper, with my verses being cut on paper?

3

Tonight the sea is like an advertisement, book after book shining.

My shadow is running down to the sea. My skin is red and green.

Who wrote me? Who is making a poetry of advertisements from my bones? I will raise my blue fist to them. – 'A stout Highlander with his language.'

4

The circus has gone home. They have swept the sawdust away. The pictures of beasts have gone. The rain is falling on the bay. The wheel has gone off by itself. The season is over. The lion is running through sunlight. He has left the rain behind his feet.

5

The big bell began to toll. The church has been opened. I sat down inside it in my mind and saw on the window, instead of Nazareth and Christ, worn earth and sawdust, a lion moving in the explosive circle of Palestine without cease.

Sighting the Mountains of Harris

Sighting the mountains of Harris I saw neon on every street. An Eventide behind the wall, and the gold sailors swimming on the yellow sea of the cafés.

Advertisements on every hand: 'These are the mountains of Harris, this is the end of my love.' Guitars glittering with light like broken ships on the shore. Nylon girls in a doorway: the stones of Woolworths in the bay.

Sighting the mountains of Harris, an armoury of light, a sea of laughter and a green which is not the green of the sea swimming on the face of a sailor.

The Sea and the Rocks

Ballet of foam against the rocks, these are my northern dancers. A bare ignorant head that cannot understand the art of the tribe of foolish dancers who leap and leap to a salt death: like pictures thrown on a white screen, the hard beautiful lost ballet.

Song of Remembrance

Goodbye to Stornoway and the 'Muirneag' in the bay. The castle of our dream is glittering like a box full of Christmas.

O Stornoway and bare Lewis we need more iron than there is in these sails and that castle.

1941–1942

Those days, on the radio, nothing but ships sinking in grey ignorant seas. I sat in the light of the Tilley listening to Big Ben tolling on the heavy eternal bottom of the sea.

The Minister*

In the woods of Kintyre the minister began to squeak about the Amalekites and the Bible. Like a picture in the Old Testament the dew penetrating history, but his heart full of hatred and dryness. He ordered that the long swords should cut breast and skull, he wrote on them his Latin. A dry man of the silver buckles, black hose, was he not a bargain? God's servant and a devil of armies.

A high tide of blood about his shoes, wretched hands stretched out towards mercy, but he in the sun of happiness, and the dew falling, drop by drop, on the Amalekites beside him, like the murder of deer among the heather. And the crows from a blue space slanting to the rich manna among the trees and alighting on moustache or Bible.

The Rain

The rain pouring on the street. The rain pouring on my heart, on the lonely bridges of my heart, on the busy roads of my heart, the screen of red lights blazing about the blue cinemas of my heart.

* It is said that the Duke of Argyll's chaplain ordered that five hundred prisoners be put to death after they had surrendered. He did this because he was comparing them to the Amalekites and giving a warning that the same thing would happen as happened to Saul if they weren't killed.

Song

I got up on a morning of May, and the radio playing loudly. I looked out on a window of shirts and the children shouting on the street. Radio Luxembourg blaring, O Young Girl of the Million Loves, ghost of nylon and ceilidhs swimming among the blue cookers.

Love Song

'You left me and my mind was heavy,' your macintosh over your arm. I do not understand anything but this, the smell of your perfume: and your bones in the calm window of a supermarket.

The Highlands

So much land, so much sea, this is a land for a poet who has lost his love for his fellow men. His pen is like a gull writing the screaming of loneliness.

Luss

Roses swallowing the stone, a picture of a village instead of a true village. Beside the crouched cemetery there is one horse raising his old head out of time like an engraving of tranquil grey steel. And the children running among the graves and the sun. A picture of the roses of Scotland lying asleep in the picture of the windows which are heavy with heaven.

Bareness

It is bareness I want, the bareness of the knife's blade. And the words to be going away from me like ducks settling on the sea when night is falling, their wings folded on the sea, and the night falling.

On the Street

An old woman crying on the street. That is what I thought as I went past with my basket full of wine and bread – an apple, an orange, a banana, an old woman crying on the street, from world to world, under the Planet of the Old Woman.

Innocence

The blue sea is like diamonds. O world, O world of innocence, how much destruction there is at the bottom of the sea, though your smile is so eternal – like God above and the Devil below.

The Island

There is an island always in the spirit so that we can flee there when the way is hard.

But they hit Malta from the sky in the ancient sea in the middle of the day. And Crete also suffered agony. Its guns were heard speaking. And Singapore was safe from the sea though it was broken from the north. And even on Lewis and Islay the aeroplanes of our time will burst, and angels and devils from the clouds descending through desperation or hope.

When We Were Young

When we were young it would be raining and we throwing stones at the telegraph poles unceasingly.

One horse would be standing against a wall, drenched by the rain, his skin slippery with the grey rain.

When we were young we would be playing football, with the moon in the sky like a football made of gold.

When we were young old women would be telling us, 'Don't do this, do that' for fear of the owl.

When we were young the sky would be empty, and pictures in the book, and the earth green and distant.

When we were young, there would be lies, when we are old the lie is that youth was without stain.

Poem

Liberal, Labour or Conservative, what business have they with us? The dark dry questions are breaking heads. And what have the red and blue to do with that dark river in which we swim, and the stars of Labour or Tories so dim among our oars?

My Poetry

Well, I did not learn love from you. What I learnt was the truth. And without doubt the truth is hard as they will tirelessly tell us. But I remember a frosty night and the world open, south to north. O the sparkling sea was my choice. Who said that the truth is hard?

One Girl

One girl I saw who was both intelligent and beautiful. That was two gifts from God. He opened his two fists over her.

I saw many who are intelligent and have learned many griefs. And also many a one has been seen who learned evil from beauty.

But truly the temptation will be sore when the two are together. For the world is full of thirst, and many, without either, pursuing them.

Freud

Great man from Vienna who opened the mind with a knife keen with sore efficient happy light, and who saw the seas sweating with the blue-green ghosts of plague, and uncountable riches.

I follow the beasts with a joy that I cannot tell though I should be fishing from dungeon or from prison, as they move on that sea-bottom in the freedom of truth with their great helmets.

Cancer took your jaw away. But you were scanning with profundity the bottom of that sea where there are horrifying shadows. Father, mother and daughter fighting entwined together in a Greek play, in a strangling of forests.

The letter that I will not send, the letter that I will not keep, the poetry that my head cannot put together, the history that I would not want anyone to tell of my planets, the star is below in the seaweed of the skies.

Goodbye to the laughter of nature and the seas, goodbye to the salt that will bring tears to thoughts, goodbye to death which opens valuable countries, our rings are early in the weddings of our gifts.

O miracle of the waves and I tirelessly scrutinising you like a gay porpoise leaping in my country, it was you who gave us these new waves – your monument is on the bottom, and the seas are your pulpit.

The White Swan[*]

The white swan is always there, even in the Great War, especially in the Great War, the white swan is swimming, on a river that they will never reach, those who die and those who return, at the far end of what happened to them, the white swan that will never die. With her long white neck, with her curiosity fishing among the canisters for clean water, where a house will be growing and the little children will be running, and the grey lark rising above distant chimneys.

The Little Old Lady

The little lady with the black hood, that snake among the heather, with her little sighs, O hi o ro, with her little sighs O hi o raobh, the little old lady of the communions, as clean as a diamond and on the side of God in the battle of sin, sniper of hell among the trees.

Conversation

'You are old and I am young, let me go, let me go. Do you not see the rockets of our time? Do you not see Venus glittering?'

'Let me go, let me go, there are new birds in my heart. Will you not hear the young music? Will you not see Venus shining?'

'That was also what I said, "Let me go, let me go." But age and death are coming. And the dark sky is so far away. Goodbye then and may things go well with you. Venus is shining white. Age is withering her face like a little old lady with a little face.'

---

[*] *The White Swan* is the title of a Gaelic love song about the First World War.

The Melodeon of the Spirit

E hi o ro, e hi o ri, dance dance on the road, O melodeon of the spirit, dance dance at the end of the garden. O melodeon of the spirit, O distant hands faint and white in an autumn moon, O the active rash feet. O melodeon of the spirit, green and red and green again, there are ghosts at the end of the garden, our tears are falling.

There is a new music at the tips of our fingers, dance, dance on the road. O melodeon of my tears, the new music is shining over the ripening moon of the barley, the golden moon of the long night, the moon of boys, the moon of Lewis, the moon of the shoes of the new fashion.

Predestination

If I had done that, if I had done this, if I had read Calvin all day and into the small hours.

If I had attained my dream, if I had a million dollars, if it weren't for that long shadow that is always at my feet.

Calvin tells us that we are lost. Freud tells us that we are deceived. O my long thin hands why then are you writing?

And that great question in the shape of a snake moving on the lands of my father.

O my long thin hands, the world was lost when I was still a child.

And that long shadow in my bones from the very first day that I cried. Freud and Calvin come together like black angels and devils about my skies.

For Derick Thomson

1

We were brought up in Bayble together. There are many years since then. There were ghosts at the edge of the dyke and heather on Hol, and the stone round it. And an owl in the wave, and a wind shaking Mary Roderick, and the hen being blown to the moor. At the tips of our fingers was the dream. But the wind took low Bayble away. The boats are coming towards uncultivated soil and the terrifying corn. What is that cloud with the scowl?

What is that cloud on the Muirneag? What is that Bible opening and the leaves with wind and rain on them? What is the shadow that is troubling me? Whence is the thunder of the river? Who put these fish on the park? That eagle is high above my memory. Whence are these winds, Derick?

2

There is a tall mountain, the mountain of poetry, there is a tall mountain, the mountain of life. Which is the more difficult, which is the higher? The white ghosts are waiting.

Their large eyes are laughing, the helmets of Aignish catching us. O my guilts, O my shame, streets of names, row after row of them.

Above the mountain, mocking, is the sun of the spirit, waiting. Above Bayble, above the horizon, above the wells of life.

Above the great lights of the streets, above Homer, Aberdeen, above the white moon of my friends, above the crayon books.

Above the autumn of nuts, and that tall tree that is waiting. Like hens scattered across moorland, those Greeks who taught us life.

3

Bayble and Athens, isn't the compass strange and strict? How locked the lock is! There is a broken door in the glen.

Greek is on the broken door. There is a hawk on a chimney singing and saying: 'You are laid by. But I will open you to the chest.'

O beautiful hawk, O key of fire, teach me your beautiful poetry, your beak as innocent as a child's and as skilful as the work of intelligence.

4

In his beak he lifted Lewis and Bayble. In his beak he lifted me up. I saw Jupiter with its shadow steering heaviness over my sea.

And Mars and Venus going past, all the planets singing with the sweet choir of the thousand lights.

The Mod of the universe so sweet, bitter and sweet, that white choir, and the poet being crowned in the heavens, his face carved like a hawk's and his wings open, star on star.

5

The cuckoo is in the hawk's mouth. The chicken is in the crow's mouth. (The sore wind is in a great hurry.)

I will not put on my silken coat, my summer coat, in the bad weather and my fool's coat in pieces.

This century is throwing enough water at us like that great coloured tall bus that makes holes in the roads.

I will not leap from it, it is going too fast for me, it is putting the earth upside down. It is putting joy and hate on me, and my hair streaming to that wind, and my white face becoming a diamond against elegies and hymns, against the Iolaire and Holm, that song amongst the psalms, against the darkness and the blue and we now in our time with white lights, smooth lights on us, and Stornoway as small as a pin, but a golden hawk in that high sky like God, looking in a mirror.

The Prodigal Son

Under the stars of grief, the thin glass in his hand, like ice which grows on pools, he listened to the dance. He listened to that music, the melodeon of his loss, he listened to his wounds in that golden distant country. His father running like a bird on tiptoe of joy, his brother breaking up the troublesome soil of dislike, the neighbours winking: 'What happened to you, dear? Wonderful the prosperity that has come on the little boy of our song.'

What sort of place were you in? Is it beautiful, is it new? Is it wine that is in the well, whisky instead of water? Is there reaping without labour, is the autumn to your wish? Will corn be found in the barn on the great morning of the dew?

And the dance goes past, the dance of the planets and the people. He looked down inside the glass that was foolish and thin. He saw the stony eyes and he was filled with a sort of shivering and he sat there like a kettle on the dishonourable fire of the world.

And he heard the thunder of feet, the dance of past fashions. He felt again the rainstorms that spoilt the seasons before his step. He felt again the locks, the dangerous prison of lies. 'O God, who put this spark in my breast in vain,' he shouted in the unsteady winter and he threw the glass from his hand.

It turned over beneath the moon. It broke on the uncultivated soil. He got up and went home: 'This place is as good as others,' he shouted through the untellable music and the planets of a million laughters.

The Poppy

The flower of Flanders is red in the blue sky. That blood is still strong amidst the storm.

That red star is on my calm jacket. The hands are folded and the eyes are shut.

The potatoes are growing and the roots are so white, the dead bones among the water and the dew.

And the cows with their helmets and their great horns tasting grass that was cleansed by them and each skull quiet under the plough gently fertilising the earth from heaven.

Saturday

Here on Saturday evening, nothing but a dark tiredness in my soul, nothing but a blanket on my eyes or the two Greek coins, nothing but a seagull going past the narrow window of the stone, nothing but an earth that has gone to waste on us and left me with this tiredness.

For the soul needs blossom as the potato does, the soul needs a thistle woven in peace and turmoil, it needs renewing and restlessness, it needs more than the graves that I see at that stone church with those long narrow windows, with the steeple that is rising to an empty sky that is in pieces with black heavy slow clouds, the rainy bare sky of sheep, sky of cows, sky of that weariness, sky of the moon as she rises from the poor broken bodies of the heavens, a broken woman in her nightgown seeking a world that has gone astray on her.

Deirdre

O Glen Etive, O Glen Etive, Deirdre made her way over the sea. The whistle of Naoise took her to Ireland, the beautiful girl of our songs and instead of berries her eyes rested on the red blood of the wrong spring. The dagger descended through the room like a beaked seagull into the sea.

O Glen Etive, O Glen Etive, you did not save her when she left the innocent hollow of lies and followed the whistling of death.

The Heroes

There are some whom death will not break though the graip goes through them: and a man will eat cut potatoes, for that wound is simple.

I prefer them to whole potatoes with their faces full of hope, so stolid and foolish and so white on the plate of bad sweetness.

Autumn Song

They have taken the corn in, they have folded up the mountains. The moon is in the back room on an old prudent sideboard. You are sleeping in your autumn and I in my mind am walking street after street, my talent beside me.

O sleep easily and quietly, sleep without turning and do not listen at night to my feet wakeful in your world.

The Fool

In the dress of the fool, the two colours that have tormented me – English and Gaelic, black and red, the court of injustice, the reason for my anger, and that fine rain from the mountains and these grievous storms from my mind streaming the two colours together so that I will go with poor sight in the one colour that is so odd that the King himself will not understand my conversation.

To My Mother

You were gutting herring in distant Yarmouth and the salt sun in the morning rising out of the sea, the blood on the edge of your knife, and that salt so coarse that it stopped you from speaking and made your lips bitter.

I was in Aberdeen sucking new courses, my Gaelic in a book and my Latin at the tiller, sitting there on a chair with my coffee beside me and leaves shaking the sails of scholarship and my intelligence.

Guilt is tormenting me because of what happened and how things are. I would not like to be getting up in the darkness of the day gutting and tearing the fish of the morning on the shore and that savage sea to be roaring down my gloves without cease.

Though I do that in my poetry it is my own blood that is on my hands, and every herring that the high tide gave me palpitating till I make a song, and instead of a cooper my language always hard and strict on me, and the coarse salt on my ring bringing animation to death.

The Old Woman

The postman will come tonight with the Christmas letter. The postman will come tonight with light on his clothes. Does anyone know what will be in the letter? 'The sharp star of the Bible,' said the old woman who was waiting alone in a dream.

On a Beautiful Day

From the stone the wildcat is watching the world. The hare shakes like a lily. The hawk and the lark are in the same mirror and the sun shining and the grass growing. The wildcat is drinking champagne over his teeth. The hare is halted, listening with ears like doors. The hawk is sitting on its wings drinking the wind, and the lark singing like a record in a Gaelic cloud.

The Stone

I will tell you, my dear, the words that the stone told me. The stone has never heard of Lewis or about songs. The stone is a prisoner under the lightning. The lightning is weaving a light around the stone like an old woman who has gone mad.

The stone is inside the prison thinking about darkness, about clouds, about shells, and about other stones.

But at the end it is thinking of itself alone.

And because of that and because of poetry which is weaving a swift light about the stone, this is what the stone said to me on a

winter's night or a summer's night far from the moon and the restless
sea that will not find sleep again but is walking the world at three
o'clock in the morning.

This is what the stone told me: 'I am waiting. The longest river
will reach its end. The brightest spirit will reach its conclusion. And
at the end of the matter I will rise in front of it and in the middle of
the thunder I will be like a king.'

Raven

Writing the last words I gave my pen to a raven. 'What have you to
say to them? What story is in your heart?'

He looked at me with cold eyes. He put ice on my sight. And then
he wrote with permanence: 'Tell them that I will be paying a visit.'

'But our music,' I said to him. 'Our poetry, book after book. O
miracle of the northern lights, the imagination of Dante and Homer.'

'I know,' I shouted to him, 'the Odyssey of greatness. They kept
you in mind but swallowed you with hope.'

And he threw down the pen. The window was hard with marvel-
lous and strict light and the raven lost in my comfort.

On a Misty Evening

On a misty evening
I raised my luggage
on my shoulder
and I went aboard the
Kaiora.

The guns began
to thunder
about Europe
on that large sea

where I was striving,
for Garrabost.

How red the water.
How red the brine.
No one told me
about those roses
about these roses
that are swimming

about your son's cap, mother.
Your head of bone
is looking out to Salamis.
You are weeping ceaselessly.
The *Kaiora* is going down
at Trafalgar, at Bataan.

The TV

1

The sun rises every day
from moving shadows –
on the TV.

2

We did not believe in the existence of Ireland
till we saw it many nights –
on the TV.

3

He knows more about Humphrey Bogart
than he knows about Big Norman –
since he got the TV.

4

Said Plato –
'We are tied in a cave' –
that is, the TV.

5

A girl came into the room
without perfume without expression –
on the TV.

6

At last he lost the world
as Berkeley said –
there was nothing but the TV.

7

He bought *War and Peace*,
I mean Tolstoy,
after seeing it on the TV.

8

When he switched off the TV
the world went out –
he himself went out.

9

His hands did not come back to him
or his eyes
till he put on the TV.

10

A rose in a bowl on the TV set,
the things that are in the world,
the things that are not.

11

He found himself in the story.
He was in the room.
He didn't know where he was.

12

You, my love, are dearer to me
than 'Softly Softly'
than 'Sportsnight with Coleman'.

13

'In locked rooms with iron gates' –
but, my love,
do they have TV?

from THE NOTEBOOKS OF
ROBINSON CRUSOE AND OTHER POEMS
(1975)

My Uncle

In '18 the M.O. said:
'You've got six months to live,'
demobbing him among the dead,
issuing him with a civvy shroud,
a kit for the churchyard.

'I'll piss on your grave,' he answered
and strode into the raw
postwar 'twenties, then 'thirties,
almost collapsing America's
green twilight of the hurt cities,

marrying a Scottish 'lass',
growing richer, settling down,
tending his large garden
when the Rising Sun of Japan
parched his adopted nation.

This year at eighty-six
he flies home for a while
to the Scotland that he once left
to fight against old Kaiser Bill,
his melodeon in his case.

Back home he drives a Plymouth Fury.
Here he'd hire a car.
'But all my schoolmates are dead.
It's entertainment to read
the obituary columns.'

'Reading is your life,' he says
shrewdly and then adds,
'We couldn't speak English good
but we got by, goddamit.
We had to, in them days.'

Says, 'At my age you're not afraid
of dying. You just wait.
That goddam M.O.s dead.'
Like an old craggy laureate
he talks on till midnight.

'I never use them damn pills.
What's happened to this place?
Why does no one ever dance?
Son, I use to be a prince
with my melodeon.'

I see him off on a large plane.
He waves. He will arrive
at midnight in his own house.
Having outlived his wife,
'I'll have to do a few chores.'

The plane climbs. We'll not see
either the other again.
I've bought him an Alasdair Maclean.
'I always read books twice, son,'
he says as he turns away.

The Prodigal Son

'All day,' he said, 'I've been trying to write a play
about the Prodigal Son and how he came
home after twenty years on a fine day
to where his brother laboured in the corn
with his huge curving scythe that was the same
as he'd used the day the Prodigal Son had gone.

I tried each way. The Prodigal Son had prospered
while the farm slowly decayed as the huge scythe
steadily harped at the stalks where the wind whispered.
Or perhaps the Prodigal Son turned at the gate
and headed, humping his case, for the hated south
because his arrival was that much too late.

But somewhere in my mind there was a boulder
I couldn't climb or pass. A day so pure,
the weight of failure on each dusty shoulder,
the large forgiveness of that simple weather
seemed so beyond the power of literature
I couldn't focus on the happy father,

his outstretched arms grasping a changing ghost,
a harvest of images that the autumn brought
home to wherever home is for the lost.
It wasn't possible that the Son should come
or if he came that his grave wandering spirit
should settle there after delirium

as each new day perched on the rusty fence
and rotting posts and, radiant on ponds,
revealed more sparklingly unchanging essences.
Would he not leave once more when useless growth
barrenly blossomed, when the lying diamonds
momently flourished as ever from the scythe?'

Ceilidh

Some ragged tartans hang above the stage.
There are wooden trestles and they all come in,
the villagers, to listen to their past.
Some finished passion has removed all haste
and granted courtesy instead of rage.
The years have taught them how to lose not win.

Such sleepy faces gather for the dream.
Of this pure ceremony what might aliens think,
this late communion of the dispossessed?
Are they the best, or have the fiercer best
abandoned for real things the things that seem,
the suns that rise for the old suns that sink?

The music starts. Exile begins again.
They leave the mountains and the glens in song.
They are lost sailors on a moving mast.
The girls they sing of are all sweet and chaste,
herbs of the mountains, sighs of a dear Amen.
The stream of elegy receives all wrong.

The common dream unites them as they gaze
into the tender surfaces. They hear
the bagpipes playing from the wars they've lost
historically, daily. At what cost
would they awaken now and taste the day's
sharp bitter victories, barbarous and dear?

The overbred and overcivilised...
The accordions and pipes are packed away
into their boxes and the songs are finished.
The decorated hall seems quite diminished.
Their souls return to what their souls have prized
too little against exile and decay

and they set out to real glens and hills
depleted townships and the gathering roar
of midnight streams, the moonlight on the sea.
They come together – Art and what they see –
but, should they leave, what new dream strikes and kills
knocking forever at a lustrous door?

The Sound of Music

After the *Sound of Music* we mooned out
into the street again. Glasgow by night.
The pavement and the road were blue and wet.
There wasn't a single rainy close without
a couple kissing. They wore narrow tights
and clung together in the plaguey lights
infecting their white faces. It was not
what one would call a fine attractive sight.
It was a whimpering wolfish appetite.

It wasn't really like the *Sound of Music*
with all those Viennese waltzes and the like,
the roomy castles, staircases, the stock
of trilling nuns more musical than Catholic,
their sudden warbles, eloquent technique,
but everyone so cheery and so slick.
They seemed to sing whenever they should speak
and all so nice and pricey as in *Vogue*.

Through the blue and green of Glasgow we strolled on
by Indian restaurants and Chinese ones.
Cropped youths stalked past us in their mottled skin,
their glinting eyes expressionless as stone.
There was a dance-hall coloured violent green
and slogans six foot high made yellow stains
on rotting tenements. I could see no nuns
and nowhere marbled halls or chanting children
but swaying drunks so miserably alone

that convents could not reach them, nor God's ways
which chimed with Hollywood's refined arias
that even the gauleiters could not suppress.

The screen, uncracked by bottle or by vice,
reflected perfect flawless families.
I did not walk in fear but saw each dress
as in a radiance which I must prize
not freshly laundered nor as Viennese
but stained with sweat to a more tense repose.

Incident

She watched him with her children and she thought,
'They're not his flesh. What am I hoping for?
They are my flesh and mortal, of myself,
they grew in me and by me, we are all
a chain of common growing, or a ring,
and of the days a wandering company
cohered in pain and happiness. But he walks
distant yet dear, not one of us. They run
together down the road. He sees them as
I see some other children, how they are
is not to me responsible, their grave
or playful motions not so far from me
as stones might be, but they are not my care
in sunshine or by lamplight, they are less
deeply embedded in me. So with him.'
She watched him walk, she knew his mind as clear
observer of the clouds and of the sky
and of the pale white moon that slowly rose
into the frosty winter afternoon.
The children ran ahead, competitive
in matching clothes, the fair one and the dark,
cowboys and transient tenants of that space,
their merciless energy inveterate

and normal in the day. She closed her eyes
and when she opened them she saw the three
bending over a pool of mottled ice.
She saw him break it tenderly with his shoe
pointed like a dagger while they stood
beside him watching. Then he turned and smiled.
His smile was white as the ascending moon
of equal delicacy and equal light.
Her smile strengthened to his, two partial moons
converging on the full and harvest moon
which lights the autumn corn. Then with rare joy
she heard them running towards her, and he
was walking steadily not away but to,
and she was the centre of the untidy chain
whose light was for the three, whose light was not
meagre and bristly but ubiquitous,
on them as always but on him as well,
and then on them, and him who from the clouds
had turned his eyes on her and the common earth.

Chinese Poem

1

To Seumas Macdonald,
                           now resident in Edinburgh –
I am alone here, sacked from the Department
for alcoholic practices and disrespect.
A cold wind blows from Ben Cruachan.
There is nothing here but sheep and large boulders.
Do you remember the nights with *Reliquae Celticae*
and those odd translations by Calder?
Buzzards rest on the wires. There are many seagulls.
My trousers grow used to the dung.
What news from the frontier? Is Donald still Colonel?
Are there more pupils than teachers in Scotland?

I send you this by a small boy with a pointed head.
Don't trust him. He is a Campbell.

2

The dog brought your letter today
from the red postbox on the stone gate
two miles away and a bit.
I read it carefully with tears in my eyes.
At night the moon is high over Cladach
and the big mansions of prosperous Englishmen.
I drank a half bottle thinking of Meg
and the involved affairs of Scotland.
When shall we two meet again
in thunder, lightning or in rain?
The carrots and turnips are healthy,
the *Farmer's Weekly* garrulous.
Please send me a *Radio Times* and a book
on cracking codes. I have much sorrow.
Mrs Macleod has a blue lion on her pants.
They make a queenly swish in a high wind.

3

There is a man here who has been building a house
for twenty years and a day.
He has a barrow in which he carries large stones.
He wears a canvas jacket.
I think I am going out of my mind.
When shall I see the city again,
its high towers and insurance offices,
its glare of unprincipled glass?
The hens peck at the grain.
The wind brings me pictures of exiles,
ghosts in tackety boots, lies,
adulteries in cornfields and draughty cottages.
I hear Donald is a brigadier now

and that there is fighting on the frontier.
The newspapers arrive late with strange signs on them.
I go out and watch the road.

4

Today I read five books.
I watched Macleod weaving a fence
to keep the eagles from his potatoes.
A dull horse is cobwebbed in rain.
When shall our land consider itself safe
from the assurance of the third rate mind?
We lack I think nervous intelligence.
Tell them I shall serve in any capacity,
a field officer, even a private,
so long as I can see the future
through uncracked field glasses.

5

A woman arrived today
in a brown coat and a brown muff.
She says we are losing the war,
that the Emperor's troops are everywhere
in their blue armour and blue gloves.
She says there are men in a stupor
in the ditches among the marigolds
crying 'Alas, alas.'
I refuse to believe her.
She is, I think, an agent provocateur.
She pretends to breed thistles.

The Notebooks of Robinson Crusoe

Extract from Log:

Labour will sustain me, to permit my soul enter iron, steel, wood. To swim, ransack ship, assemble impedimenta, build raft, negotiate currents, investigate territory, seek water, build shelter, watch for wild beasts, to scrutinise sun and stars, to cut notches, representing days, weeks, months, to protect against earthquake and storm, to plant seeds, to make chair and table, to invent ink, to construct shovels, plane ironwood, to find eatable flesh.

All these, to forget soul.

To use body, and let mind commit itself to the materials.

To be busy without mirror.

To let the day invent itself.

Today I wished to write a story. It would be of a man wrecked on an island many years, feeding on fish and flesh, limes and oranges, who rushing down a long slope to meet his rescuer (in punctilious blue) would run through him bone and sinew to the other side.

Instead I opened my large double-columned Bible, its pages stained with rum and tears, and found written in faded ink on the leaf before Genesis the words, 'To my dearest son from his mother.'

I could not elucidate the date.

> Evenings: the sea monotonous:
> swishings: sousings: vaporous ululations:
> tenuous jelly: askance gulls.
> Sea different from us: its trade
> observing different currency, varying levels,
> emptying and filling of exchanging shelves.

The wind blows in my chimney. How mournful it is! I can hear in it voices of exhortation, of warning, and of regret.

They speak of partings, wrecks and exile. They remind of crimes inflicted on others and on oneself.

O that I were a man without memory, a machine renewed by the days, a tree that forgets its autumn leaves, its winter dispossessions.

O that like a cock I could crow in the morning, my red hackles duplicating the sun's rays, my head fierce and singular, my brassy extended throat dispersing the rack of clouds.

Last night I drank much rum. I dreamed that you were in my arms.
Later I talked without ceasing.
Waking from my dishevelled bed, I entered a world so tidy that I wept
as you wept. If I had my mother's clock, with the two Dutch figures,
I would stay in the dark to watch you step out in your green sabots.
But you are not there, the climate is constant, and the only speaker is
Pretty Poll who speaks beady eyed and without humour the words,
'Crusoe… Cruise… Crew,' from the world of his squalor, riffling his
feathers, regarding me from his red cage as I walk by the ruffled sea.

Today I stupefied myself with rum. The world became rum-coloured.
The grass became red, the masts, the last peel of sails.
The earth swayed like a deck under my feet.
My eyes stared helplessly out of their large portholes. I saw the sea
heaving past.
Strangely it had trees, goats, a dog, a hammer, and an antique pot with
a wrinkled face.
I remember cursing the sky as if it could be merciful. How childish to
expect justice from a wandering story book.

In my leafed chapel I pray to God.
I say to myself: I am better than spastics, idiots, physically ruined men.
I do not have TB, cancer, heart disease, or any plague.
My heart, lungs, kidneys, liver are sound.
I do not suffer the tremors of the bank clerk or the tempests of the
manager
I do not pace up and down in a hospital waiting for the doctor to tell
me about my wife and whether the haemorrhages have stopped.
I do not hear the crazy white-haired violinist scraping in the attic.
I am not feverish with love.
I do not phone my sweetheart at midnight from a squalid bar, nor do
I see her raising her shadowy lips to her lover's, behind a closed
curtain.
I do not stand by a stretcher watching the pale mouth hardly breathing.
I do not see my children returning from the arena beaten.
I do not stand before the blank wall of my disabilities.
For all these things I give thanks to God.
Why, then am I not happy?

I dreamed that a girl called Lavender had captured me: that she led me to her mother in a flowered cartwheel hat, that her father, sunk in shadow, welcomed me with a greenish smile.

I dreamed that, brisk by cooker, she walked in a godly light, and that when at night she turned from my vulgar hairy arms I lay with eyes wide open, stumbling from pit to pit like the moon.

I dreamed that, laden with the honoraria of duty, in a mild clank of medals, I pottered in my shed, concealed by foliage from my cardboard house, steadily repeated along the avenue.

I dreamed that on all fours I howled and barked nightly at the moon, feeling long fangs in my jaw, gnawing aspidistras, baring my teeth at the shadow on the blind.

I dreamed that the sea had become sand and that the universe, an enormity of possibilities, had diminished to a match box from which my hand struck shaking sparks.

There is no other world but this: no posterity at which, crowned with laurels, we arrive breathless.
The eternal page is a leaf twinkling in the breeze, in the here and now of our own drama.
Singer of TV, flashing your artificial smiles, their insincere punctuation, you are made of light and you make the light.
Gather your photons while you may, your dewless bouquets of the altering present.

> I shall clamp my teeth.
> I shall not bleed language.
> If my condition is absurd let it be so.
>
> Let me be steel, irony's not enough.
> I shall go down into my grave
> below these foreign blooms.
>
> Starlight dangles towards me. Let me wave
> my handkerchief to the universe.
> This is no place for rage.

I am the parrot of a lost routine.
I have a splendid cage
central to this green.

This is a comic place.
I shall carve my name on the trees
over and over.

It is possible that I shall grow used to this as a knot to wood and that,
were rescuers brisk with pity and self congratulation to emerge from
the sea I should hide in the woods and like an animal peer at them
fearfully between the slats of leaves.

It is possible that, aware of my kingship here, I would not return
to anonymity there but that, breeding hauteur in my solitude, I should
recoil from the momentary and dramatic solicitude of others.

For the oyster in the depths of the sea has its pearl as I my arro-
gance and, constant to my own sufficiency, I would disdain the million
wandering fish sliding past, each on his own level.

It is possible that, my own god worshipping my own images, I
would not wish to enter, unshaven and hairy, the monotonous climate
of the mediocre, but would prefer my extreme pain to their temperate
ordinariness.

O Lord, let me know my mortality: let me cast myself on the
common waters. Let me be resurrected by the cheap tarnished
glorious tinfoil light.

Island, what shall I say of you, your peat bogs, your lochs, your moors
and berries?
The cry of your birds in the fading evening.
Your flowers in summer glowing brightly where there are no thor-
oughfares.
The perpetual sound of the sea.
The spongy moss on which feet imprint themselves.
The mountains which darken and brighten like ideas in the mind.
The owl with its big glasses that perches on a late tree listening.
The mussels clamped to the rocks, the fool's gold, the tidal pools
filling and emptying.
The corn that turns from pale green to yellow, my scarecrow rattling
in the wind

The smoke that arises from my fire.

This I say:
One man cannot warm the world.
This I say:
The world of one man is different from the world of many men.
This I say:
Without the net, the sweetest fish are tasteless.

I have read them all, Sartre, Wittgenstein, Ryle. I have listened at midday to the actresses popstars authors in 'Desert Island Discs' speculating happily on islands among the traffic of London ('Am I allowed dettol and bandages? Voltaire?')
And as I remember hell, the choice of staying by the communal inferno where we feed on each other or going alone into the middle of the dark wood leaving behind me forever the Pickwicks and the iced candles of Christmas, I hear now clearly in the hollow spaces of the valleys, in the roar of the waterfall, in the appearance of the birds of spring and their departure in the autumn the same phrase repeated over and over:
    Language is other people.

It is not with sorrow that I stand on deck and leave behind me the island and the thirty years of my life there.
It is rather with puzzlement as if a dream were beginning again, the dream of officers in white, seamen in blue, television cameras, the manic unblinking eye of the announcer.
The enigma of the dream persists as the jovial captain at the head of yards of white lines quizzes me, between draughts of wine: as the sailors weave about me their human erotic legends!
As the ship steadily steers towards the cameras providing rich merchandise for my new dream and I emerge from the world of sparse iron into the vast cinema of sensation.

from IN THE MIDDLE

(1977)

In Yellow

The Chinamen sing Chinese songs
as they go round the bamboo tree
and their faces are all yellow
and the tunes of their songs are very strange

and the canary settles on the washing line
and sings all morning
its sweet canary song –
while the shapeless clothes are drying.
It is a fine day for everyone,
for canaries and for Chinamen
and for the clothes slowly gaining their shape.

When Day is Done

Sorrow remembers us when day is done.
It sits in its old chair gently rocking
and singing tenderly in the evening.
It welcomes us home again after the day.
It is so old in its black silken dress,
its stick beside it carved with legends.
It tells its stories over and over again.
After a while we have to stop listening.

The Torches

The newspapers create news.
The poets create poems.
Everyone illuminates his acre
with a hugged torch.

And the skeletons clash in the wind
like a wash of old clothes.
The horizon chases its tail
over and over.

My Child

My child, where are you?
The woods are waning
and I am seeking you among the hedges.

I am still wearing my stiff gown
which often sustained you
among the stones and thistles.

I bring you the right shape of things.
I bring you the warm bread
with the crust on it.

I bring you the bottles
with the white milk in them,
the knives and the spoons.

I bring you our house with the rigid roof on it,
the cupboards with their groceries,
the wardrobes with your ironed clothes.

I bring you the made bed,
the fire with the red voice,
the rectangular windows.

Child, I am looking for you.

They tell me you are in the rivers
growing haphazardly
dabbled in water.

My voice comes to you across the cornstacks,
across my completed harvest,
across the sharp stubble.

The Chair

The tall green-backed chair
in a room with brown walls
and all the old questions
start here.

If I had met you elsewhere
if you had dried your tears
with a different handkerchief
in a different hand —

and the tall green-backed chair
seems so fixed and solid
like a family lawyer
in all the thunderstorms.

The Scream

The scream rips through the forest
tearing the trees down.

'Love me love me love me,'
cries the scream at the railway station
with its hair streaming backwards.

It's like a train flashing
at two hundred miles an hour
blowing the birds from the hedges
and bending the iron rails.

It ends up at a cottage
deep in a secret wood
searching the pale windows
for the kind iron face.

It staggers across the flowers
and beats on the warped door
which opens like a cloud
onto its sudden rain.

It crosses the bare floor
like a single moonbeam
and lies in a straight line
on its exhausted paws.

Women

Bewildered and angry is the sap of women
as if the tree were to fight against itself
in a hurt greenness, in a swaying current,
in a wrestle to put out flowers or thorns.

Man often strolls down an avenue of ideas,
his hands in his pocket, cool and lenient.
It is the morning for a cigarette
or for a joke from his worn pack of cards.

Woman sees no humour in the sky.
Earth is a purse which feeds us.
The tidied child is heading towards marriage
and then a fixed place in the earth,

or perhaps in astrology, that favoured village,
which sheds names sensibly and certainly.
The girl walks in the steps of Pisces,
in the chains of Virgo, in its green lanes.

Man measures the stars' heat and incidence,
their probability, their constituents.
Their naval and other councils are formal.
Their disentangled language is of weather.

Women follow the moon down yellow pages,
their bodies shaken by winds, teeth chattering.
Their roots whine and sing. They grip their acre.
Sometimes they float out on eerie tides.

Tears Are Salt

Tears are salt like the sea.
How reality breaks in on us
while we are acting so well
on our tiny stages,

dressed up so sunnily
wearing our brooches and belts
considering the world
as just about our size.

Suddenly reality is there
with its large crude torch
shining it into our eyes
and into our guts.

The sunbeam just passing
is carrying a coffin
as a bee will carry pollen
home to its hive.

In the centre of the tear
is a small inverted man
gazing down at the sky
and a pair of dusty shoes.

Tears are salt like the sea.
Standing together
we look out from the headland
at a mouth burbling with foam.

The Old School Books

Do you remember
the old text books
the old jotters
that we used to have?
What has happened to them?
I cannot understand it.

In those days they were so confident
telling us about countries
about electricity, about Latin,
each reflected the other.
They were like marble
they were like commandments,
they were so dull and
so deadly accurate.

They were like our elders
old and grey and dull
standing so foursquare
against our skyline.

In them no scent of roses,
in them no scent at all,
as green as arsenic,
linoleum acres.

And now they have gone away
not even buried
they have gone to some attic
beyond our frontiers.

Like old film stars
like those who have once been famous
they are lying in old rooms
with their outdated message.

Clouds

Black clouds in the sky
drifting about in the evening.
They are like the ashes
of burnt-out major poems.

None Is the Same as Another

None is the same as another,
O none is the same.

That none is the same as another
is matter for crying
since never again will you see
that one, once gone.

In their brown hoods
the pilgrims are crossing the land
and many will look the same
but all are different

and their ideas fly to them
on accidental winds
perching awhile in their minds
from different valleys.

None is the same as another,
O none is the same.

And that none is the same is not
a matter for crying.

Stranger, I take your hand,
O changing stranger.

from THE EMIGRANTS
(1983)

Translated from the author's own Gaelic

Lewis

From the War Memorial
we see Lewis entirely.
For this place they died,
the new houses, the smell of seaweed,
the rivers,
an old woman walking about her croft,
the wind on the Atlantic,
a seagull lying dead on a bare headland,
the sea breaking whitely on the long sand,
flowers among the stones,
a minister on a Stornoway street
on a cold wet day.
For this place they died.
Prayers are exhausting
the old sick people.
The wind is beating against the headlands
with its lonely song,
the moor yellow with flowers
the small elegant lochs
like blue rings, there they used to walk
when they were children.
The loom of the wind on the headlands
with its eternal whine.

The Herring Girls

The herring girls,
where did they go to
with their necklaces of salt?
They would come home with presents,
small yellow rings,
sweets,
dresses of water.

Where did they go
with their long skirts,
they who never had a rose
or shadow of poetry,
were they drowned in time
sinking deeper and deeper
till nothing was seen
but their wet rings?

Climbing and Climbing

Climbing and climbing
what do we see?
A girl's thighs at the top.
A blossom on the summit of the mountain
of hungry bones,
sleep in a bed
that is shaking ceaselessly.

And now in two chairs
on each side of the rainbow
we are sitting
eating salt herring.

We Will Walk

We will walk between two verses
where the words will not catch us.

We will walk between two waves
where the sea will not reach us.

We will talk between two languages
where the guilt will not ravage us.

We will walk between two graves
where we will avoid death.

Berries

We gathered berries on an autumn day
from trees that grew beside the road.
The ripe ones were behind thorns.
Why is that, you said.
The day was so calm and beautiful,
the berries were like black bells
from which no sound rose.
I looked for my hands, they were entirely red,
as if there was blood on them, bright red blood.
The evening was so calm that I could hear your thoughts
as you walked so carefully among the thorns
with your red boots, with your legs so tall and white.

When I am Reading

When I am reading
the literature of my people
I think,
We have no Homer

no poet as great as that,
at all as great as that,
in that way
in that marvellous way.

But now and again I read
about a particular girl
who died of love
in a ragged dress

or an eagle will rise
crying, I was eating
noble dead soldiers
who were lying on a battlefield.

And now and again there will sail
on the sea towards Canada
ships with salt sails,
songs that are white with pain.

On an Autumn Day

On an autumn day the children are returning to school
with their new bags,
in their blue uniforms
with their fresh hopes.

The teachers return as well
and they know about autumn

that the leaves wither,
that the birds depart,
that the hair grows grey.

And because of that, spring meets autumn.
Between the two seasons
as if on transient clouds
the chalk is writing.

Vancouver

In Chinatown
you and I.

The kiosks with Chinese writing on them,
the prostitutes walking by
with their wine-dark cheeks,
and their short skirts.
Another country
(Skid Row is not far away).
You are aiming your camera
like a gun at a battlefield.
The drunks ceaselessly
curse the world
that is mocking
the lost ones.
Looking at my watch
it occurs to me
that your brother at home
is lifting his scythe
and setting off to cut the corn
in Garrabost
which is at rest
in the camera of your mind.

You

Your face is wrinkled
with the roads you travelled,
the vows you took
to the plates.

Your beauty
shines with age
like a boat in the bay
fishing in the blaze
of a last sunset.

Let us Raise

Let us raise, let us raise
the language of our poetry
in the dew
like a flower
on a summer's morning
and around it
the wild beaks
of the birds.

from THE EXILES
(1984)

Returning Exile

You who come home do not tell me
anything about yourself, where you have come from,
why your coat is wet, why there is grass in your hair.

The sheep huddle on the hills as always,
there's a yellow light as if cast by helmets,
the fences made of wire are strung by the wind.

Do not tell me where you have come from, beloved stranger.
It is enough that there is light still in your eyes,
that the dog rising on his pillar of black knows you.

There is no Sorrow

There is no sorrow worse than this sorrow
the dumb grief of the exile
among villages that have strange names
among the new rocks.
The shadows are not his home's shadows
nor the tales his tales
and even the sky is not the same
nor the stars at night.

Sometimes he sees his home in the stars
the light from its window
his village trembling and vibrating
and the old white faces
mumbling at the fire.

But the strange names stand up against him
and the dryness of the earth
and the cold barks of dogs
and his sails are folded in this harbour
which is not his.

Poor lost exile
For you there is nothing but endurance
till one miraculous day
you will wake up in the morning
and put on your foreign clothes
and know that they are at last yours.

Next Time

Listen, when you come home
to see your wife again
where the tapestry stands unfinished
across the green brine,
sit among the stones
and consider how it was
in the old days
before you became a king
and walked hunchbacked
with decisions on your shoulders.

Sit among the rocks
hearing the sound of the sea
eternally unchanging
and watch the buttercups
so luminously pale.

The cries of the dead
haunt the gaunt headland
and the shields clash
in that astonishing blue.

Simply enter the boat
and leave the island
for there is no return,
boy, forerunner of kings.

Next time, do this,
salt bronzed veteran
let the tapestry be unfinished
as truthful fiction is.

The Exiles

Translated from the author's own Gaelic

The many ships that left our country
with white wings for Canada.
They are like handkerchiefs in our memories
and the brine like tears
and in their masts sailors singing
like birds on branches.
That sea of May running in such blue,
a moon at night, a sun at daytime,
and the moon like a yellow fruit,
like a plate on a wall
to which they raise their hands
like a silver magnet
with piercing rays
streaming into the heart.

Always

Always in the same way the poets die
when the girls on horses irretrievably
cross the horizons that are slowly closed,

when the ravens no longer dip their pens in ink
and the winds bring no treasures from the west
in stubbly autumn, of sharp absences:

when cafés that in corners once were lit
round pale-faced waitresses tenderly subside
to pavements crowded with bowler hats and furs;

and the manuscripts of spring are whirled away
from cloaks of the sad monks and thinner nuns
when prayers are points of meagre icicles,

and the late evening skies are lost sails
beyond all feeling's mercy, beyond lights
trembling and yellow of the unmown wake.

In the Spring

In the spring, air returns to us,
wide, with a sense of windows,

and our ruinous virtues sparkle once more
like old cans in a ditch.

On such a day Hector set out
in leaf upon leaf of blue

in the spring that surged windily over Troy,
its banks with their whipped green swords,

before the fire sizzled, and the bones were given to the dogs
and the sea pink reddened the shore.

Youth

When the wind blows the curtains wide, do you not remember
the green trams on their wires and yourself young
singing on a street that no one can now find.

It is as if the book opens, showing the parts you have played
in a theatre more precious to you than the Globe
with its ghostly flag flying in an Elizabethan wind.

Australia

1

In Australia the trees are deathly white,
the kangaroos are leaping halfway to heaven
but land at last easily on the earth.
Sometimes I hear graves singing
their Gaelic songs to the dingos
which scrabble furiously at the clay.

Then tenderly in white they come towards me,
drifting in white, the far exiles
buried in the heart of brown deserts.
It is a strange language they speak
not Australian not Gaelic
while the green eyes stalk them
under a moon the same as ours
but different, different.

2

Naturally there are photographs of Ned Kelly
in his iron mask in his iron armour.
His iron body hung stiffly in the wind

which blew past the ravens.
In that dry land his armour will not rust
and the hot sun flashes from it
as if it were a mirror, creator of fresh stars.
However dingos leap at it they will not chew him
for he is a story, a poem,
a tale that is heard on the wind.

3

No, you will not return from Australia
However you may wish to do so.
For you have surrendered to its legend,
to its music being continually reborn,
to the eerie whine of its deserts.
Somehow or another it entered your soul
and however much you remember Scotland,
its graves sanctified by God,
its historical darknesses,
you will not return from it.
Its dust is in your nostril,
its tenderness has no justice,
its millions of stars are the thoughts
of unbridled horsemen.
With blue eyes you will stare
blinded into its blueness
and when you remember your rivers,
the graveyards the mountains,
it is Australia that stands up in front of you,
your question, your love.

4

All day the kookaburra is laughing
from the phantoms of trees,
from the satire of nature.
It is not tragedy nor comedy,

it is the echo of beasts,
the bitter chorus of thorns,
and flowers that have names
that aren't easily remembered.
The kookaburra laughs from the trees,
from the branches of ghosts,
but the sky remains blue
and the eyes glow green in the night.

Prince Charles

To the Highlands he came, boyishly running.
There was clear water there, greenery without form,
a waste of stones, nature's academy.

And so adventurously he rode and fought.
This was a fresh land to put his stamp on.
This was in the end his hoped-for home.

He marched and marched and then turned back and marched.
The dizzying snow blossomed against his face.
He was the ghost so powder-white and dumb.

He turned away, his horse obscured by snow,
his torn shirt a sail, the sun so warm
and still adventurous on his secret boat.

But he fattened steadily far from that gaunt waste.
To love a home is not to find it true.
He drank and drank in that intriguing blue

of Italy, the rich luxurious land.
Thin sheep cropped the rocks, the tinkling streams
flowed to the sea, the port, the bitter wine.

No Return

No, really you can't go back to
that island any more. The people
are growing more and more unlike you
and the fairy stories
have gone down to the grave in peace.

The wells are dry now and the long grasses
parched by their mouths, and the horned cows
have gone away to another country
where someone else's imagination
is fed daily on milk.

There were, you remember, sunsets
against which the black crows were seen
and a moonlight of astonishing beauty
calmed at midnight by waters
which you're not able to hear.

The old story-telling people
have gone home to their last houses
under the acres of a lost music.
These have all been sold now
to suave strangers with soft voices.

It is a great pity, that your cottage
preserved in January by clear ice
and in June surrounded by daisies
has been sold to the same strangers
and the bent witches evicted.

If you were to return now the roofs
would appear lower, the walls would have no echoes,
the wavelike motion would be lost,
the attics where you read all day
would be crammed with antiques.

No, you cannot return to an island
expecting that the dances will be unchanged,
that the currency won't have altered,
that the mountains blue in the evening
will always remain so.

You can't dip your mouth in the pure spring
ever again or ever again be haunted
by the 'eternal sound of the ocean'.
Even the boats which you once rowed
have set off elsewhere.

The witches wizards harlequins jesters
have packed up their furniture and guitars.
The witches have gone home on their broomsticks
and the conjurors with their small horses
and tiny carts have departed

leaving the island bare, bleak and windy,
itself alone in its barren corner
composed of real rocks and real flowers
indifferent to the rumours and the stories
stony, persistent.

Reading Shakespeare

On a dark day in winter I read Shakespeare.
The birds set off to branches of the south.
I tremble in the branches of the mind.

Summer is finished. Shakespeare always remains,
tree on tree for ever fragrant, young,
leaves that never fall out of the leaves.

Forest of Arden, you are my best south,
the lightning wit in this locality,
the cloudless sky, the rainbow tunics there,

and thunder too. We have the best of it,
so many weathers, changeable, intense.
Farewell to the long-necked geese that cross the sea.

Speech for Prospero

When I left that island I thought I was dead. Nothing
stirred in me. Miranda in jeans
and totally innocent was standing by a sail
and all the others happily recovered talking
in suits made of brine. But to return to
the gossip, the poisonous ring, was not easy,
and many times I nearly tried to turn back
feeling in my bones the desolate hum of the headland,
my creation of rivers and mist.
Still we went on. The corruption had put on flesh,
the young were hopeful again, all was forgiven.
Nevertheless the waiters were scraping and bowing,
the rumours beginning, the crowns of pure crystal were sparkling,
the telephones were ringing with messages from the grave
and the thin phosphorescent boys glowing with ambition
in corners of velvet and death.
Still I went on. The ship left its wake behind it,
shining and fading, cord of a new birth,
and over by the rail Miranda gazed at her prince
yearning for love.
Goodbye, island, never again shall I see you,
you are part of my past. Though I may dream of you often
I know there's a future we all must learn to accept,
music working itself out in the absurd halls and the mirrors,
posturings of men like birds, Art in a torrent of plates,
the sound of the North Wind, distant yet close,
as stairs ascend from the sea.

'You'll take a bath'

'And now you'll take a bath,' she'd always say,
just when I was leaving, to keep me back.
At the second turning of the stony stair
the graffiti were black letters in a book
misspelt and menacing. As I drove away
she'd wave from the window. How could I always bear
to be her knight abandoning her to her tower
each second Sunday, a ghost that was locked fast
in a Council scheme, where radios played all day
unknown raw music, and young couples brought
friends home to midnight parties, and each flower
in the grudging garden died in trampled clay.

Standing by her headstone in the mild
city of bell-less doors, I feel the sweat
stink my fresh shirt out, as each gravelly path
becomes a road, long lost, in a bad bet.
Once more I see the dirty sleepy child.
'The water's hot enough. You'll have a bath.'

And almost I am clean but for that door
so blank and strong, imprinted with her name
as that far other in the scheme was once,
and 'scheme' becomes a mockery, and a shame,
in this neat place, where each vase has its flower,
and the arching willow its maternal stance.

Autumn

Autumn again. A wide-eyed absence in
the woods and skies. The trees once berry-ripe
are cleared of weight and in the midday shine,

forlorn perhaps. Triumphant. It is true
that exile, parting, is our earthly lot,
though roots cling tight below the green and blue.

O handkerchiefs wave free while the full heart
is squeezed of purple, leaving the wrinkled skin.
Depend on everything, depend on art,

your crystal table set with paper, pen,
such simple instruments. Begin once more.
Spring in its fury breaks on us again,

frizzle of summer, winter with its snow,
and also autumn beating the hazels down
from trees enriched by taste and by red hue.

Art feeds us, famished. It's the heavenly crown,
the earthly crown against the dazzling blue.

Owl and Mouse

The owl wafts home with a mouse in its beak.
The moon is stunningly bright in the high sky.

Such a gold stone, such a brilliant hard light.
Such large round eyes of the owl among the trees.

All seems immortal but for the dangling mouse,
an old hurt string among the harmony

of the masterful and jewelled orchestra
which shows no waste soundlessly playing on.

'Iolaire'

On New Year's Eve 1918 a ship called the Iolaire *left Kyle of Lochalsh to bring three hundred men home to Lewis after the war was over. On New Year's morning 1919 the ship went on the rocks as a result of a navigational error at the Beasts of Holm, a short distance from Stornoway, the main town on the island. About two hundred sailors were drowned. In the following poem I imagine an elder of the church speaking as he is confronted with this mind-breaking event.*

The green washed over them. I saw them when
the New Year brought them home. It was a day
that orbed the horizon with an enigma.
It seemed that there were masts. It seemed that men
buzzed in the water round them. It seemed that fire
shone in the water which was thin and white
unravelling towards the shore. It seemed that I
touched my fixed hat which seemed to float and then
the sun illumined fish with naval caps,
names of the vanished ships. In sloppy waves,
in the fat of water, they came floating home
bruising against their island. It is true,
a minor error can inflict this death.
That star is not responsible. It shone
over the puffy blouse, the flapping blue
trousers, the black boots. The seagull swam
bonded to the water. Why not man?
The lights were lit last night, the tables creaked
with hoarded food. They willed the ship to port
in the New Year which would erase the old,
its errant voices, its unpractised tones.
Have we done ill, I ask, my fixed body
a simulacrum of the transient waste,
for everything was mobile, plants that swayed,
the keeling ship exploding and the splayed
cold insect bodies. I have seen your church
solid. This is not. The water pours
into the parting timbers where I ache
above the globular eyes. The slack heads turn
ringing the horizon without sound,

with mortal bells, a strange exuberant flower
unknown to our dry churchyards. I look up.
The sky begins to brighten as before,
remorseless amber, and the bruised blue grows
at the erupting edges. I have known you, God,
not as the playful one but as the black
thunderer from hills. I kneel
and touch this dumb blond head. My hand is scorched.
Its human quality confuses me.
I have not felt such hair so dear before
nor seen such real eyes. I kneel from you.
This water soaks me. I am running with
its tart sharp joy. I am floating here
in my black uniform. I am embraced
by these green ignorant waters. I am calm.

For Poets Writing in English over in Ireland

'Feeling,' they said,
'that's the important thing' –
those poets who write in English over in Ireland.

It was late.
There was dancing in the hall,
playing of pipes, of bones, of the penny whistle.

They were an island in that Irishness.
'Larkin and Dunn,' they said. 'Now Dunn is open
to more of the world than ageing Larkin is.

What room was Mr Bleaney in? It's like
going to any tenement and finding
any name you can think of on the door.

And you wonder a little about him but not much.'
We were sitting on the floor outside the room
where a song in Irish waltzed the Irish round.

Do the stones, the sea, seem different in Irish?
Do we walk in language, in a garment pure
as water? Or as earth just as impure?

The grave of Yeats in Sligo, Innisfree
island seen shivering on an April day.
The nuns who cycle down an Easter road.

The days are beads strung on a thin wire.
Language at Connemara is stone
and the water green as hills is running westwards.

The little children in the primary school
giggling a little at our Scottish Gaelic,
writing in chalk the Irish word for 'knife'.

To enter a different room. When did Bleaney
dance to the bones? This world is another world.
A world of a different language is a world

we find our way about in with a stick,
half-deaf half-blind, snatching a half word there,
seeing a twisted figure in a mirror,

slightly unnerved, unsure. I must go home.
To English? Gaelic? O beautiful Maud Gonne,
the belling hounds spoke in what language to you?

In that tall tower so finished and so clear
his international name was on the door
and who would ask who had been there before him?

I turn a page and read an Irish poem
translated into English and it says
(the poet writing of his wife who'd died):

'Half of my eyes you were, half of my hearing,
half of my walking you were, half of my side.'
From what strange well are these strange words upspringing?

But then I see you, Yeats, inflexible will,
creator of yourself, a conscious lord,
writing in English of your own Maud Gonne.

Inside the room there's singing and there's dancing.
Another world is echoing with its own
music that's distant from the world of Larkin.

And I gaze at the three poets. They are me,
poised between two languages. They have chosen
with youth's superb confidence and decision.

'Half of my side you were, half of my seeing,
half of my walking you were, half of my hearing.'
Half of this world I am, half of this dancing.

Lost

Lost, we go from street to street
past the cinema showing *The Deer Hunter.*

They are playing Russian roulette,
red bandages on their eyes.

Where are we? Is it here or Saigon?

What street is this, that the soldiers are in the water with the rats.
Who are you, drunkard with the black cap,
swaying?

We want to go home. A safe wound will be enough.
He is putting the gun to his head.
The gooks are watching.

I think we are in a maze of green
and there is a rickshaw coming towards us
with Death in red riding in it.

He bows deeply. We are in the middle of his dead eyes
and the bloodstained chopper takes off.

Hallowe'en

Someone was playing the piano when quite suddenly
there they were standing in the room.
They would not sing or speak or tell their names.
Their skull faces blankly shifted round
as if they were studying us implacably.
'Yokels,' one said. 'Rustics,' said another,
and truly they had come in out of the rain
with their masks tall and white and bony-looking.
'Macbeth,' someone said, and someone, 'Hamlet'.
Or perhaps at least the 'Elegy' by Gray.
The rain drummed on the roof and they were gone
in their muddy boots, squelching past cowering doors.
We looked at each other. It was graveyard time
as our black ties on our white shirts might say.

Poem

It is always evening in a German poem,
the moon shining on the shell-like houses
and the roses like swans' necks bowed over lakes.

Something is always about to happen,
a crouched being rising over the horizon
with fur on its hands and fur about its cheeks.

Past the water it comes, out of the moonlight,
heading steadily past the little church,
the tavern that resounds with loud tunes.

And it stands, turning its head in the moonlight,
slowly, purposefully, in the pure light
among the roses with the necks of swans

while somewhere in the distance a bell rings
very gently, humbly, and a milkmaid
sings to herself, the warm pail in her hand.

The Survivors

How can they survive the days
those who have no talent
how can they face the sharpness of the morning star?

Those who have no direction
who have nothing they can do well
whose days do not form a book

or even a particular style
such that it feeds on the clouds
and on the big spaces between them.

Admire them most of all
those who built the pyramids
but were too close to them to see.

Those who died
before the road was completed
before the bridge spanned the water.

The hyphens the dashes the strokes –
those who see the sunsets
as wheels that return and return.

These I think are the true heroes,
they push stones away from their breasts
when they rise in the morning.

The 'Ordinary' People

The 'ordinary' people sing on the edge of the grave.
When the hero howls and cries they are humming
in the middle of ropes, griefs, the deaths of roses.

The 'ordinary' people are not stones.
They are revengeful, bitter, quick to strike and laugh
and they buy oranges at the market-place.

The 'ordinary' people say, 'I'll not be put upon.'
They spend their money freely on food and drink
and then they have no money, only hope.

Where does the hope come from that they see,
who live precariously by the deaths of roses,
and hang their washing among tragedies?

I begin to think there are no 'ordinary' people.

Or rather that they've learned about tragedies
from birth and can simply pass them by
or walk through them clutching food, bottles.

I believe there is no such thing as tragedy,
that the hero has deceived us, is the red infant
howling and screaming from his wooden cage.

At the Funeral of Robert Garioch

Something about the April day
touched me
as they slid your coffin onto the trolley
in the Crematorium.

More and more often it troubles me
this wind my sails have missed
which is still around me
fluttering the bluebells.

'The Lord's My Shepherd' we sang.
It was time for the burning.
The minister blessed it
dressed in his white gown,

his voice fat and voluptuous,
his enunciation pure.
You slid down into fire
in your yellow coffin.

In half-way April
the breeze was vulnerable
straying among the warble
of the first birds.

Poet, the flowers are open
even when we are dead
even when the power has gone
from our right arms.

The flowers open in flame.
The coffin slides home.
Fugitive April becomes
a tremendous summer.

Who Daily

Who daily at the rickety table
writes and sings, writes and sings,
Venus with the one arm,
Apollo with the one leg,
the stuttering rainbow that hirples
like early crayons into the sea.

Envoi

        There are
more things in heaven and earth, Horatio,
than bones, roses. There are windows
        through which gaunt faces peer
            and there are children
        running through great doors.
                            Consider
how the sea roars mournfully at the edge of
        all things, how the seaweed
        hangs at the sailor's neck, the crab
        shuffles in armour, Horatio,
    the punctual dead visit us, rise
            bird-voiced from the grass,
                and the owls
            are scholars of the woods.
        Horatio, I remember
        a kingdom and a kingdom's diplomat,
        a girl floating tenderly down stream,
            a crown on her young head.
            These are portents, warnings, ominous
            reflections from the mirror.
                Horatio
            my eyes darken. Tragedy is
            nothing but churned foam.
            I wave to you
        from this secure and leafy entrance,
            this wooden
                door on which I bump my head,
            this moment and then,
                that.

A LIFE
(1986)

Lewis 1928–1945

1

'When did you come home? When are you leaving?'
'No I don't... don't think I know...'
The moonlit autumn nights of long ago,
the heavy thump of feet at their late dancing.
'We'll sail by the autumn moon to Lewis home.'
'I think I know you...' But our faces age,
our knuckles redden and webbed lines engage
eyes that were once so brilliant and blue.
The sharp salt teaches us. These houses, new
and big with grants and loans, replace the old
thatched walls that straggled in a tall lush field.
I lie among the daisies and look up
into a tall blue sky where lost larks chirp.
The sea is blazing with a bitter flame.
'When are you leaving? When did you come home?'
The island is the anvil where was made
the puritanical heart. The daisies foam
out of the summer grass. The rigid dead
sleep by the Braighe, tomb on separate tomb.

2

All day she sleeps but often in the night
she calls on her dead mother, her live son.
Her pills and bottles shine in the harvest moon.

She who was once beautiful hangs on
to her frayed thread of being: will not die.
She speaks in two languages in the night,
will dance like a light cloud, as once she did
with the luminous others at the corner of the road.
The stunning moon is cruising overhead,
the stacks of corn are gossiping in the field.
There was a time when she would starve for bread.
'Mother' she cries, 'mother' and that shield
of cloth bends over her. My child, my child.
She runs home lightly to her thousand pills,
her clouded marbles. And the daffodils
spring upward once again behind her heels.
The hills are cardboard blue, the skies are red.

3

Our landmark is the island, complex thing.
A rock, a death, a house in which were made
our narrow global seaward-going wings,
the rings of blue, the cloth both fine and frayed.
It sails within us, as one poet said,
its empty shelves are resonant. A scant
religion drives us to our vague tremens.
We drag it at our heels, as iron chains.
A winsome boyhood among glens and bens
casts, later, double images and shades.
And ceilidhs in the cities are the lens
through which we see ourselves, unmade, remade,
by music and by grief. The island sails
within us and around us. Startled we
see it in Glasgow, hulk of the humming dead,
and of the girls in cornfields disarrayed.

4

You will not find a Rubens, Rembrandt here,
nor my revered Vermeer. You will not find
the velvet-lined
hound faces of aristocrats: the blind
blank mask of genius with its gravid stare.

The meagre furniture appals me here,
the props of rock, of heather, and of sea,
the constancy
of ruined walls and nettles. A humming bee
is smartly burning round an absent pier.

Life without art, the minimum. I hear
a sermon tolling, for your theatre is
the fire of grace,
hypothesis of hell, a judging face
looming from storm towards boats and sea-drenched gear,

the thrifty fields, monotonous, austere,
where poppies are superfluous, and the rose.
The thistle grows
its thorny purple crown: and Sunday flows
with its burning transient girls through psalm and prayer.

5

Once famous footballer, he's alcoholic now.
He'll speak to no one, crying through bare rooms.
O what has happened to that fragrant bough?

Shin-guarded and striped-stockinged, he ran out
to fields of local shadow and of sun,
was wasp in quickness and in freshness trout.

And poked the girls at night among the stacks
in his horned majesty: the moon a clear
ball that was spinning through vast cloths and racks,

discarded knickers. O spread legs of white.
He staggers past the mirror in his room
and dribbles helplessly. His early strut

on studs descends to shuffle. In this globe
the sunny whisky burns. The shadows ray
across him pitching towards his moony ebb.

He kicks right through the mirror. Is it day?
The spidery keeper hurts him in the rib.

6

O hi ro O hi ree,
dance the reel beside the sea.

The wedding dances out three days.
The roads of moonlight are a blaze

across the strait. It starts again.
The red breeds red, the green breeds green.

The brilliant boxed melodeon
squeezes out a husky tune,

and legs are twined with legs, while one
sucks whisky with a baby's grin.

The red breeds red. It all begins.
The bridal gown's a wheel that spins

among the rocks. The river roars.
In darkness at the play of horse

he jockeys home. Triumphant sails
billow the firth above hard keels.

7

In school it was, each morning, and her bum
divine and rounded. Mr Cicero Trill
burns on his pyre and hears its ceaseless hum
in sizzling Carthage while that ruined sail –
his cloak – hustles him Rome – and duty-wards. O love,
who but Catullus could inscribe those pains,
or exiled Ovid. At each window pane
the leaves are rustling. In carved white she sits
behind a desk that's scored beneath her tits.
Her bum is glorious, stern of the boat that rides
his tourist Mediterranean. So fresh and young.
The fire is flickering its viper tongue.
Virgil is burning with a wealth of brides.
The chalk trills crazily down her fleshy sides.

8

Beside the library, I smelt the salt
as once I used to do,
the island boy with the *Tatler*, *London News*,

in their black leather covers. Shooting grouse
was not his special thing. Nor was the wine
red in his cup, nor the marbly and 'divine'

bare shoulders his. The snouting drifters drowsed
beside the pier. A sailor wove a net,
green among orange buoys. The hull was set

exactly on its shadow, and the gulls
were streaks of avarice. It was the drowned
slept neatly in their hammocks without sound

in the plain water among salty shelves.
The knickerbockered gentlemen expel
their smoky bubbles, and they come to heel,

the obedient beagles, then set out in line
into the crumbling sunset, and their haul
the dripping dead, so foxy-faced and tall.

9

Remember how the War brought the News home,
John Snagge and Belfrage… The new wireless was
a huge mahogany. Each HMS

sunk in the Mediterranean might be ours.
Always 'the next of kin have been informed.'
I see them sheltering from the random showers

in seas they hadn't heard of, and the guns
defend the poor thatched roofs. In hollow booms
our HMS Accumulator runs

deep down to zero. In the box they see
young bodies hearsed. A vibrating Big Ben
tolls out their deaths, in the inconstancy

of an ocean named, unfathomable. They come
running from the playing fields which are blue.
They stutter out in classrooms words and sums.

That bitter water schools them through and through.

10

Roses, I think there is salt on you,
and on the headland I hear the exiles' songs.

The thatched roofs, woven by dead hands,
are sunk among the superannuated school buses,

in a field of daisies and lush grasses.
The buzzard slants over the untilled ground.

Varying perfumes taunt me. In church I saw
the fifty-year-old girl I used to know,

her face curdled and gaunt. Bibles
are open in the churchyards, marbly white,

and the sea sighs towards the gravestones.
On the moors

the heather is wine-red and the lochs
teem with unhunted fish. The sky

is an eternal blue and God drowses
momently from his justice. Singing,

the drunk sways among poppies, missing
the rusty unused scythe. The boats are

a frieze on the far horizon, smoking gently,
and almost motionless. The cornfields were

a nest of snaky legs: and now it is
the butterfly that wafts there. This is not

a haunt of angels. The devils kneel at night
offering whisky in a bottle to

those who despise church windows in their reds.
Gaunt girl I walked with in the long ago,

sleep gently in the beams of the red moon,
whose claws are crablike in your drained breast.

11

They get off the buses at the ends of roads,
walk the rest of the way. The vague butterflies

are wafting all around them. In the ditches
whisky bottles, empty lager cans.

The windows of the school are red shields,
the sky a waste of embers. Soon the stars

will begin to swim among oblique scents.
The spirits of sailors sigh along the walls

returning home at night from Canada,
where paunchy men with sky-blue suits and ties

flourish on memories of their Scottishness.
Slowly the moon rises like a ball

that was once a vague horn. You hear the moos
bring you home to your extended house

beside the old one which your grandfather
when still a boy signed with his careful name.

12

Stubs of pipes in teeth, the old men
predicted good weather. It was our annual

visit to the town. Red apples
nested among their straws, as if birds

we did not know of hatched them. And the cones
were cold on icy teeth. Hardy, Laurel,

plunged out of windows on their rubbery ladders
in thin or baggy trousers. Errol Flynn

wearing smoked glasses had the Japanese
pilot in his sights. On Wake Island

we left the wakes behind, and strode, blinded,
into the brittle sunlight. This town is

too small for both of us, bowlered minister.
The colours of the cinema warmer than

your plain clear window. Till we reach our homes
we ride the gulches of these starved fields.

Aberdeen University 1945–1949

1

The glitter of the water and the wake...
Heading for University in Aberdeen.
It's an autumn morning. I am seventeen.
Above the Isle of Skye the dawn's a flag

of red infuriate ore. I see the train
for the first time ever steaming from the Kyle
beyond the screaming seagulls, in the smell
of salt and herring. There's a tall sad crane.

The landscape, rich, harmonious, unwinds
its perfect symmetry: not the barren stone
and vague frail fences I have always known.
I hold my Homer steady in my hand.

All day we travel and at last dismount
at the busy station of that sparkling town.
A beggar with black glasses sitting down
on the hard stone holds out his cap. I count

the pennies in it. Should I freely give?
Or being more shameful than himself refrain?
His definite shadow is the day's black stain.
How in such open weakness learn to live?

I turn away, the money in my hand,
profusely sweating, in that granite blaze.
Unknown, unlooked at, I pick up my case.
Everything's glittering and transient.

2

The prim historian talks of Robespierre.
Shakespeare's *Othello* is a mineral play
suited to granite and the wide North Sea.
Each subject has its scrupulous compère.

The guillotine cuts sharply between me
and that far island nesting in its waves.
Roof upon roof creates collapsing graves.
'Put up your bright swords.' Dewy Italy

and Aberdeen and Lewis all collide.
The sea-green incorruptible sustains
the sodden salty flesh. I shake my chains.
Europe is glowing like a flowery bride

with her fresh bouquets; and that ring recedes
mile upon mile away from me. I hear
the sharp quick yelp of tight-frocked Robespierre.
Some wound within me bleeds and bleeds and bleeds…

3

'Youse students with the cash,' says Mrs Gray,
our iron landlady with the Roman nose.
(Her stuttering husband is a paler ray.)

What art, what music, troubled even once
her brow that's wrinkled by the thought of gold?
She fills the space around her, holds her stance

against the world's obliquity. She stakes
her confident site out, while the scholar ghosts
through a double landscape of new streets, old Greeks,

a sturdy lady not to be put upon
by tragedy engendered in the soul,
nor by her husband who drives buses down

familiar roads, and who at night attends
religiously the 'flicks', whose bedroom is
the moony attic that her greed commends.

4

Beowulf dives into mysterious depths...
The girls on Union St in cruising pairs
clutch shiny handbags, and wear Woolworth rings.

He swarms in armour towards an old death.
In Hazelhead their legs are white and bare.
They swim in twilight wafting vague soft scents.

His bubbling armour frays and leaks and dents...
Their breasts at evening swell, their short skirts flare.
We are such fleshy fiery tenements.

The salty hero strides about his tents...
My dear pale girls with permed and lamplit hair...

5

Bicycles sparkle past the market place.
The cafés glitter. Love O Careless Love.
The statues cast their shadows across parks.

The velvet-jacketed pensioned Major moves
a piece on the draughtsboard in the open air.
This is a mimic and yet serious war.

I lie in Duthie Park with the *Aeneid*,
in my white flannels. All the epitaphs shine
in the adjacent overgrown graveyard.

LOVE O CARELESS LOVE. The Odeon towers
in its white marble towards a blue decor.
Its transient images are what etch and burn.

And in the café a small radio plays.
Everything passes, everything is weighed
with a random music, heartbreakingly sweet.

6

Aberdeen, I constantly invoke
your geometry of roses.

Your beads of salt
decorate my wrists

and are the tiny bells
of grammar schools.

There are no deaths
that I recall

among your cinemas,
in the shadows

of your green trees.
Aberdeen,

I loved your granite
your salt mica.

Your light
taught
me immortality.

7

No library that I haven't loved.
My food is books.

The grey-haired twittering lady climbs the steps
to drag a heavy Spenser to the floor.

She is not made of crystal but is mortal.
An old professor is bent over a chair
drowsing perhaps sleeping.

How reconcile
the market to the library, the till
to strict Lucretius?

The foam of flowers in Duthie Park, the page
blazing in its whiteness, in this sun
whose sleepless socket is perpetual.

The grey-haired lady lugs a tome across
a library floor as polished as a glass.

O she will die but this book will never die.
The Faerie Queene; this pale dishevelled one.

8

In winter, ice and frosty Aberdeen
inscribes its images on window panes.

The Polar Star is miles away from us.
It glows on towers and ghostly lighthouses
and on the spiky Latin in my room.

This is your weather, strict Lucretius.
How can religion stand it? How can Pan
with his hairy tropic legs? That animal?

The frost an exhalation of the mind.
The icy planets keep their rectitude.
Religion dies in temperatures like these.

And God the spider shrinks in his crystal web.
The gravestones bloom with ice. The city is
a constant shrine of probabilities.

National Service 1950–1952

1

The corporal struts briskly up and down,
moustached, Hitlerian. 'You play fair with me
and I'll play fair with you. Otherwise…'
We stand at attention in the barrack room
beside our beds. There's a black ancient stove.
The sentry at the gate had glassy boots
and glassy eyes. The reapers in the fields
waved towards us as we trudged the dusty road
in the last hot July of our free youth.
We lay in our grave sheets as the Last Post

wailed through the room, a lost mysterious soul,
the bugle music of our homesickness.
The lights of our windows faded towards the square
where the RSM, a brutal cockerel,
had shouted as we trudged towards the door
which shut on Milton and on Shakespeare.

2

'Listen, you poof, I'm standing on your hair.'
The public schoolboy smiles, superior
to this old patter. He's an officer
already in his mind, he will not fail.
The plumber's mate is shaking as his shots
miss the ringed target, small as a postage stamp.
His eyes are wells of weeping. The ball-cock
rises, a perfect circle, buoyant, light.
The public schoolboy registers a bull.
Last night he played some melancholy jazz
while we spat on boots and burned them luminous black.
The plumber's mate was reading *Dracula*.
The public schoolboy casually turned a page
of *Murder in the Cathedral*. The shots slam
into the distant circles. The red flags
swell in a breeze that's cool, civilian.

3

Education sergeants, lowest of the low...
Our NCO looks hunted, vigilant,
bearing fresh files wherever he will go.
We teach the recruits about NATO, UNO,
drowsy from ten mile marches. No one more
soldierly, crisply creased, than our NCO.
His badge is shiny, he's meticulous,
We teach letter-writing to the illiterate
easily unearthed, in spite of shame,

since they're the ones most charged. Unreadable,
Company Orders, but particular
their sense of personal honour, and their name…
The poster says, *Make the Army Your Korea.*
The burly RSM shadows the camp
red-cheeked and bulbous-eyed. We are the grit
of education sticking in his eye.
The haggard Wracs pass by in khaki skirts.
'I'll get that skiver Morrison,' he says
of our librarian. For BAOR
he pines at evening into his tearful glass.

4

'Love O careless Love', Irene, 'Good Night'.
The corporal actually talks to us, smokes our cigs
obsequiously donated. Brute mugs
often turn handsome as the gunfire fades.
Alone, the plumber's mate engilds his badge.
The Glasgow boys who masturbate at dawn
below gigantic sheets appraise their bints.
We are now bowed to these harsh elements.
The plumber's mate is exiled from his kind,
obsessed and jumpy. The omnivorous
witticisms tear him limb from limb.
The corporal approves, in sleepy calm:
our lotus land this squalid barrack room,
the harmless rifles stacked along the wall.

5

We marched so beautifully, cleanly, then.
It was a perfect music wrought from pain.
EYES RIGHT – the general serenely shone

medalled and ribboned, a commissionaire.
The organ rose in blue… How strict and bare
the square at morning. Stony birds will share

its perfect stoniness. The reapers fade
into their corn and poppies. Sheared, I tread
this glorious echoing stage, exude

a rich fine scent of lotion.
               It is done.
I enter the barrack room out of the bright sun.
It is a well of shadow. I lie down

extended on the bed, and see the blood
rolling along the floor. The head, the head…
The plumber's mate unrecognisably dead

but for the comic with its bleeding fangs.
The victim bubbles gently and the wings
turn ugly on the Quisling. A bee sings

thinly on a pane that's turning red.

Clydebank and Dumbarton 1952–1955

1

The adjective clause, the adverbial and the noun –
how would these boys consider them divine
as the bell-cheeked monks had done

in mediaeval gardens? In pale neon
where tenements sag brokenly: or at noon
where they burn like cages; how could these girls shine

with laurel, not with lipstick? Random buses run.
How could that stairhead bowl be the carved urn
of shadowless Greece or Rome? Those pipes a vine

twisting and turning on that barren stone?
They're taught by what they are. That barbarous wine
boils over grammar and will not decline.

2

Alliteration, simile. He composed
his yellow booklet when day's work was done.
Such careful bureaucratical fine prose!
Metonymy, synecdoche, the pun.
Over this grimy grid he superimposed
the texts of Greece, the scholars' monotone.
Beyond his window a cloud snottily flows.

A cage for bees and wasps! A lined fine school!
The chalk's a ghostly dust for such as these.
O somewhere else they find the beautiful,
the unpredictable flashes of girls' knees,
the curves of football that transcend all rule,
the poetry of the Clyde so silvery cool –
down sudden avenues green crowns of trees.

3

The flash of trains on rails, the Cenotaph,
how shall these meet, collide?

Pale girls at evening on neon roads –
the marble halls of Rome.

Cloth-capped Glaswegians with their spotted hounds –
great Homer in his pride.

The vested hairy-chested boilerman
soaping his body in the kitchen sink –
the libraries and tomes.

And yet as legionnaires they once set out
thump thump on knife-straight roads,

creating once their strong geometries
to link damp hot and hut.

4

Seen here from green Argyll, the city is
a yellow labyrinth where each winking house
composed a bracelet of pure randomness.

The emptiness and hollows of the street!
The scholarly lamp-posts each with their viperish light
reading the stone. Each pack had its own suit

like grape flies gathered in the evening.
The sallow girls imagined a red ring
blazing on their fingers. The trains sang

and whined like wolves along predestined rails.
Among these garish ads the spirit fails.
The watery twilight of a million souls

composes jesters' colours. Where is home?
Not in this place with its tubercular bloom.
The city is a painted yellow room

for actors without denouement. I stand
inside the Underground. There's a hollow sound.
The whooshing train casts papers to the wind.

Oban 1955–1982

1

Oban in autumn, and reflective Mull
cast on the water. How the snowy gull

pecks at waste herring bones on the scaly quay.
The central glitter of the boundless sea.

Like pots that boil on Sundays, engines find
their drumming destination, and the mind

its fixed direction. By tall cliffs I see
the jackdaws playing. On green benches the

tourists repose at evening, while the tide
whispers and chuckles. O I see you, bride,

Gaelic, mysterious: and this radiance is
the extravagant presence of the sea's abyss

extending to Iona and its graves.
The very stones are green. The sea is sheaves

of endless blue on blue and lucid crowns
of jellyfish drift lazily. No one drowns

in this amazing light. The War Memorial burns.
One soldier helps another through the stone.

2

A Roman rector, measured gravitas,
a Gaelic scholar too. He knows each child.
Our own names honour us and each one salutes

us from his sparkling bicycle. The school hums,
directed engine. Black-winged he comes
along the shiny corridors. In the hall

appointing prefects he quotes from Paul.
The race is to the kind, not to the smart,
to Brutus not to Antony. The clear art

of human Homer is our constant aim:
whatever's comely. Casually he says,
'It was Housman taught me in my Cambridge days.'

And behind him Macintyre and William Ross.
Where's Eliot and Auden? Horace glows,
each marble phrase, the clarity of prose.

'Transposing Greek to Gaelic is no toil.
They had their clans, their sea terms. And the style
of the great *Odyssey* is what Gaelic knows.'

Easily he chats to the crofting man
who sucks a straw: as easily as he scans
those vast hexameters or the pibroch.

                              Does
what's comely and what's right by natural rule,
by Roman cheerfulness and harmonious Greek.
Propounds a human yet a rigorous school.

3

To find the way!
The raindrops glitter,
Lucretius's idea.

To let the light
sway through the marble –
temporal appetite.

To keep the mist
about the grammar
in the amethyst

bloom of violet.
Sheep's eyes
cast greeny jets

and grass waves —
itself how lightly
over graves.

4

That sunny Gaelic world! That Roman rule!
Addison and Lamb. And Keats who died
in perpetual autumn with the nightingale.

To be centred in a place where the pure tide
renews its treasures: and each misty hill
is real yet poetic. There abide

the famous dead who walk the promenade
at watery evening when the world is still.
Around the moon the scholarly stars reside,

survive our light. I know the miracle
of the perfect bridegroom and the perfect bride
chiming exactly. Sometimes there's a style

we wear at moments, almost deified.
We see in others what ourselves compel,
inscriptions of our happiness. There's a wide

ocean, yet a margin of the will.
The prefecture and others. The divide
is what moans nightly as tides ebb and fill.

5

Around the library
there is a cry,

unauthorised, casual.
They toil

to build the marble.
They scribble

their transient names.
Tattooed arms

scandalise the Forms.
In dreams

they're famous and see
in the huge screened smoky cinema

themselves enlarged. In beds
become immortal. O words

how stamp these wrists?
They pay for visits

to castles they themselves raised
in winds swayingly composed.

6

Spinsterish teachers, missing the apples, die
quite abruptly, or in Homes
sleep beyond plasticine and nursery rhymes.

After retirement they venture
into Geography into History,
posters and labels of the day,

from the simply presented alphabet.
Their grey hair is combed white.
The wind and tenements confuse

with random uncorrected news,
scraps of jotters in the gutter,
homeless incorrigible litter.

I think in ashen corners they
suffer for their innocence,
the prim precision of their stance.

Their children swarm far afield.
Among projects they grow old.
None shall repeat his circumstance.

7

Come towards me, immense millions.
From the carved desks I see you rise:
and you, ghostly inscribed blackboards,

be the red shield of a new sun.
I constantly see the stain
spreading on my calm jacket.

I constantly see the braid
unwind, unseam. The million dead
illuminate the million tides.

The feathered quill
is stained with red. The terrible
agonised cry infects the page.

Your helpless rage
shakes the tranquil gold board
on which the Duxes' names are scored.

8

The unpredicted that I prize
blossoms in a furious
dishevelled spring.
                    Around the lectern
the plebs, candle-white, arise.
Sir is shaken. His gown flows
along a suddenly turbid Styx.
The red marks on his rigid index
recall the blood of those who've died,
anonymously. The outraged dead
stand up in rows. The sparsely fed
gnaw at his prose and will not hide.

9

Peasant that you are, realise
that you belong with them.
Your village is hideous

with the blood on the door
and your grass
is their grass.

It is the same wind
that blows everywhere,
and islands

howl with the same seas,
the white
foam on the lips.

It is the rigour,
exactitude, appals
without mercy,

and the homeless ones
rise on waters
unjustly flamed.

Peasant,
I order you
stand with them

when the epauletted one
ticks off on his register
their names.

Consider
that the loved chimneys
are for all of us,

and the castle
reflects the blood-red rays
of the diligent

whose epitaphs
are the torn washing hung out
on ropes themselves have made.

10

'Please, sir, I don't read books…' she says to me.
Who on the Tiber Bridge were the famous three?

'Horatius, Stout and Lartius…' It is true
the fabulous Elvis with his 'Blue Suede Shoes'

sways in their stony garden, 'Paper Roses'.
At intervals they comb each other's tresses

with sleepy tenderness. 'I'll be a pilot, sir,'
says one to whom all writing is a blur,

'an engineer, an architect.' The girls yearn
for glamorous hairdressing, where helmets burn

as if on space men. Through neglected terms
they dream of dances and of wavy perms.

11

Sometimes in supermarkets at the till
I see them tapping. Sometimes in hotels
I see them serving – all these Annabels,
these Floras and Fionas! Such sweet skill!

They tolerate, I think, my puzzlement,
conspirators together in a world
where life has been partitioned: and the blood
thinned down to chalk. Somewhere I see my pent

bourgeois persona, individual,
thornily investigate the rose
which raggedly pushes through pale slabs of prose.
The human flesh and the reflective jewel

to be combined and unified! The fixed
and unpredictable to sing as one –
the pale-faced girl chained to the changing moon,
and Venus smiling from her marble text!

12

The teachers are growing old,
their faces whiter,
their eyes disillusioned and sad.

How long ago it was
when they played on their pupils like violins,
and *Macbeth* was a green field.

How joyful they were in those days
well-scrubbed and youthful
just as rich as the clouds.

Now their faces are chalk white
and the blackboards are singing
with a graffito of sour thorns.

13

There was a time
when they could read Tennyson
to docile classes,
when poems rhymed.

when clad in their gowns
they seemed to be masters
of a finally colonised globe.

Now there is hubbub.
They are the chancy
scouts of the frontiers
and the chiming pentameters
have forsaken them.

They are no longer bearers
of messages from Rome and Greece,
the police
of the poem.

Unprotected, knobbly-kneed,
they must learn to bleed
their own, not Caesar's blood.

And in the marketplace
listen to Antony's address
with bitter grief.

For the chalk is like scrawls of lighting
on the blackboard,
and the sacred and abhorred
real poem has a waspish sting.

14

'Sir, we are the stupid ones,' they say.
The football on the field invents a plot,
random and unpredicted. Who has taught
the inner rhythms of this outward play?

The English master with the grey moustache
watches from the touchline. 'Fodder, these...
But after all they rescued Rome and Greece
for the lucid talkers who turned pale as ash.'

Bewildering gyrations! On the wing
they flash fresh plumage, and the goal appears.
A ghost with gloves protects their universe.
The net behind him is a complex thing.

O graduate from this to Tennyson!
You fail at fences which the others raise.
We are practitioners of choice ideas.
It is our turn to listen and to learn!

Taynuilt 1982–

1

Alone with my old typewriter at last
astronomy of letters I aspire
beyond its teaching to make literature.
Away from ghostly chalk I stand aghast

in this cold marble cell which will forgive
only the best and truest. Truant boys
from breezy woods, I hear your careless noise.
It is not by negligence that I must live

though not forgetting human voices too
in my study of the vases and the stone.
Beyond the sane and steady monotone
I listen patiently and must pursue

what shines beyond the grasses and the shade.
The leaves are trembling past my window pane.
By some fixed justice everything is weighed.
The truant boys are harried by a chain

that exactly measures both the loss and gain.
The value of the vase is always paid.

2

What have I done today?
Read some of Aubrey's
Brief Lives, walked to
the newspaper shop and saw
the tenant below
feeding his golden cat
on a raw
plateful of meat.

A vast crowd
of seagulls landed to feed
on the mouldy bread
set out for the tit and the wren.
My table
rose towards me like a ruby
containing white sheet after sheet.
Was it this way
that Beethoven wrote his music or Mozart
dealt with his perfect art?
Did Homer, say,
shepherd the clouds to his roof
or suddenly laugh
at a joke made by the stone or the wood?
Life, life,
you are not respectable,
you are the sudden glance
of frilly knickers,
the unrepeatable
ray on the untidy work table
a drunk man saying his prayers.

Or according to Aubrey
'the worthiest men have been
rocked in the meanest cradles.'

'I'll have an umbrella invention
to retard a ship in a storm'
or of the Marquess Hamilton
(a beheaded lover of carps)
'would bring his fish into England
in barrels from Scotland
but their noses all turned green
from gangrene
by bobbing against the tub.'

Who is this poor worm then
who stands among apples and wine?

3

for Donalda

So I come home to you
as the one I didn't leave behind
as the quick diligent
drawer back of curtains,

lest the house should be seen
as too much slept in
when there is so much wind
among the sunlight:

so many rainbows
trembling among news
of the daft old glasses
twinkling together:

so many owls
sucking to their eyes
the moon-struck mice
in the leafy classroom,

and the world a skirt
turning a corner
altering pleat by pleat
its breezy sculpture.

4

If everything is contingent
how can the poem
be made necessary?

Like the summer rose
exact and perfect
in a coronation of dew.

Some come to the jail
of the inevitable sonnet
by unique suffering

demanding to be heard,
the song of the bird
in a metre of new thorns.

5

The joy of the author is beyond speech.
His characters come dancing back to him.
They sing in the morning in his happiness.

Like the morning stars they are innocent,
enigmatic, diamond-like, without denouement.
They have such hope, they shine among dewy roads.

The joy of an author is beyond speech.
God, what do you think of us? Do you regret us?
Have our journeyings been sufficient justification?

The devil walks about the country in green,
colour of nature, suave, impenetrable.
You had to allow him his own perfect will.

And therefore the complainings of Job were heard,
the head becoming ashen, the pride dying,
the fire fading behind the black grate.

Are you happy with us, supreme author,
as other authors are in the evening
who scrupulously dine with their imaginings?

Such joy, such joy! Do not recall us to You.
Let us go on our way rejoicing
down all the possible avenues we can take.

Life is a sublime gift, supreme one.
What can it be compared to? Nothing.
Your stars are like the words that burn on carbon.

Let us go justly to our just denouement.
All that we ask of you is consistency,
not the arbitrariness of the partial one.

Only that the axioms should generate
the correct justice. Only that the ending should be
a perfect rainbow sprung from genesis.

6

Never trust the author, trust the tale.
Out of the autumn mist it swims out to us,
a strange exhalation from the past
which is the tale remembering itself.

It is an affair of crows and of trees,
of clouds which bloom round chimneys, and of skies
that wear at once the first and last embers.

The author is not important, the author dies.
The tale lives on. It is the long river
heard at deepest midnight, in the day,
with berries hanging over it, subsumed
in a sweet water that is not a mirror.

Set out, set out, on your bare autumn soil.

7

I think you will die easily.
You have been a book reader all your life.

You will not fight the imagination.

There have been so many deaths, denouements,
resolutions of plots,

and marriages at the ends of books.
We are always told of them
especially in the empire of Victoria.

So your death will be like a marriage,
as a return of the lost boy
to the house where he originally belonged,

after he had been punished in an orphanage,
forced to climb sooty chimneys,
to put varnish on coffins.

You will die in a cloud of roses,
the pages quietly finished,
the last disentangling chapter

putting all the characters in their places,
the marriages and deaths blossoming
from the final arranged words.

8

Your brain is a thorn
that starves for meaning
as the thin cactus
with its single red flower.

Headaches remind you
of the vast distance
between your pale hand
and what your hand touches.

Headaches are the fields
of the thriftless thistles,
the rose which rises coolly
in a hiatus of pain.

9

Don Quixote, through appearances
you stubbornly ride, a fragile skeleton,
ideal of the perfect and the true.

Common sense beside you, carnal, limited.
'Tell me if you were knight would you pee –
if to enchantment you were truly captive?'

The rusty voice creaks out against the proverbs,
wisdom of ages. Book-compelled
you kill your library of fictional villains.

Madman, idealist. 'Is this helmet, jug?'
A vase may be the armour of the poet.
Creation abhors wisdom, common sense.

You'll always be there, Sancho, by the wayside.
But for the other one who fights coffins, windmills,
let him be bridal to us, a fresh breeze.

10

for George Campbell Hay (1915–1984)

The vulnerable ones die many deaths
but if they are poets they rise again.

Kintyre, your adopted home, will have fresh leaves
in double April of the sun and showers
even when you're dead in your honey-coloured coffin.

The Middle East where you learned about man,
his beggary, nobility, still shines
with oil and violence, and the noise of war
prolongs itself beyond Tobruk, Bizerta…

And your country, Scotland, still remains the same
passive and hollow, the imperious thistle
nodding above a black and empty grave.

The vulnerable ones are the most precious
if from the desert they bring back reports,
with shaking hand record their victories –
no generals more valuable than they.

From lost Culloden towards Africa.
The judge condemns the beggar and the thief
but you recall the glittering, generous
waters, and the trees that do not fade.

Sweet gentle spirit, proud and breakable,
the mast is shaken but the boat survives.
The constant lyric of the possible
obsesses, the brief eternal wind
that trembles among leaves, and is the soul…

The Sahara, saffron, inescapable,
does not wholly burn you, nor the stars,
scatter of sand make you indifferent…

For though we are sand we are diamond. The slim waist
of the vulnerable hourglass brings such tears
as in the morning of your joyousness
when Kintyre was no mirage but the will itself
upthrust in mountains, towering and green.

11

'We authors,' she will say, who has written nothing
but a single poem in a local paper.

'We authors,' she will say, so carelessly,
as if she were saying, 'We doctors' or 'We lawyers.'

Are you listening, Tolstoy, do you hear her, Burns?
Such a clear day, such a small coffee cup,

the statues being folded into leaves.
'We authors,' she will say and the earth is churning,

a thunderstorm swallows her white coffee cup,
and the lightning seals her lips with a blue flame.

12

The jet plane leaves a trail in the blue sky.
The trail I leave is far more tortuous,

hesitations and false starts and grief and pain.
That plane with one explosion's far from us

in another country, almost another time.
I rhyme and sing in the ambiguous

but straight as a ruler is the trail you leave,
ambitious pilot, and conspicuous.

And mine is invisible and quite tentative.
Shall others find it straight, to the blue grave?

13

Poet, you arise from the dead.
Among stones your shroud is palpable
changed into web, hung in the fragile day.

Nothing ever dies and you do not.
Leaf upon leaf is deathless and becomes
new forests for the climbing hectic tribes.

Leaf upon leaf, first green then white then green.

Nothing abhors you. You abhor nothing.
Even the spit of snails your soul loves.

The spirit uncrushable and breakable.
You die in green and you arise in purple.
The hills of evening remember you.

Your hand is the script of millions, of the dumb.
In you they live. Through you their blood returns.
Away with statues and remembrances!

Consider rather the bread of the spirit
imperishable wine. The changing shadow
of April is the soul, shy and yet public,
the private and the general at play.

14

Such joy that I have come home to
after all that measurement.

A redbreast cautiously stutters
towards the bread cast on the lawn,

the cherry tree
mistily in blossom:

the swallow teeters
tenuously on a twig:

the roses
unfurl themselves.

The vole
noses in the garden:

and at its pail
the calf nuzzles.

We are part of this world,
tremble on the same ladder,
our flesh is beguiled
to the same soil.

Those who have lived here long
walk among old stones
lightly: and the clouds
are not strangers.

See how at night the moon
anchors among branches.

The dog barks from winking lights.
The crofthouses
have their roots deep in the pasture,
the straws smell of this air.

Blackbird
with the bracelet of worms
in your beak,
weasel
with the squeak
of the rabbit.

There is no storm
scrawls more locally than here:
its slant lightning
and the tackety boots of the thunder
are known.

Under the stone
the worm is a slow train
unwinding its carriages.

The lark's beak flashes.
The lark spirals and sings.

15

Latterly the sea would cast them up,
all your tragic heroes, doomed princes.
In their blue tunics they would all rise

with belts of green seaweed about them.
Better than statues were these human hands,
the eyes surprised by the luck of nature.

The earth that echoed with its antique armour
gave way to the various language of the sea,
its furious onsets, sunny promises,

its bony headlands softened by spring flowers,
its billowing robes, its briny theatre,
betrayals forgiven, sunk among iron keels.

16

There is no island.
The sea unites us.
The salt is in our mouth.

I have heard the drowned sing
when the moonlight
casts a road across the waters,
fine and luminous,
and each house sways
in its autumn light.

'The moon that takes us home to Lewis.'
to the dancing
to the phantoms of evening
to the charmed wells.

The island, as our poet said,
is an iceberg.
We bear it with us,
our flawed jewel.

As the sun sets
over the mountains
I see the homeless ones
forever rowing.
Their peasant hats mushroom,
like foundering bouquets.

The wakes
are for everyone
and the large sun
glints on the excised names
of the exiles.

'No ebb tide ever came
without a full tide after it' –
precious ones
whose flesh is my own,

and who arise each day
to a new desert.

The island, my vase, knows you.
Your inscribed faces
burn out of the brine:
this is the sharp wine
that educates us.

As we change
so the island changes,
we are not estranged
by the salt billows.

'There is no ebb tide
without a full tide after it.'
The tall white bride
accepts the fresh waters.

THE VILLAGE AND OTHER POEMS
(1989)

The Village

1

My house of music,
I have left you behind
    for this garden
    blossoming in the country,
this sky
    plain and guiltless.
The busyness of feet,
    the drama of projects,
the distant city smile,
    all have been left behind
for this open ploughland.
    Here no shadows
slant from lamp-posts,
    the long black rays
of city clocks.
    And the beggar
does not doze
    under his newspaper:
and the chipmaker
    dressed like a stoker
    does not shovel chips
    out of his container.
Here, the bay
    is not a hive of yachts,
    wasp-striped, stingless:
and the wind-filled skirts
    do not breed tales.

My house of music,
    I shall not forget
    the debt I owe you,
    the flash of windows,
    the thresh of shadows,
the tree-lined avenues
    that never have an end.

2

Graves invent nothing
in a country cemetery,
    aged and mossy:
and the stone bibles
    shine with ancestry
under the flicker of birds.
The minister winds his robes
    decently about him
as he shakes hands
    with all the live people
who at Easter time
    wear their flowery hats
in unchiming envy.
    Overhead, the clouds
    head for distant countries
in their changing marble:
    and the wheel of crocuses
returns each year
    above the mouldering chests.

3

Gemeinschaft –
Katag at the bookstall
exchanging weather.
Everyone naming each other
in this calm air

through which the water
glides, reflecting trees:
the weasels however anonymous
and the hares
  at whose throats they suck.

Smoke
  rises from bonfires
of bracken. Ash
badges the rowan tree.

     4

While the birds sweetly twitter
  I visit the old lady
  who reads Ouspensky
  and whose blue radio
converses among the glitter
  of random sunlight.
'I am frightened,' she says.
  'of what I do not know.'
  Is it of Death
with his negligent scythe
  familiar as Hugh
  under a blue sky?
'I do not know,' she says.
  Just, 'I am frightened.'
  Her horned cows stare
  out of her meadow,
and the rabbits race through dew
  towards the weasel.

5

At night
    I put out the ashes,
       and stand amazed
    beneath the blaze
       of a million million stars.

6

The fox sings
    his songs of slyness,
and lopes easily
    by the hedge:
and the spare hawk anchors
    by a cloud.
    By rabbit-watch
I walk clothed among the naked.
    Not by lamplight
does the harsh buzzard read his book,
    nor change from black
    will the ragged crow
whose language does not frame the No
    of the soul's delicacy.

7

Each morning
I cross the railway line

towards the kiosk
to collect my newspaper.

Summer,
how lovely you are,
how leafy,
just like a newspaper
composed of coloured paper.

And also the rails hum
towards the future
in the midst of such news returning,

those reds and greens.

8

She walks,
mumbling to herself
    down this street,
big-bellied, round-faced.
She has found no one
    other than herself
    to talk to,
and her discussions
    are infinite.
Beyond her
the sea keeps its own music
    obsessive, self-absorbed,
    omnivorous.
Her lips move
    soundlessly,
    endlessly,
in that continuous gossip
    that never surprises.

9

She has filled
    her life's emptiness with furniture.
'That chair is too good to sit on,
    and the carpet
    cost me five hundred pounds.'
There is a vase
    of paper flowers on the television:
her suite
    is made of rich red velvet.

'Look at the view,' she says.
    The sea, the sea,
stretches emptily to the horizon.
Envy is too simple a judgment
    for one who sits in her kingdom
    like a queen
whose servants have left her.
    It is autumn.
    She sees us to the door.
    I remember
the coffee had no real taste
    and for her talk
it was so full of chairs
    I stumbled over it.
Where there is emptiness
it has to be filled somehow.
This autumn fills it with leaves,
    which storm about her legs.

10

The little red van
buzzes about the village.

Letters from England, Canada, New Zealand.

We communicate with each other
    because of a driver
    with a small black moustache.

Little red van
    at the edge of the ocean
dodging among the trees
    with no salt on it.

11

The nest
    with one green egg in it
is suspended among the trees.
    The thrush has deserted it.

It is a tiny earth among straw,
cold now, without the throb of life in it.
Who has touched it with his hands
    and left the smell of man on it?

For the bird flies away
    and will not return.
I imagine how its wings mourn
    an absent greenness.

12

I should have loved Paris
    when Picasso was there
    or Braque,
when they stuck morsels of news
    to their paintings:
    when the concierge
was a cube
    like a French mountain:
and in gaunt attics
    the easels
thirsted for the paint.
    Excitement,
    discovery,
    a new world,
quotations from Africa,
    triangular faces like deer.

But I have to live
    where the black bibles

are walls of granite,
where the heads are bowed
over eternal fire.

                              13

Last night
you attended a lecture on Vermeer
on the Island of Mull.

How clear
the mountains are,
and these rooms in which symmetry was humanised!

The deer
are elegant,
though the men have been prised
loose from their moorings.
In these pictures
such light, such light!
Remember the girl with the jar
pouring milk into the ewer,
her arms are so muscular!
Or at a table the soldier
talking to his sweetheart.
Dutch maps on the walls.
The echoing bibles and the sails, the sails!
Under the green hills,
the exiled bodies.
Open the windows!
Let the light flood through!
Space, such endless space,
so framed by joy.

14

The old lady is dying
among the roses,
    and at night
she hears the hoot of the owl,
the fluting of the blackbird,
the excited cry of the thrush.
    Doctor,
she knows well what is wrong,
she is adjusting her shoulders
to the stone cloak.
    She has put out the ashes
for the last time.
    And yet, who is dying
in this summer of stunning splendour
when the rhododendrons are ablaze
by the hedge,
    when the pansies
are bowed in thought,
    and the azaleas
are a constant fire?
    We are part of the earth,
its blackness nestles about us,
    and the rowan
is a constellation of blood drops.
    There is no sorrow
in the song of the blackbird,
    and the rabbit
runs easily towards its death.
    I have seen a cat
stiffly dead on the road,
    the crow pecking at it,
its eyes staring upwards
    in an illusion of agate:
and I have seen the children
    in their butterfly frocks.
    Summer, we love you,
there is no end to your manifestations,

to the freshness of your plots.
    The white curtain
in the bedroom of the old lady
freshens the window.
    A man is ploughing the land
with a red tractor.

15

Today
    as the trees sparkle
    in the sunshine,
I remember my university days,
    the historian
who lectured on the French Revolution
    with exact primness.

Robespierre died in Aberdeen,
    and so did Danton,
    a whole structure
    of chandeliers fell.

And also
    Lear died on the moorland,
his crown melting
    in reality and age.

The trees sparkling,
    these tales I remember,
    and the clear
cemeteries also I recall
    on whose slabs I lay revising
Virgil's *Aeneid*.

16

This morning,
the snow falling,
the children

are building a snowman.
How white it is.
How they toil

to shape it
behind the schoolhouse
with its chalky blackboards.

This blank squatness,
Buddha of silence,
beyond questions,

sitting in the world,
temporary art,
a structure of water.

17

I read of *Sevastopol*
   by Tolstoy
   in a train going to my village.

This Russian is my contemporary,
   though my sky
   is Gaelic.

I hear the guns
   in the holy silence
   of your prose
   which casts its shadows,
just as it was,
   bravery and cowardice.

All the aristocrats
whom I never knew
in peasant Lewis
dying like lilies
which are unable to bend.

18

Writing
is easier than experience.
        In Halifax
you suffered the tax
        of exile,
and in dosshouses
        you nailed your shoes
        to the wooden floor.
        There is no sorrow
worse than the sorrow
        of the exile,
for he wakens early
        with ash in his mouth,
and there are only shadows
        in the world around him.
Open your purse
        to the shadowy exile:
        as for my book,
        leave it.
For pages do not starve,
        do not die of
the thirst of salt.
They can easily be remade,
        though not so the sails
        that reflect new sunsets.

19

Bags over shoulders
      the kids make their way
to the country school.
      There is a smell of roses
      and an untaught sky.

Geography is here
      in the wandering perfumes
and the chalk-white roads:
      where the larks sing high
above the scrawled bushes
and the dewy rowans
wear their red dresses
in these parishes of green.

20

The raspberry tree
      arches the garden,
the crocuses
      are bent by the wind.

      The small birds beat the rats
      to the bread,
among all that red
      and yellow and white.

Sun, you are shining
      from your old socket,
as Peggy carries her bags
      of groceries home.

How calmly the dead
      lie in their worn ground,
      wrinkled like carbon
      above which the clouds call
      briefly, whitely.

21

Death strides freely across the countryside,
    swinging his stick.
Sometimes he stops at a cottage
    where an old woman
is fraying fresh water
    from a bucket.
Sometimes he watches a weasel
    sucking the throat of a hare
    beside a rowan tree.
Sometimes he watches a cat
    trotting with a lark
    through the shrubbery.
He takes out a cigarette and smokes it,
    a small cloud at his mouth
    and listens to a radio
    playing Greensleeves.
Sometimes he knocks on a door
    of a large house
    where a man with white hair
    is reading Everyman.
Death is a polite fellow
    who loves azaleas
    and the blur of bluebells.
'Without me they would not exist
    without my sickle and scythe
    without my empty circles.
And what would the shepherd be then
    singing of his sweetheart?
    And as for Greece or Rome,
    beyond the Dark Ages
they shine like jewels of fire.'

22

Days when the rain brims
    the teeming barrels,
and plain wet windows
    reflect no drama:
and the small birds peck
    at the soaked bread.

Days when the clouds loom
    over the chimneys,
and, like old women, the trees
    forget themselves

    in demented stories.

23

It is a fine morning,
the frost is sparkling.
It is said of you, Raphael,
that you learned
    from Michelangelo,
from the study of armies.
    So happy you were,
contented creator,
    whose Virgin and Child
calmly foresaw their fate.
    It is a fine morning,
the frost is sparkling,
    glittering diamonds.
    Let me open my hands,
to the visitations of clouds.
    Let me see Florence
in these mountains of pure white.

24

Hang out your washing
    like paintings
in the calm day.
    Raphael,
    Botticelli,
each beside the other
    in a gallery of blue.

Rag-darned goddesses,
    the sweat of the present
drying towards Venice
    and its fine cloudy towers.

25

Sundays, how awful they are.
    All day the grass does not change
    and the clouds that visit us
    drift off elsewhere.
    We try to think of
the beauties of religion but
    in fact we feel aggression,
    inward furies,
the torment of silence.
    Dear birds,
    flying from the south
can you bring us contentment?
    Can we hear in your tones
    the dry classical voices?
    Sundays,
when will the dead abandon us?
    When will the living
    no longer be a sacrifice
    to the gnaw in the bone?

The gates are open,
>   let the stranger enter
>   with dust on his feet
>   all the way from Galilee,
>   that serene profile.

26

At Easter we sit in church.
>   The organ pipes
are pointed like missiles.
>   The minister
assails all nuclear arms (pushing
>   a curl back from his brow).
What does he know of it, they think,
>   the crofters, the wives.
>   His passion
is, they would say, indecent
>   among these calm grey graves
where their forefathers lie
>   so placidly
having travelled their single rut
>   on a bony cart
towards the cemetery.
>   See,
the women's hats are like wheels,
>   blue, green, purple,
>   as the ball
sparkled high in the sky
above Japan,
>   that 'foreign'
unintelligible region.
>   His plan
is, for the good, heaven,
>   for the bad
an earth converted to ashes,
and the bushes
wearing their blossoms of grey.

27

The cat
    brings the rabbit
    home between his teeth.

It is a gift
    to the lank god
    who feeds him,
to the magic
    that renews his dish.
    The rabbit mews
    piteously
more winning than the mouse
    with its tail of string.

    Stunned, it lies
under the cat's negligent gaze.
    To rescue it
    is, now,
    out of the question.
    That fatal blow
    has brought it low
for this is a savage circuit
    on which the cat, lazily blinking,
    thornily turns.

28

These roots stretch
    deeply into the soil
almost unpullable.
    White and tough,
    how can they know death,
    aged lady,
    who too die
    very slowly
so that you have to be tugged

out of your chair
which is burning there
    in a priceless sunset.

                    29

Today,
    you send me a letter
    from Lewis,
    saying
how much my writings mean to you,
    the tragedy, the comedy,
    the child who remembers
    and the man who grieves.

Island,
    you are moving away from me,
    and yet
    there is a mirror
    with images in it,
the headlands
    which wail of exiles,
    the stiles
over which ghosts leap
    like angels,
the daffodils
    that will yellow the moors,
    my remorse
for not being word perfect.

                    30

    Altogether
you take twenty-two pills,
to keep you sound.
In your calm weather
you have little to do

                but, like water,
pass time in talk.
                Animals,
we are talking animals,
                gregarious.
Without gossip
                we fade and die.

And sometimes more than gossip
                there is Homer,
                the very high stair,
                towards azure,
the former monkey can climb.

                        31

                Our brains bulged
to differentiate us from the animals,
                and our eyes became bifocal.
                We could stand upright
and clutch the sharp stones.
                Fate
was on our side; to the local
we weren't tied, but could explore
by entering foreign doors.
                Tigers
we sank in pits,
                and we ate
                the marrow bones
of mammoths.
                O, the wind brought stories
to us, and in the fires too
                we saw the shadows of flesh,
and on the walls of caves
                we drew the first trembling strokes.
                Oaks
bowed to us.
                In the sunshine of April

we limped in rain. We prayed
to the clouds above.
      And then
galleries we made, draughty paintings.
      Food they became to us,
         poetry,
epics and tales on the breeze.

32

Clumps of bees built
      their fences of sharp stings
      to protect their honey;
and the ants too
      learnt their grades and classes
on a fine morning.
      Hermit, you are strange
in your soiled blanket,
singing to yourself
under a slum of cloud.

33

On a breezy morning
we visit the market.
The lady at the cosmetics stall
      is making up her face,
and another is trying on the opal
      of a new ring.
Clothes hang on rails
      above the dry people,
and the fiery curtains
      flutter bravely.

Pick up the toy horseman
who rocks backwards and forwards
      on his metal horse.

'How much in this world we don't have need of,'
    said bald Socrates,
strolling through the market
    on a Greek morning.

    I, on the contrary,
    love the sly
cries of the salesmen,
    who have to live, don't they,
    just like us
on this plenteous
    market most various
among white dishcloths and rings.

34

Tonight the moon's so close
I could almost pull it towards me.
And I hear the dancers' feet
on the hall's bare boards.

The moon of autumn,
unrustable and red,
in which the sailor sees
his mother's exiled face.

35

The village has its own sky,
    its own river,
its paths are unrepeatable
    among the tangle
    of bracken and fern.

It is visited by birds
    from the horizons of Africa,
    who return annually
    to build their own hammocks.

It has its own sun, its own moon,
    those unstable rings
    that remember it.
    Its cemetery is a treasury
of previous coffins and bones.
    On its gates stone lions
    snarl in silence,
    and its roses
    redden the air.
    Echoes everywhere,
    prints and resonances;
a single cloud
    is part of the narrative,
    of the story
    which bursts in fragrance
    from the dewless tips of bones.

36

The sun goes down
and is then reborn
    above paths, ruts:
under its rays
    the boys run
    towards their graves
    on bicycles:
    and girls too
    graduate to kitchens
    and the fierce breezes
of bedroom curtains.

All this has happened
    day after day,
    year after year,
    the sun a red
    ball that's returned
    every morning
    from over the wall.

37

From Italy
you come to our bare land,
from Venice
prodigious
with paintings.
Here the sky is clear,
lacks the fierce fire
of the Renaissance,
and the villages
sleep among sheep.

The drunks sing
'Flower of Scotland' to you
in echoing stations:
and the purple-crowned thistle
vibrates with thorns.
Tender Virgil,
dead in Mantua,
in the ice of perfection,
this is not your land,
you, exquisite saint
of the compassionate metre,
sleep elsewhere.
Our sun shines
(not burns)
beyond a grille of cloud,
and winter
is our typical season.
From Italy
you come to our sky.
It is like shifting
from a warm flat
to a lonely castle
hissing with ghosts.

38

The rainbow arcs
at the end of the water:
it is a frail bridge
prepared by God.

In this field I find it,
then in another,
its fine colours anchor
among the sharp corn.

How strange it is
that angels can walk
among the cornfields,
the tares, the poppies,
the frail hint of blood.

The rainbow reminds us
that heaven is present
among the maggots,
the brown carriages of worms.

39

Last night
I saw a snail
eating the cat's food.

Its mouth was busy
like a miniature snake,
its delicate horns
were tiny aerials
above the red plate.

Such a strange feeding,
this being from wet grasses
in the dry kitchen,

an alien entering
our warm kingdom,
with its black body
questioning our food.

40

In the garden
among the birds
my typewriter chatters,

It too has its own voice,
its astronomy of letters,
its interpretation of the world.

It too guards
its own territory
with ignorant metal.

Such happiness
among the green leaves
with its derived foliage.

41

Cathy walks past,
and I am writing:
she sees through the window
my infirm hand.

'The corn is doing well,'
she told me this morning.
'After all, I'll take
the bread for my hens.'

Such a marvellous light
that binds us together,
even I who grow
words on the page.

42

Cat, today you caught a bird,
I found its feathers in the lobby,
and that, I must admit, disturbs me.

That the song should be stopped,
that the wings should be stripped,
from the slim body.

I don't mind you impaling mice
on the sharp protruding vice
of your claws.

But that you should have chewed the lark.
That you should have sent to the dark
the quick linnet.

I consider you, rising humpbacked,
a witch of the beautiful fact,
a thorny shadow.

And a white hunter, along the trench,
of the orange-breasted bullfinch
bitter-toothed one.

Who will nuzzle my shoulder
affectionately later,
bird-murderer,

feather-scatterer in the porch.
O let not in March
my songs be silenced

by that prowling inquisitive doom
which will devise harm
in a ring without mercy.

43

You died
more a connoisseur of Latin
than of English.
    The rabbits played in front of your house
    but you did not notice them
    and as for the buzzard
    he was the unseen Caesar
    of your farm.

In togas they chatter among marble
    who were your obsession
    and the fountains of Rome
    jetted out of your garden.
    Virgil
    has written for your gravestone,
    and Ovid sings of exile
    in the depths of your library.
    It was a life of quotations
    that you lived,
    and an absence of mind
    your biography.
    It was only latterly
    that you really saw the sky,
    changeable:
    the wind of your century.
    As for the rest, footnotes,
    the relentless boredom of the classicist,
    the verb at the end of the sentence
    revealing at last your fate.

44

The fire sparks up the chimney.
It is a hedge of thorns,
bright, purified, and simple.
Without it the art galleries
would have foundered in the marsh.

With it, the logs ignite
Rubens and Vermeer.
Statues replace glaciers,
and books, water.
Ghosts are born in fire.
They run about the world
breeding.

45

In summer
the blur of warm mist
    over the water,
    and the tall girls in green
    riding horses
along the level road,
clip-clop by shop-front.
Such mornings
    opening like books
fresh and novel,
    such fresh black shadows
humming among the leaves.

46

The dog runs away
with the hen in his mouth.
Catch him!

He must not be allowed such traffic.
What bundle of feathers will be safe from him?
He will snatch the cockerel from the dawn.

Solid and meaty have been some of our poets,
our theologians, philosophers.
They can feel in their teeth
the theme of a new world.

Eat them thoroughly,
the bouquets of new stars.
Leave the bones, Copernicus,
to the starving Jesuits.

47

The cat mews at the window
trying to get in.
It rears on its hind legs, like a stoat.

Beggar of the wind,
this is your house,
your fire is here.

It has the red sparks
of furious claws.

There were ghosts on my island
that chewed at the pane.
They were the many exiles
with their teeth of ice.

Why therefore should you not enter
with your eerie white fur,
having prospected all morning
for the absent mice?

48

Art, how marvellous you are.
You bring us a birth,
a second birth in reflection,
and these reflections
seem more real than the real,
O wine red sky,
I burn in your vase.

O grave book,
I travel your winding road.

49

Art,
   it is in the city
that you flourished,
were cherished
against the thirst of grass.
Redder than skies
   your reds,
and your greens
greener than mountains.

Your windows opened
on to a banded rainbow
that absolutely sang:
and nature does not know
your perfect circles.
   Breughel,
you brought your proverbs
   home in the evening;
Chagall, your bride and bridegroom
   waft through the air.

50

Put out your paintings:
someone will notice them,
even in the passing,
in the wind of everyday.

Nothing Will Happen

Nothing will happen surely in this village
except adultery, sickness, harmless lies.

Listen, I watch the suns in their redness,
winding imperially around our stone,

and the absent-minded minister taking a walk
through these green clouds of his philosophy.

Nothing will happen surely… What's that?
Our crayon books are torn by strange shell fire.
A voice is shouting. There is nowhere safe.

And a dog digs for its bones under the holly.

The deer look down with their clear questioning eyes.

Not in Heaven

No, it is not in heaven that we find the dry
fine winds of fact,

but in the stones of March, Holy One,
in the knots of their essence.

Galilee, wind-dark sea, miracles,
there is no miracle greater

than the literature of April,
the manuscript of crocuses.

Shine, Holy One, from your narrow yellow niche
which has no clouds.

And let me have the ambiguous dapple of April,
the sigh of a forked breeze.

Helensburgh

I return to Helensburgh
where I used to see the green girls on horses
clip-clopping down the street.

Towards the Glasgow day trippers
with their breathless dogs and children
the tide rose slowly like silver.

At the fair,
the dodgems, painted with dragons,
turned in the salty air.

The retired pensioners
discussed their vague lives
through shrunken jaws and teeth.

In the spectacular evenings
the late sun touched
the Old Folks' Home with gold.

This is the town
of the mobile executives
to whom the Fair was a vulgar glare,

on a safe horizon
where nothing threatens
their gardens sheltered by walls.

And the old ladies with sticks
tottered up the brae
to the library to exchange romances.

And the Clyde lapped the shore
like an excitable dog
grey and masterless,

while the discontented young
toppled the benches
in the direction of the infinite sea.

The Drowned

It is true that the drowned return to us.
In the blue eyes of children we see them,
in a slight eccentricity of gait.

They spring actively out of the water, seeming
smaller than they were, bearing
large smiles, corn-coloured crowns.

Where the rocks are and the crabs manipulate
their bodies like toy tanks
in waters green and teeming like soup

they arise, clear-winged, articulating
sons and grandsons of themselves, stumpy
authentic chimes,

echoes, reflections, shadowy
waves that speak through the new waves,
underwritings, palimpsests,

a ghost literature behind another one,
carbons that have faint imprints on them,
blue veils of a fresh breeze.

Villagers

So many of those that I once knew
drowned in the Atlantic or the Pacific,
that unignorable and unknown blue.

Fishermen and part-time footballers,
inadequate scholars, starers at dusty maps,
now forever locked in the sea's purse

with a miserly snap, while the guns tolled
over these restless acres, not to be ploughed,
at sunset fading into a foreign gold.

These guns which defended an empire
which wasn't, isn't, yours, who have drowned
ignorantly in sharp salt and fire,

who were once big figures in the twilight
where the river gently ran and chimneys bloomed
with a smoke sometimes grey and sometimes violet,

bone of my bone, my villagers. You have met
with the foreign-spoken stranger who has pulled
you inwards to his boat, his teeming net,

a random catch, I think not predestined,
gaping, slack-jawed, stubbly. Yet I sing
you breathless in the meshes long enchained.

Photograph of Emigrants

Your faces cheerful though impoverished,
you stand at the rail, tall-collared and flat-capped.
You are leaving Lewis (Stornoway) behind.
Before you the appalling woods will rise
after the sea's sharp salt, your axes hack
the towering trunks. What are you leaving now? –
The calm routine of winding chimney smoke,
the settled village with its small sparse fields,
the ceilidhs and the narratives. Deceived
by chiefs and lairds, by golden promises,
you set off, smiling towards a new world,
Canada with its Douglas firs and snow,
its miles of desolate emptiness.

Why do I weep
to see these faces, thin and obsolete,
these Sunday ties and collars, by the rail,
as the ship moves, and you move with it,
towards your flagrant destinies of sharp
bony starvation, ruinous alcohol.

All shall be revealed but at this time
your faces blaze with earnestness, and joy,
as if you were coming home instead of leaving.
Nothing will save some, standing by the rail,
others will come home in tartan caps,
a fury of possessions, and a love
of what's disappeared forever when they left,
themselves not being able to be there and here,
and therefore growing differently towards pictures
which frame them where they stand, thus staring out
into the inscrutable waters of their fates.

Incubator

The tiny baby sleeps in a cage of wires.
Lights blink on and off:

its legs are thin as matches, and its hair
a fuzz of limpid gold.

Sometimes it arches its tiny body,
stretches itself and yawns,

delicate as an egg in that machinery
which sings its own quiet tune.

Machine, you are my mother now, you feed
with the slow drip of time.

It is warm here, sleepless mother,
raise me to run one day

with my leather schoolbag among blossoms
on a day of lessons and fire.

Wakeful machinery, be good to me,
hear me if I don't breathe,

and ring your alarm bell, the panic
of your kind breast of steel.

Machine, let us sleep together,
on the bosom of the night,

till I grow tall, till I leave you
and seek soft human arms.

The Story

This is the story that I've always loved.
A little girl is running towards a bridge.
She leaves her tiny footprints in the snow,
and then suddenly becomes invisible.

Like the reader who leaves off reading the page,
Like the dying who have still some way to go.
There are first the footprints, then the unfathomable.
The Muse hasn't finished the good poem.

Perhaps it isn't good enough; perhaps
another poem takes over, yet another
better and more invisible song will come
out of the snow with a flaring of red banners.

Perhaps one day the ending will come back.
Now we aren't finished, but some day
after fresh experience we will find it,
having first tumbled from the bridge,

which is a rainbow from white heaven to here.
The little girl is ageing somewhere else.
She has run through a mirror to a new country.
Drenched and flecked with snow, she has changed.

What is the future? Suddenly it breaks off.
This is a part of freedom, isn't it?
Years later she appears, no more a child,
but adult, unperplexed, her own mother.

Rainbow I love you, you are composed of light,
primary colours, hiatuses, a bridge.
Athlete and artist, you have perfectly curved
into the rich ignorance of the future.

At the Party

At the party everyone is talking.
Suddenly silence falls and you are alone
among the plates, the wine-glasses, the cups.
And there is no one to talk to but a limping man
who comes in late smoking a cigarette.
His face is gaunt and his frosty hair is wet.
And he coughs repeatedly and he says,
'This is my fifth party tonight.
I am rather tired and my appetite
is not as good as it used to be.'

And there he is, graduate of frost and snow,
coughing repeatedly and saying No.

After the Edinburgh Festival

The Festival is over,
the Chinese acrobats have gone home
tumbling over piles of chairs across Europe,
dangling from the autumn skies.

Hamlet, wrapped in his black cloak, is brooding
among the colourful courts of the clouds,
hearing behind the curtains of leaves
a mortal song.

The Finnish poet has stopped reading
and is back among the pines
which stand like masts beside the lakes
in the country of the strange tongue.

The paintings hang in a gallery of the wind
showing harbours, people,
squares of an autumnal colour,
on which the night is falling.

The black troupe has returned to South Africa
and the sour smell of prisons,
their passes held humbly in their hands
in the debris of desolate camps.

Autumn remembers art
and the pipers who played at the castle
in a swish of sculpture
among the historical deaths.

Listen, is that the dry cold music of Stravinsky
bony, intellectual,
and the king in his suit of plague
bleeding volubly from the eyes.

Clowns, acrobats, actors,
you are our marvellous doubles
you keep the autumnal ice away
from the pools of evening.

You sing so high that the ice will break,
you put the dazzling crown from you,
your power is different,
yours is the glitter of cloaks,

the tinsel that illuminates the meagre,
the masks that face both ways,
the Januaries of ambiguity,
the consolation of defects.

And the acrobats on the edge of disaster
are saved by strong wrists,
and the lady who was sawn in half
jumps to her feet.

Resurrections, deaths, resurrections,
who is that black blind visitor
who sits patiently by the fire,
mortal ventriloquist,

whose tenement is falling apart,
while the stuttering landlord
is hopelessly free of his speech
in a room that is bordered with leaves?

Stupidly

Stupidly we stared down at our own hands
in the country of stupidity on a day
of autumn mist which wreathed about the trees.

We were the Bottoms with our asses' heads
among the miniature wristwatches which ran
smoothly, impeccably, among the leaves.

We missed the small bright eyes that ruined us,
the purposeful, ambitious, colourful wings,
the fans of sunny morning in their zeal,

remembering only tales of a sweet justice,
the doors of mercy, wide poetic doors,
where tiny weasels pulsed at the throats of hares.

In this Pitiless Age

Somewhere in this pitiless age
I see the head of Dante leaning out of
the city of unemployed stars,

just, vigorous, condemning,
assigning to his three-line bars of flame
the loitering phantoms.

The thrifty system! Your justice killed the worst,
and not that Beatrice in a scent of rose
whom your soul rose towards so immortally.

Beyond it all the fragile climbing stairs
and that tremendous sentence luminous,
'The Love that moves the sun and the other stars.'

Slowly

Slowly we are adopted by the words… slowly we are other,
We are the aesthetic critics, not the ethical.
The play is a playful event.

Even agony becomes beautiful.
Even the broken heads are questionable.
Even the dictator's talent is in doubt.

No sounds from the street reach this theatre.
The torturer is a genius, or he is not.
The drapery on the coffin a lovely red.

The actor walks out on to a cold street.
Someone arrests him… someone tortures him.
His scream is no longer an actor's scream,

and yet the one from the theatre sounds like it.
The two screams meet where no one has a name.
They meet where all the walls have fallen down.

Meeting

I'm sure you don't know me, she said,
putting out her arms to me. On a wet day
in Lewis this was, among the dead.

Surely I know you, and she smiled.
You're Jessie, I said, and you stayed
in my village when I was a child.

So glad she was I remembered her, though dead,
her hair combed with salt, her hands
remembering the clothes' pegs she would fit

to the line once with her gallery of frocks.
Woolworths where we stood shone red.
I grew tired, she said, of the white clocks,

but you, you're different. And her mouth spread
like a seagull's in the wet and briny day.
I emigrated to the sea from dry land,

the waves attracted me with their energy.
But this is spring, isn't it, she said,
if you remember that clear cloudless sky

with no clothes in it. Yes, don't shed
tears, I answered. There is memory.
And took her fading hands. We are wed

to springs, autumns, visible and solid.
And watched her fade and fade past Woolworths' red
imitation jewels, like a seaward bird.

Marx

The ghostly superstructure reared up in front of you
from the time that the expropriated peasant
was turned into money.

From the time that the city became freedom's grave
and the usurer fattened on the farm
and the mortgaged fences.

All this grew more defined until one night
the structure of death reared up in front of you
disinheriting you:

the inevitable and determined one
who set out in the most beautiful urban evening
with a sickle in his hand.

The Women

See, the clouds are strolling along towards the sunset
in no hurry, almost unemployed,
except for the times when they are heavy with rain.
Sometimes they look down on the land
and admire the hills and the plain
before they are pregnant with rain.
Handbags, wristwatches, sheer stockings, it was another country.
The milk makes us heavy. Now no lightning strikes
and there is the thunder of bottles on the stairs.
Give me my purse.
I shall set out
on a summer day. I'll spend the money I've not got.

In Belfast

The years' lessons are written on the walls –
No Surrender – Ulster Says No.
I see in the sky a Presbyterian rainbow,

orange and unforgiving, woven of fire.
To tear apart what oneself owns!
The nun strides through the city like a whore.

The present seethes about the Holy Book.
And drums tap on the coffins of the slain.
The tanks will ride tall through Genesis: masked men stalk.

O Rose of Sharon, modest and demure,
when among broken stones will you bloom once more
into an ordinarily guilty future,

Among the waste of broken iron, doors.
And men rather than angels greet across fences
the scoured tired eyes of pity and remorse.

Girl and Child

Trudging through the air of Homer for a sight of the bruised girl
                                        with the child
who stops at kiosks to wait for a telephone to ring
with his voice out of the clouds that have grown suddenly callous,
and a ring which she has not yet sold winking on her finger,
and the child's blue eyes staring out of its temporary nest,
I found only the scene where Andromache holds her child up to
                                        Hector
and with small fingers it touches the big shadowy helmet
before his death in a whirl of vulnerable dust.
And the battle is different and for the girl there is no Homer
and there is no memorial among the slums and lights of the city
as she stares into the windows at the bridal dresses and the furs
and slowly licks her lips as if she was tasting the last of her milk.

Speeding-up

Even the pace of the leaves seems to have accelerated,
even the children grow up more quickly:

even our dreams turn into nightmares
and the statues are stalking away,

even the nights seem to have become one night
and the poems one poem:

and in all the airports of the world
the terrorists are reading the same books.

TV

This is your rectangle of narratives.
This is the voice that saves you from silence.

This is your scroll of perpetual images.
Listen, is there time for the poem to grow
in this incessant noise?

Is there time for that which is secret
to blossom?

Privacy must be paid for.

The blessed room, the refuge, the well, must be paid for.

When the comedians fade like ghosts grimacing in water
when the clowns remove their eyes,

the silence must be paid for, like water,
and the cell be precious

with silence, with fragrance, with the stone of privacy.

For the din is dreadful, the confusion of narratives is merciless,
the screen is vicious, it is a stadium of assassinations.

We need the bubbles of our own secret recesses,
the scent of clear water.

The narratives overwhelm us, they have no meaning, they have no
                                       connection with each other
We need the sacred light of the imagination.

We need the sacred cell and the pen that lies on the table.
We need the paper, that cool rectangle of white.

For one is heaven and sometimes the other is hell,
the world of frustrated murderers, the advertisements, the elegies

without echo,
the questioners bending down to the bandaged ones,
the smiling humourless clowns.

The narratives overwhelm us, we need the white paper, unclouded,
we need in that furious hubbub a space for our names,
the sanity of prudent distance.

Christmas

This is the time when the egos struggle for air,
when the television screen is a mishmash of narratives.
The children gather round the tree in simple greed,
and a horror film reproduces the agony of the Christ.
Love and goodwill are hard, there are so many contradictions
in the behaviour of those who are trying to be saints,
and then there are the others, bizarre in their avarice.
The too-often-sung carols lose their witchery,
even when the snow beautifully frames the windows,
and the hills are voluptuous with its whiteness.
Listen, what happened to that poor inexpensive manger
when so many are travelling towards it in newly-bought ski-suits
and furry collars which sparkle in the starlight.
This is the time for the family to assemble
and as on a treasure hunt dig up skeletons
and quarrel about hatred which illumined their childhoods.
Where is there perfection? Even the child will be corrupted
by those who say, Why wasn't he given the proper family name?

The cameras burn holes in the fragilely human,
and lust and greed are perpetuated on the sideboard.
Who did not send us a Christmas card this year?
We shall have our revenge on them. And who sent
a cheaper card than the dear one we sent them?
See how on the father patiently slicing the turkey
the son's eyes are fixed. Soon I will be your master.
I already feel the power refreshing my arm.

You neglected me often, he shouts to his exhausted mother,
I wasn't ever your darling, your jewel was really my sister.
Plain light but not love shines on the table.
Better to be alone with a cold compress on the head
lying on a bed and staring out at the stars
which are limitless, spendthrift, unused to pain or to ennui.
The riders of the past are coming with their treacherous parcels.
There are more than three of them and none of them wears a crown.
The whole white world is rented by the ambitious
and the noise of the television overwhelms literature.

Privacy may be metred like electricity or gas.
Dear night, someone is composing a carol
in Germany perhaps, in the heart of the Middle Ages,
far from the tables loaded with pheasant and wine,
and in the world of the mind, protected from all this racket –
the rotating narratives of films – the angels are flying
in the absolute country of the imagination, sustained
by the most terrible effort, trembling
in the middle of the night when no cries of the animals are to be heard.

The Country of Pain

In the country of pain there is the whimper of degradation,
and the man on the tall horse looks down on the defeated.

And the sir who has no imagination cannot suffer sorrow
since the land around him is a dazzle of mirrors.

He who sharpens his knife at the breakfast table and does not hear
                                               the cry
of the deprived and insulted dies the death of eternity,

and he who sings in the bathroom while the child drowns
will choke on the suffocating garbage of his own soul.

Listen, can you not hear it, the hum of Pain is everywhere
it whines over the tilled fields like the wires of telegraph poles,

and he who cannot see the dead for the flutter of silken flags
lies in a coffin of his own devising.

The soaked hats in the fields are like mushrooms,
and the careless whips return on the lightnings of time

to lie like snakes at the foot of the luxurious bed.
Stronger than poison is the venom of selfishness.

How shall the seasons forgive you and the songs of nightingales
and the glamour and splendour of roses, the humility of lilies –

how shall you correctly hear the notes of music
or scan with consonance the harmony of poems –

for all must be atoned for, the debts will some time be paid
and history will commemorate the coins that yourself have made.

Poor Artist

You who live on the dole and haunt the Oxfam shops,
how do you survive?

In the galleries there are paintings by Vermeer,
there are portraits of the opulent.

But how shall angel feathers spring from worn shoes,
and how shall the Madonna smile at you?

You have no room for a studio,
you must starve for your fresh paints.

And the landscapes look back at you without mercy,
and the still-lives have no serenity.

Let you paint the wine bottles of others,
the sweet apples on their plates,

Let you paint space without boundaries,
the sombre faces of the great.

How should art rise from the pavements,
sparse, moneyless, dizzy.

How should you not be troubled by the smile of the Mona Lisa
by her expensive raiment?

The mystery is in the stones,
the mystery is in the ungovernable,

the desire for permanence.

So that clutching your paints you descend
to the Hades of the chaotic,

and in your mind a table without knives on it,
a table of perfect colour,

and on your feet the worn shoes you must paint,
the remedy of the actual.

Against Apartheid   1

Those who beat the children
will die in the enchanted forest.

They will forever hear the whisper
of the leaves that will not fade.

Those who prepare the false mirrors
and the brews of poison

will turn into icicles,
in the caves of unknowing.

As they make rainbows from crayons
under the eyes of the stepmothers,

the children will be painting a history
that shows the tyrant as black,

obese, unhistorical shadows.
In the gardens of remembrance

the fountains will be sweet and merciful
only to the innocent and the wise.

Against Apartheid 2

For you who have died in the silence of prisons, what prayers are
                                                                enough?
For you who have been beaten to death,

who will never see the blossoms of your pain, the fruit of your
                                                        broken bones,
the open and scented windows…

You are the alarm clocks that have been hammered by tyranny,
you are the complex wristwatches that rough hands cannot bear,
you are the imaginative ones.

I see you in the concentrated lights, blinking, exhausted,
I see you staring into the ardours of the future.

You have been accused of arching your bodies through windows
                                        like rainbows,
you have been accused of loving death.

Who loved life too much, its perfumes, its radiances,
who hated the cruelty of boots.

Who stared into eyes that have communed with stones
and for whom the human body is plasticine,

a pliable instrument from which all the music has been squeezed,
a careless melodeon.

You who have died in darkness may the future brighten,
for you who have died in silence may there be applause.

I say that your coffins will blossom with roses
when the earth will have devoured your enemies,

and that your bloodstained scripts will outlive their graffiti,
and that your triumph will be heard in the cells of violence,

and that your meagre calendar will be the beginnings of seasons
which will glow brilliantly in your broken spectacles.

Snow

Snow brings the soul to our land.
It brings the whiteness of eternity, it brings
a book with no print.

Snow, you are so lovely, you frame houses,
you lie in little white hills on the roofs,
you are the genial dictator of the night.

Slowly, gently, you transform the world
as from evil into good,
as from graffiti into origins.

The slums have disappeared, the rivers are silent,
the farms on the moors have become magical houses,
at which we call with white maps on our coats.

Only the spires out-soar the snow,
only the planes which travel sparkling,
only the sun which glows like a forge.

See, she plunges her hands into snow
who belongs to Africa,
whose poverty has not been hidden by it;
she drinks of its coolness.

And the children too enter this new country.
They build snowmen,
they put pipes in their mouths,
red buttons for noses.

Who does not love you, snow?
Magician of the night,
radical reformer,
instant utopianist.
Let us imagine you are eternal,
marvellous painter and sculptor,
let us sing your praises,
forgetting you are common water.

Cat and Mouse

The mouse's purple guts lie in a corner.
There was a battle of the innocent.
The cat threw giant shadows over the leaves.

To meet death with such immediacy
In a smell of roses and of buttercups.
To feel the teeth deep inside your throat,

and, shocked by such a death, be paralysed
in a forest of tall grasses without music,
in a stadium of hot justice and of dew,

and a final meeting so unfortunate,
and somewhere the moon turning over and over
like a coin thrown carelessly by a distant hand.

The Leaves and Us

Running through the leaves we are not leaves.
Living among roses we are not roses.
We are the forked indecisiveness of history.

There are a million roads which we can take.
On each of them there are leaves and roses,
not the same roses but not so different,

as we are, the clever double ones,
in the scents which are pungent everywhere,
in the snow and ice which are everywhere the same.

Yet our summers are not theirs, nor our winters.
They do not see the role we give them
as part of our legends, of our history:

a certain leafy moon, a certain leafy night.
A story's made of transient foliage,
and forever afterwards we thirst for it.

In the Garden

I am bitten by the thorns of the roses.
They hang about my jacket in a fierce
clutch of claws, invisible and catlike.
My knuckles are a red astronomy
Such stars, such stars, such a new galaxy!
Prudence, my friend, does the rose mean so much,
and is perfection worth the sour thorns?
Somewhere I can hear a dog barking
at the invisible cat high in the rosetree.

Rose

Your exclusive shine, rose,
your colour that transcends relevance.

Blood of the inmost heart, triumph,
that which is transposed as it is:

in precise shape, fragrance. Nothing
is as exact as this:

the inmost torture astonished
into statement without history,

but itself, itself, itself,
rising from prison entire.

Autumn Stubble

The corn has been cut:
the stubble remains.
It is sharp and intense
in spite of the fences.
It will cut bare feet
not like the various
happy hilarious
seethe of the waving summer.
It has the crucial
bite of bright teeth,
this exciting satire.
Its rich dryness
invites us delightedly
as the swaying gossip of stalks.

The Cat

You were eighty-five when the cat appeared
one night at your door. It was perfectly white.
You wouldn't let it enter the house but you fed it
on scraps of fish which you placed on a blue plate.
It reared at your bedroom window like a stoat
mewing to get in: but you refused.
Sometimes you would threaten it with your fist.
What a strange white bony animal it was!
It would stare at you intently from the grass
and you would think: This thin beast troubles me.
My bones too are shaken as if he
were a sinister part of me, that had gone
hunting inquisitively about the stones.
The night before you died, it stared fiercely
in through the window, a tall vertical eel.
Its concentration was unshakeable.
And your bones melted and you lay at last,
a plate beside you, while your stubbly beard
had a fishy tang, wild, perilous, abhorred.

Early Spring

The primroses are out already
at the beginning of January.

And I have heard the birds sing.

Like Chaucer,
like the beginning of an idea,
like the hinge of a horizon.

Like happiness.
Like hearing the click of your heels
on the road outside my house.

And then as you climbed the stairs
your dress of yellow.

The Black Chest

When I opened the black chest there it was —
the pure diamond of the sweet alas
shining quietly like a teardrop.

In the distance I could hear
the fall of great houses, and the fire
of wills clashing in a new idea.

And also I could hear the scurry
of mice around the big tree
whence the cat glared down with green eyes.

Nevertheless there was a fragrance
from the black box: and a consonance
breathing from the lucky perfume,

though the gaunt face of the actor glowered
and among the waste moors shook the white beard
of the mad king, unfriended and defunct,

and though from the black box she rose
with white wings, throwing away her purse
of contradictions, and her candid verse.

The Traveller

The gates are open for you, stranger,
come in with your packet of narratives.

The wind has refined you
on your long journey.

What have you not seen? My imagination
cannot invent your stories.

For there is nothing more imaginative than life,
or more fortuitous.

And its epics have more fluctuations
than there are in Homer.

It was in another country entirely
that you recognised your fellow villager,

it was in a bar in Auckland
that you met your brother.

It was under the stars of Australia
that your mother drifted towards you

in a nightgown of dew,
in a bridal web of remembrance.

Life has mysterious corners
that the imagination doesn't know of,

and someone will enter at the denouement,
who wasn't in the dramatis personae,

and so it is that you may unpack your stories,
stranger, messenger of the wind,

and remove from it clouds,
waterfalls with well known portraits,

while the imagination will sit in a corner
listening like a pupil

to your stories of transformations,
the authentic detail of life.

Farewell my Brother

'Farewell my brother.'
The seas separate us,
a history of salt.

It is as if I had dreamed
that on an island ringed by waves
we once walked

when the buttercups blew in the wind
around the ruins of houses
in a blank sea-gaze.

The Bible was a hard wall
which we climbed over
to touch the consolations of the heart.

Eternal voyaging!
Among the civil wars of Africa
you spent the best of your days.

You will lie in a different earth
far from Lewis
unlearned in your history,
with its own legends.

In the early morning
I heard a raven
squawking above my ground,
a rancorous wanderer
in his bad-tempered province.

Forgive us our misunderstandings.
'Life is not like strolling,
carelessly through a field.'

It is not sunset
over a stubble
colouring the sharpness,
a perfection of swords.

The earth shakes
often when we are surest
of the prosperity of our fortune.

Even when the moon
is round as a coin,
our achieved gamble.

Even as I wrote
you were absently sleeping
like an alien on this earth.

My distant brother
with your own casket
of joys and tribulations.

Barer than the mind
is the soil of Lewis.
It is in the keeping of the wind.
It has the sea's resonance,

that constant music
that enchanted cottage
which enhanced our residence,

our hunger for the unknown.
If we could speak again
would we know better?

I offer this bouquet
from the oceans of salt,
my distant brother.

I send it across the seas
to the spaciousness of Canada,
my flowering poem,

to let its fragrance
be sweet in your nostrils,
though you are now unable
to converse with me.

My distant brother,
in the shelter of my poem
let you be secret

till we are children again
in the one bed
in the changing weather
of an inquisitive childhood.

The roads separate:
see, I wave to you,
you turn away completely
into your own cloud.

See, I wave to you
you are disappearing forever.
Tears disarm me.

Now you stand like a statue
in the honour of goodness.

My pride and my tears burn me.

Farewell, my brother.

Listen

Listen, I have flown through darkness towards joy,
I have put the mossy stones away from me,
and the thorns, the thistles, the brambles.
I have swum upward like a fish

through the black wet earth, the ancient roots
which insanely fight with each other
in a grave which creates a treasure house
of light upward-springing leaves.

Such joy, such joy! Such airy drama
the clouds compose in the heavens,
such interchange of comedies,
disguises, rhymes, denouements.

I had not believed that the stony heads
would change to actors and actresses,
and that the grooved armour of statues
would rise and walk away

into a resurrection of villages,
townspeople, citizens, dead exiles,
who sing with the salt in their mouths,
winged nightingales of brine.

from THE BIRLINN
(uncollected, 1977)

Translated from the Gaelic of Alexander Macdonald
(eighteenth century)

The Storm

Sun unhusking to gold-yellow
    from its shell,
the sky growing seared and lurid,
    amber bell.

Thick and gloomy and dun-bellied,
    surly curtain,
vibrating with every colour
    in a tartan.

Rainbow in the west appearing
    tempest-born,
speeding clouds by growing breezes
    chewed and torn.

So they raised the speckled sails
    wind-tight, towering.
They stretched the stiff ropes against
    her sudden flowering,
timbers of the resin red
    tapering proudly.

They were knotted with fierce vigour,
    neatly, firmly,
through the eyes of iron hooks
    and round the ring bolts.

Every rope of their equipment
    was adjusted.
Coolly each took his position
    as accustomed.

Windows of the heavens opened
    blue-grey, spotted,
with the banging of the tempest
    fierce and haughty.

The sea gathered round about it
    a black cloak,
a rough, ruffled, swarthy mantle
    of ill look.

It swelled to mountains and to valleys
    shaggy-billowed,
the matted lumpy waters rearing
    up to hillocks.

The blue waves were mouthing chasms,
    horned and brutish,
fighting each other in a pouring
    deathly tumult.

It needed courage to be facing
    such tall towerings,
phosphorescent flashes sparking
    from each mountain.

Grey-headed wave-leaders towering
    with sour roarings,
their followers with smoking trumpets
    blaring, pouring.

When the ship was poised on wave crest
    in proud fashion
it was needful to strike sail
    with quick precision.

When the valleys nearly swallowed us
    by suction
we fed her cloth to take her up to
    resurrection.

The wide-skirted curving waters,
    bellowing, lowing,
before they even had approached you,
    you'd hear roaring,

sweeping before them the small billows,
    onward sheering.
There'd be a massive deathly water
    hard for steering.

When she would plunge from towering summits
    down pell-mell
almost the ship's heel would be bruised
    by the sea-floor's shells,

the ocean churning, mixing, stirring
    its abyss,
seals and huge sea creatures howling
    in distress.

Impetuous tumult of the waters,
    the ship's going,
sparking their white brains about –
    an eerie snowing!

And they howling in their horror
    with sad features
pleading by us to be rescued,
    'Save your creatures.'

Every small fish in the ocean
    belly-white
by the rocking violent motion
    killed outright.

Stones and shell fish of the bottom
    on the surface
mown by the relentless threshing
    of the current.

The whole ocean in a porridge
    foul and muddied,
with filth and gore of the sea-monsters
    red and bloodied,

the horned splay-footed vast sea-creatures
    clawed, misshapen,
their many heads in ghastly screaming,
    mouths jammed open,

the deeps teeming with hobgoblins,
    ghostly pawing,
monstrous crawling, phantom seething,
    vague out-clawing.

Loathsome their abhorrent groaning
    and their raving:
they'd have driven fifty soldiers
    wholly crazy.

The crew entirely lost their hearing
    in the maelstrom,
the screaming discord of the demons,
    beastly wailing.

Crashing of water and its smashing
    smiting planking,
the prow's rushing as it dashed
    the ghastly monsters.

Breezes freshening from windward
    from the west,
torment everywhere from ocean
    and from beast.

Blinded by the pouring spindrift
    sky unbrightening,
incredible thunder during nighttime
    flash of lightning.

Fire balls burning up our tackle
    and our gear
acrid smell and smoke of brimstone
    everywhere.

The elements above below us
    seeking slaughter,
water, earth and fire and air,
    a hostile quartet.

But when the ocean could not beat us
    make us yield
she became a smiling meadow,
    summer field.

Though there was no bolt unbending,
    sail intact,
yard unwrenched or ring unweakened,
    oar uncracked.

There was no stay that had not sprung
    or gear undamaged
no shroud or halyard without ripping.
    Snapping, cracking!

Each bench and gunwale all gave witness
    to the storm.
Every timber, every fitting
    suffered harm.

There was no angle-piece or rib
    which wasn't loosened.
The wale and stern sheets all were damaged,
    smashed, unfastened.

from THE BIRLINN (uncollected, 1977)   391

There was no rudder without splitting,
    helm unwounded,
sob and groan from every timber
    sea had pounded.

There was no tree-nail left unpulled,
    or board in use,
every single well-clinched washer
    had been loosed.

There was no nail that was untwisted,
there was no rivet without bending,
there was no part that still existed
that wasn't worse at the storm's ending.

The tranquil sea benignly saw us
    in Islay Sound,
the bitter-voiced breezes were appeased
    by God's command.

They left us for the upper regions
    of the heavens
and made for us a noiseless even
    level plain.

We gave thanks to the great Father
    and Creator
that Clanranald came unharmed
    from brutal water.

But we furled then our thin sails
    of linen woven
and we lowered her red masts
    across her floor boards.

We put out melodious oar blades
    finely tinted
of red pine that had been cut
    on Isle of Finnan.

We rowed with smooth and springy motion
        not neglectful
entering harbour at the heights
        of Carrickfergus.

We anchored easily and calmly
        in that roadstead
and we ate and drank, unstinted,
        and abode there.

ROMAN POEMS
(uncollected, 1979)

The Invasion

'When will the Gauls invade us?'
I hear the city whine.
'They're bayonetting children
along the Apennine.'
Time for the newscasters, I would say,
to scribble their memoirs
and recall our ageing generals
to fight in earlier wars.

Our gardens in uneasy calm
wait for the boots to stride
over élitist blossoms
to the works of art inside
hung by illiterate millionaires
as safer than our coin,
insurance from the crippled men
who died of cheap red wine.

No statement anyone can make
but breeds its opposite now.
The gods have left us howling.
The fabled Golden Bough
shines on young killers in the wood
tracking the infirm king
who's brought to bay by end of day
and dies within their ring.

Before the riders ever towered
above the gates of Rome
our nerves had snapped like bowstrings
we'd fashioned our own doom
in poems, paintings, politics.
The Left struck at the heart,
and joined with Rightist ignorance
in their contempt for art.

No longer shall our buildings stand.
Without, within, we quake,
we went to sleep in careless dreams,
in nightmares we awake,
and when the shadowy conquerors
guzzle at thinning shelves
we recognise them from our sleep
as portraits of ourselves,

the violent Ids that we have seen
from pillows calm and white
projected on demonic screens
in the long boring night
arising to devour us now
in reality gone wrong,
as Tiber's waters flood the world
and raise their nightmare song,

disoriented, sharp and pure,
with the amoral child's
wish to possess his mother,
destroy his father's shields,
and live forever by itself
in the waste it calls its own,
the total freedom of its wish
and the smashed toy of Rome.

Marcus Aurelius Speaks

I have to leave insomniac Rome
to guard the borders, so
farewell verse and farewell prose,
and farewell, spare philosophy,
I go to the sleet and snow.

Patricians and plebs have fought.
Many-talented Caesar struck
At Pompey's men, 'Strike at the vein.
It will cause the greatest panic to
open them like a book.'

And crazed Augustus cried all night,
'My legions, where are they?
O give me back again those men.'
And the swan-breasted blue-eyed Gauls
rushed on us day by day.

Nero and Caligula,
insane dictators both,
saw seething Rome as a boring home.
What pathological disease
was present at Rome's birth?

And so we build our creaking walls
to keep the madmen in,
and to keep out those without doubt
who crave the marble and the trees
even Hannibal couldn't win,

who learned one day that the mile of ground
on which his camp was built
had just been bought by a Roman fraught
with such an immense confidence
it made the great man wilt.

And I march out with legionnaires
to defend a dying day.
('Who hasn't seen great Rome's demesne
has never seen the sun itself,'
or so they used to say.)

I shall post myself in my cold tent,
last Stoic of my kind,
and watch the rain fall over Spain
and steadily and malignantly
watch to the very end,

voyeur of our obscenity,
and the future's confident waves.
Show them the flag. Far back there dig
the gnomes who are undermining
their defenders' sleety graves.

The Carthaginian women wove
bowstrings from their hair.
But Carthage burned and Scipio turned
on his playful horse away from the light
and omens of that air.

I see the words DELENDA EST
as now applied to Rome
as now I gaze at the piercing stars
which know no walls or borders
of our proud imperium.

Farewell, you sordid marketplace,
and forums of quick lies,
and gladiators and realtors,
The Theatre of Cruelty,
and the silence of the wise.

I'll watch for you at the world's end
in my doubtful armour till
the nameless cohorts take your forts
and the unmarbled mishmash turn
on the unforgiving wheel.

I'll watch for the simplicities
of which Cato used to speak
and the herbs so common and acerb
on which were nursed the principles
where armies used to break,

and heroes like our Mucius
who roasted his own hand
to show how Rome had a firm bone
which like the rocky Apennines
was central to our land.

So, as the border's lost in snow,
I shall watch a new day rise
and on this field with fading shield
be dazzled by the foreigners
with the familiar eyes

of Romans out of story books
huge giants of past days
who in this present use the crescent
hooked weapons of the harvest time
that topples from their gaze.

The Atoms

The Lares and Penates by
Lucretius are hurled
out of the marble villas
to the sparse atomic world
where Neptune, Mars, and Venus
diminish on the screen
of the Roman nox with its safety locks
and the human light between.

The dead will not return again
to the forum of vast Rome
nor ever stroll at evening
by the marble of their home,
but speechless, ruined and extinct,
seethe in the Roman mould
while sunny clocks and rugged rocks
tick through the heat and cold.

Their ghosts will not revisit
the tragic or comic plays,
nor above stained arenas
watch bloody panthers graze
on gladiators with short swords
while the bored emperors lean
to crack a joke to the black cloak
Death sports behind the scenes.

The atoms clash and coalesce
beyond the Roman roads.
Their minimal shields and field of force
are stronger than the gods.
Eerie and grave in the vast wastes
where legions never go
they break, reform, attack and storm
the tents of Scipio.

Inventive, accidental,
the primitive desires
which feed the will of Caesar
and banked Cleopatra's fires,
power Cicero's orations
and the envy of the Gauls
and make the plebs howl like the tribes
which beset our city walls,

and make both Death and Love the brief
spasms of mindless will.
For there's no Hades for proud ghosts
to stroll on asphodel
but only the huge silence
which falls when Rome will fade
from a single soul – and the state will roll
to irreversible shade.

from ENDS AND BEGINNINGS
(1994)

Poetry

Poetry has nothing to do with who we are.
It cannot be explained by biography,
e.g. sickness, unhappiness.
Poetry is a swart planet
with which we are in touch, from which
we receive at certain times messages.
Nor is it a black or emerald clock –
I think it is a voice which speaks to us
at night as unquiet trembling, or maybe
a curious arrangement of stones,
poorly random and yet sonorous,
a packet of crisps beside a Greek vase
on a day with a breeze flowing from the south.

The Bible

The Bible stands like a big rock which no one attends to.
It is a novel with murders, adulteries and fears.

It is the solid TV of our human history
and God is the eagle with human flesh in its claws.

It used to be made of marble, a statue among leaves.
Now it is a record of deaths, tribal partitions.

And its victims have black faces and its saints have batons
and their diseased ethics are undazzled by rainbows.

Old Lady

1

All your sap is thickened towards survival.
About you there is no dapple of thought.
Sometimes in the evening there's a retrieval

of old rings, old bangles. Otherwise
your tale is a stubborn root against wind.
There is no narrative in your veined eyes.

Even ice can melt and become water,
adventure. No, with bitter claws
you cling to the horned stick carved from nature,

the elegant deer's head. At night
I hear you fumbling among furniture,
for beads, ribbons, dresses, moonlit rings.

2

The sea stings. It is older than you are.
Its brine is saltier than your tears.
It is a treasury of the wandering dead.

Sometimes at sunset it looks beautiful
with its strange roses among bitter green.
And in autumn moonlight how its roads converge!

Old lady, surely we are human.
But do not shut your eyes in your blindness,
nor your nostrils nor your wrinkled ears.

The crab noses the brine in the morning.
It feels through the vibrations of its shell
the constant music of the possible.

3

The lumpy wooden ones who rose from the dead,
there have been some of those. Consider the paintings
framed in the Renaissance, and still bright.

On wooden wings they rose towards feathers,
the Dutch ones too in their sabots, from their kitchens.
On their dishes a various light shone.

The lumpy ones became angels.
They sprouted from earthly dressers towards heaven.
They left a trail of bronze chains behind

and a little dog looking towards them
as their rough heels turned golden, and their bodies
filled as with water unfathomably grave.

4

To be human is to be a river
reflecting new pictures, flowing on
deftly, imperfectly, towards the future.

Loves, ruins, weddings, rest in it,
brides with white dresses descending
raptly from clouds of the minute.

Exactly so, difficult old woman,
thorny-voiced, thorny-wristed, slow
rancours seething from your waste moon.

Indignities of the posthumous.
I love tragic heroes in the storm
profiled thriftlessly against space,

but you tick like an old clock.
Useless above the grave your gaunt face,
useless the bony chair in which you rock.

As Time Draws Near

As time draws near
the end of our days
and the plates fall

away from our knees,
let us not be afraid
of the unsponsored dark.

Heavy grave sin
is weighing your head.
There are shining in darkness

panoramas of terror.
Each nightly picture
is God in his ire.

But for us in autumn
let the trees remind us
of our reasonable sequence,

that like birds we travel
from darkness to darkness
briefly through the hall,

where there remains
the clinking of glasses,
the redness of wine,

though we lie starkly
in our effigies
which will not rise,

pen or sword in hand.
It is an achieved grand
tableau that we leave,

say, turning at the door,
putting on a glove,
and entering the sunset's

enormous concert.
Surely that is better
than on stumbling feet

in the warmth of wetness
squalidly survive.
Live O live,

all you young ones
who take our places
in this hypothesis

of sun and cloud.
May it be with pride
we applaud your litheness

in this panorama,
this drama of our days.
O yes with pride

that we step outwards
into the darkness
closing our eyes

on the last flickering page.

It is time to let the birds migrate without anguish
through the skies of the immediate
towards a fated destination.

It is time to turn the blow lamp on dogma
and inhabit this blue.

Funeral

The wind tugged at our clothes
as your coffin was borne
out on to the empty road.

We were like crows
in the middle of the autumn day
as we trudged to the hearse

with that polished chest
in which you were at rest,
your eyes closed.

The box was slowly let down
into the prepared grave.
The tassels were thrown

on to the closed lid.
Beside us the sea
stormily glittered,

minerally coloured.
I summon to mind
my loved autumn wood

and the rowan tree
with its triumphant flourish
of temporary berries,

and all that is perfect
on the verge of its dying.
It was not in a ring

of dogma or prayer
that I felt that peace,
uniquely gracious.

It belonged to the season,
to the last passion
of dignified things,

to their replete goings
as without theory
even the folded wings

of a bird declines
into the dark,
as without cleric

or the windy volume
of protective stories
we take our measure

in a natural inventory.
He was so, he was so!
The transparent window

is always open.
And so you enter,
in the complex nature

of your own history,
and also you change
in an earth not strange

but always familiar,
and the tiny daffodil
will flourish later

out of your box
which the manipulative
oily worms unlock

as the natural colourful
flowers enthral
the fresh sea breeze.

An Old Man Praying

In the middle of the night I hear you pray.
'God be with me, soon it will be time.'
And then the clock begins its crystal chime.

Provenance of the Bible and its power!
Even so far from home you're on the rack.
The day is vain and then the night is black,

starless, without compass. 'I have sinned.'
Inside your head the scarlet whores patrol.
If only light would break, and you were Paul,

self-confident and literate. Christ was once
a boy like you, fishing for his eels.
Now he hangs from wood by his tanned heels.

The box must lock us, poisonous, corrupt.
Not charitable works can save us now,
not neighbours' fields that we in mercy ploughed.

Listen, the birds begin. Is that a cat
screeching from the shrubbery? The owl
ghosts through the village, like a wafting soul.

And the birds cheep and chirrup, interrupt
the speech of Genesis, the burning stench
of flesh at sunrise far from the cool Minch.

'Tremendous pigmy on my wooden chair
I shake and stutter. Paradise exhales
a foreign scent, as roses on salt gales.

Is larger than a street of jewellers,
the haunt of youth when drunk. I would abide
His scything rainbows with my ruinous pride.

Now it is full morning, and the larks
soar straight to heaven, pagan, bodiless.'
You rise from sheets, put on your mortal dress

while rabbits race and frolic in the dew.
'I must recall my chains are made of love.
This swollen arm is fantasy. Be brave.

The soul's exhaled like scent from rotting flesh,
and like pale herring shall outlive the mesh.'

Dying Man

Breathless and blue-lipped,
you thank God for His mercies
in a prayer you have learned
on a bare island.
How grand the face of God,
secure, imperious,
to whom you are a slave
in absolute fear and dread.

Dying, you thank God,
beating at His door
for an exact justice
though you do not hear
a high answering voice.
It is only history
that sweeps grandly on
in spite of your 'Rejoice'.

Pity shakes my heart
as at night I hear
your eloquent sleepless prayers,
endless and austere.

But only the birds of dawn
answer with their twitter,
or the continuous water
chatters among leaves.

And the window rises,
contingent and gaunt,
like a white picture
misty, indigent,
over the wet grass.
Out of the vast silence
there is no voice
to raise you from your knees.

In Hospital

Over your face is the grilled snout of the oxygen mask.
I bend down to speak to you.
You are a sick eagle outspread on the bed.
Your nose grows thinner and thinner.

Oh, how lovely the nurses are
in their objective uniforms.
Their bodies sing of youth and health
in your incontinent world.

You are gazing up at me
from that country which is adjacent to me
though you have not crossed the border
breathing heavily, dully.

It is only a short distance away,
less than from Lewis to Harris.
It is a question of darkness,
away from this precious autumn.

Someone is waiting for you with scales
and a book where your sins are registered.
It is like going to school again
for the very first time.

Your eyes tell us of it.
We are no longer in the same land.
Our eyes cross that unimaginable space.
The white nurses are still here.

Dogmas

Perfidious dogmas,
unremitting theses,
let the wild seas
blow through you

with their salt taste
and tang of seaweed
and all the dead
whose bones have been picked clean

by the fresh currents,
and let the rocks of dogma
be steadily worn down
till only the water

brilliantly sparkling
with its modern ships
flows always eastward
towards a temporary sun.

Come, Fool

Come, fool, and tell me of your successes
just here where the wind combs the grasses
by this cemetery with its wooden crosses.

Come, gold-buttoned fool, with your new car
shining like a crab: walk over
this ancestral ground with its white flowers,

and talk in your loud voice of your gains,
your Midas jacket. Do you not feel the presence
of the empty-mouthed dead, and the dance

of the extinct girls.
                    Come, glassy fool,
stand by this stone and see your own name

excised as in your schooldays, an address
from your poor cottage to the universe

and then to your Mercedes and your hearse.

From the Mad Ward

1

And as you wave goodbye
I know we shall not meet again
either here or earnestly
in another place beyond this pain.
I see your foxy face
disappear around a corner and
in perfect helplessness
raise my disappearing hand.

2

Dawn
The tree's inside
a nest of orange light
as if it were a brain
on fire with all the thoughts
that make it shake and burn –
you in your neat iron
infernal suit, going home
to the house where I once was
set in the green grass
but very distant now.

3

Come, take my hand,
be more authoritative. Understand
I am only a poor simple lunatic
come from the land of fruit into this brick
undernourished cage. And what I speak
has as little meaning as the creak
of a wooden door: or a bird's voice,
low, throaty, and anonymous.
I am of the world's refuse, scarecrow man
set to protect a decent field of corn
amid that autumn music. But my own
notes are a steady strawy monotone.

4

The lunatics are forking autumn leaves
into a barrow (such bare grizzly heads!).
The sky is cold and wintry and bright blue.
They work relentlessly but they speak no words,
the eternally deranged ones. Leaves at least may change
from green to gold and back to green again

but there's no change in their crew-cut hazy globes.
They're sweeping leaves away in the vast ward
of this great daylight and the clouds are still
portentous castles high above their heads.
For them there's only autumn and no spring.

5

The rain is falling. Poor Tom, poor Tom!
This is a dreadful landscape after the aplomb
of my early days. Come home to roost
are the fake alibis and the gross boast
settling on the wires. My dearest love,
wherever you are, cunning and piteous,
send me a picture I can look at, me
in your foxy eyes in miniature, now
reflected. Poor Tom, poor Tom!
Wind wanderer, rain sufferer, far from home!

London

In St James Park, the ducks
are swimming in the river, beside which
the deck chairs sit untenanted. The
policemen stroll among the bluish mist
rustling the leaves. Along the Mall
alternate lamp-posts wear high crowns.
The gates of Buckingham Palace
are locked. At Horse Guards Parade
the riders sit on their seven black horses
one of which pees copiously. The helmets
are drawn low on the faces, in a beaten
lowering gold.
        In Soho the girls strip
to bushes and bare bottoms, their eyes

expressionless as pebbles, smiling a little
into the large mirrors, where the red
sofas are reflected.
                    The guide
in the House of Commons says, 'It's
all tradition. Don't sit on the seats.'
The bad big paintings show
Charles beheaded, Nelson in his triumph.
In the cold Great Hall, tennis balls were found
used by Henry the Eighth and his ladies.
In Soho,
blue films go on all night. Remember
the flesh is not traditional, like the ceilings
of the two Parliaments. The great legs
slowly open. The body arches backward.
Over the bridge the hair of the dead head sprays.

Aberdeen

Sparkling leaves… I remember Aberdeen,
my university days. Oil's brimming now
where once I used to study Gaelic, Latin,
in Duthie Park with pale and lowered brow.

Shall oil restore us? Virgil's Hades glooms
with fictional ghosts, implacable and proud.
From the North Sea the goggled diver looms.
On Summer St, pop lyrics, clear and loud,

troubled the leaves and me while the green trams
skid down their wires. Riches, they say, now pour
from waters Arctic-cold: and Babychams
remind Americans of the wells they bore

far from their stores and states. Shall Virgil live,
and in that granite cage Lucretius
despise religion, say we must forgive
each other on a planet spinning loose

among pure leaves of ice. I have my wells
deeper than these, and see on Union St
the coupled virginal hilarious girls
with their cracked Woolworth handbags laugh and greet

the pimply boys, brylcreemed and unheroic
oiled with their sex. Riches are what we find
in what is transient, perilous, and oblique,
the random glitter of the sun and wind,

the helmets of the sunrise: and our oil
that constant energy that feeds our loves
while ghosts in lumbering suits rise from their toil
and the furious vigour of fermenting graves.

Putting out the Ashes

A night such as we have never known,
millions of stars, shooting stars, a moon.
I stand and breathe the sky. It is breathing.
The supernatural light rests on the bin

freezing it to a palpable brilliant vase
from Greece perhaps, though it is packed with waste.
This is a marvellous spendthrift universe
a poet throwing off verse after verse.

Hallowe'en

This small child has an old man's face,
an old man's clayey bleak unquestioning face.
He plays the violin and sings a song,
small, expressionless, unquestioning.

And then after he has played he pulls
the mask away, and there he stands
fresh-faced and laughing with blonde curls
and from the grave extends his hands.

The Fence

Children running and playing
outside the school
your energy is beautiful.

What bows us down
is the invisible fence
at which we buck
then subside to a slow walk

dignified, honourable,
the wiry ethics
that we have created
in the middle of the fresh air.

Welcome

The sun is flashing from the hot gate.
Stranger, do not fear to come in.
There is cool water in the basin,
and there are shadows in the small rooms.
Remove your tunic and show yourself
entirely as the Muse,
who walks the dusty road in the summer.
          Please excuse
the tiles which are not marble,
the absence of statues from the hall.
But in the very depths of the hot garden
you will find an ordinary cool well.

The Gaelic Proverb

The Gaelic proverb says,
sad is the state of the house
without a child or cat.

But sad is the state of the child
who carries his house on his back
like a trapped snail.

And the cat who cannot go out
into the deep greenery
but sits on the spinster's lap,
narrow and infertile,
as the wild sun goes down.

The Poet

Chained at his desk
like Prometheus
the vulture eats him:

dressed in its black tails
its breath furious and sour,
it's like a clock that never fails:

in its smart evening dress it towers
out of the sunset's ravening pictures.

Milton

Out of the immense darkness your voice rose.
It was a fertile spring which defied
the excised stone, and the destruction of your hopes.
It wasn't the will, will cannot construct music,
which rises in solid pillar upon pillar,
to a new temple which was not built by hands.
You hear the louts and hooligans in the night
in their vanishing velvets and cold arrogance,
the wine guzzlers who splash blood on the wall,
those who have escaped the iron individualism of your planet –
yet the music will not cease in the moving darkness,
it creates Adam and Eve in their tremulousness,
it creates the devil elegant in snakelike green,
it creates a blitz of angels falling from the sky.
In spite of the destruction of hope, the music…
In your hebraic cloth, the holiness of your inspiration,
your head is an astronomy of stars, your ardour is relentless,
the music defies the darkness, and is heroic,
it renews itself endlessly in the reclusive silence of art.

Who cannot take comfort from you, old rancorous one
for whom the exact notation of nature was not enough,
for whom there were no real elegies even of the drowned?
You sing out of your blindness like a beggar,
at the extinct silence of your hopes you will not be silenced,
the holy doves perch on your scholarly shoulders
and common humanity is forgiven by your spartan star.
Your hearse is constructed of music
and your poems are as lasting as the towers of London,
its palaces and castles.
It is the bright architecture that soars out of the dark,
marvellous blind rancorous one who submitted your theology to
death

and who are resurrected over and over in your music,
putting off the leaves, learning a classical bareness,
the handsome Apollo who wished to know all the rays of the sun
but who bumps in the end against the pillars of his own verse.

The Scholar

The bitter scholar remembers how his monographs
disappeared down a chute in the middle of his days,
how he stuttered at the interview when questioned about admin.,
how his rivals pounced on his fresh book and munched it.
The sky darkened steadily since his undergraduate years
when he sparkled like a diamond at the café table
outside which there was an orchard with ripening apple trees.
Was it his life that infected his studies
and drew his energies away from his papers.
Was it his shyness that made him fall silent
among the coteries in the Dining Hall.
Was it that everything had already been written about his favourite
author.
Did he not know seamanship well enough to understand Conrad.
Then he withdrew. And the apple-bottomed students
were moving eagerly towards fresher voices

which combined witticisms with transatlantic power.
Who could be said betrayed him? Some sinuous Judas
hiding among the trees, among the blossoms.
Let him remember his early days before his office was denuded,
before the scholars ceased to consult him,
before timidity overwhelmed him in the eternal silence,
when literature used to reflect his youthful optimism
and the leaves of the trees were the leaves of precious poems
before literature itself, allied to power and place,
became the plaything of men agile with word processors,
before idealism drained away from his heart
on a battleground which he had never thought existed
in a world which he loved once in that early café
whose owner could talk knowledgeably about Proust.

Dream

Nervous, I carry my poems
to that chair
from which I read.

Around me
there are men in black masks,
women
with ambiguous laurels.

I speak.
My voice echoes
down the centuries
in competition with, say,
Lucretius.

I lift a huge weight.
My fingers shake,
corrupt compass needles.

O Lord,
let them relent,
smile.
Their harsh faces compose
no images of the rose.

Orpheus,
I am lost among the minerals
of the god of silver.

I rise.
The interview is over.
My poems fly
like the leaves of autumn away
to Vallombrosa.

I cry.
I break like rain
like a fine fresh April
composed of nuns,
shadows.

My masters
are still considering,
among a ring
of rocks and thistles.
Later they will tell me,
much later.

Perhaps when I am no longer here.

The Young Girls

The young girls are waiting to go to university,
they are trembling on the edge of learning.

Donne, Milton, Wordsworth, they are ready to read them.
Poetry has to do with misty mornings

and beginnings, beginnings. Let the toaster click,
let the fridge hum in your new flats

and the book lie open at a page of Marvell's,
while the pale faces dream of love

in the city of buses, chip shops and the underground
where Dido said farewell to Aeneas

as history roared through the tunnels.
                                        How they tremble,
the pages in the fresh wind, as the tenements

echo with the noise of your feet running
to early lectures, and you throw your notes

into the bag carelessly slung over your shoulder.
Beginnings, tremblings… Poetry will move among

the morning shadows. All is transient
nothing is permanent but what will leave later

out of the stone, the books, notes which will tell
what a poem really means, the fixed footnotes.

Books

Books, what should I do
without you.
I should face
the meagre coarse
board of the world.
But with you,
sombre and true,
I inwardly digest
the rich feast
of learning. Rust
is far from me
as eased by you
I travel through
land after land
in which the gods burned
and the trees rose
shaggy and muscular,
tall and voluptuous,
from whose fine leaves
our pages are made.
O I'm arrayed
in brave dresses,
I am king
when I sit down and bring
your words closer.
Plots, denouements,
stories and scents,
heroes and saints
these I always find
deep in these fond
gardens of yours –
all literatures.
Nor ever alone
am I, as down
the page my eye races
into your recesses.
Eternal fountains,

lovely philosophies,
brilliant legends,
and dry discourses.
Over-shadowing mountains,
my avid companions
who will not desert
me or my art
with your dry perfume,
calm autumn bloom.
I see my doom
as being always head-bent
over the page
to the very end
like a stone statue
which also has roses.
In the deepest crises
you comfort, you ease –
my allegories!
Tiny mirrors,
and miniature tombs,
you shine in my rooms,
unappeasable ones.
My loves, my true loves,
who will walk through the shades
with me, dear comrades,
without griefs, without griefs.

Others

It is true that there are others... of course there are others around us,
like the receptionist who has to be patient in her cage,
or the garage mechanic who sets out in pouring rain to repair a car,
or the boy who went to a private school and though he wears
                                        glasses plays rugby.
Or those who come to poetry readings and who ask no questions
or the gardener who works in the hot day in a cluster of flies

and who peers wistfully into the well where there is no water,
or the male teacher who endures the taunts of children and the
                    loveliness of the short-skirted mistress in the staffroom
or the newspaper seller who claps her hands in the bitter cold,
or the librarian who, tired of books, wishes someone would speak
                                                            to her,
or the commissionaire with his blazing medals who stands in the
                                    evening like a cockerel,
or the waitress who serves at table though her engagement has been
                                            broken
or the woman who stays with her daughter and son-in-law and
                                    wishes to be alone
or the blind man who sings songs at an unforgiving corner.
All these there are and do not forget the air they inhabit
as your single will climbs the sky like a jet that's taking off from a
                                    shining airport
and leaves an ashen mark on a sky of marvellous blue
as it sets off for Canada or Australia or Vietnam or any other country
where there are still more of the living centred in their loves and
                                            their work
and for whom the world is mainly themselves and their own shadows
and who stare up at the men with guns and the cold look of the tyrant
as the rain falls on the ricefields and on the soaked hats of the peasants
and there is autumn somewhere else breathtakingly beautiful
and the apples fall from the trees in the music of the fabulous
                                    nightingale.

Insomnia

I wake up in the middle of the night and make a cup of tea.
Because of the fever of my body I can't sleep.

Because of those I've betrayed in the selfishness of my heart
I cannot sleep though the window is open.

I hear the throaty cry of the owl. I imagine its wings,
its body growing greener and greener with horrifying light.

And I remember how a decision was asked of me and I turned away,
and climbed the stone steps to my name on the door of my house.

And I shall not sleep till morning and the house will be a glaring box
and now and again I will see the rim of a garment

flickering from a bedroom where there has been no one for years.

from THE HUMAN FACE
(1996)

'That ethnic differences should'

That ethnic differences should
lead men into a darkling wood
stained with an internecine blood
    is to be mourned
when there is much beatitude
     within our bourne.

That dogmas snap at heel and head
with bitter teeth: and that deep red
dresses the bride who might have wed
    is cruel fact:
these are the tracks of those who fled
     in cataracts

of children, women. Neighbours once
they were united in the dance
of a diurnal circumstance
    of grief and joy:
but now some raise obsessive guns
     at girl and boy.

As if at Hallowe'en they wear
patches of ancestry and dour
dogmas composed from out the air
    (for Nature isn't,
O seasonal Nature's not aware
     of more than present).

Ceilidhs you held in common halls,
you had luxurious carnivals,
but now we see such crimson palls
    as scorch the gaze:
there leap across your local walls
    blood-red ideas

of kin and creed, to smash a door.
Members of an élitist corps
you tear at the colourful décor
    that men must build
to identify that they are here,
    by self beguiled.

Nature unconsciously swells
to green and red: and it compels
even human buildings to its rules,
    a passionate queen
of weeds and lilies and bluebells,
    a rage of green.

But conscious man will kill and smash
frail secret envelopes of the flesh –
hack at beard and at moustache –
    because he's armed
with ideas made of patchy trash
    that grief's confirmed,

or loneliness or heritage,
or a new-learned unfocused rage.
O he's a vulture in a cage
    that has been shaped
by others than himself – typed page
    from manuscript.

Anthologies are justified
from gods and creeds to let men ride
on tall infernal horses. Pride
    plays lovely flutes.
Who leads this troop but Homicide
    with shining boots?

Their heavenly uniform is blue,
and complex theories tattooed
are pictures of a large and crude
      comic-strip idea.
Green nature did not once imbue
      such vicious fear,

but is composed of trees and stones,
and not these merciless monotones.
Melodious birds play different tunes
      at night or day –
my lovely throstles, larks and wrens,
      multi-voiced play!

Christians, Moslems and Hindus
have built a shelter from bad news
from creeds from which they pick and choose
      lest they should die
alone in tenement or mews
      beneath a sky

unscripted by a higher hand.
They build a pure Utopian land
where there is 'neither rain nor wind
      nor mist nor snow'
from which they gaze on the unplanned
      chaos below.

I've heard one say a Catholic
is a close acquaintance of Old Nick,
a Fenian bastard fit for brick
      or knife or bullet.
The Pope wears green, a politic
      fat Pontius Pilate.

Across the now-anointed Boyne
there rides a horse – O heaven-born.
Truth sparkles from its saddle horn,
      O brightly blue,
and a flag is raised to firmly burn
      for the favoured few.

Of course Mohommedan and Sikh,
The Turk and the 'perfidious Greek',
the Jew and his 'usurious clique'
      are also shaped
to dwell in that demonic reek,
      by the inept.

The jester wore his tunic once
in double colour: he would prance
and joke for his empurpled prince
      at laden table.
He saved himself by shifty stance,
      sparkling, unstable.

But those who wear idea's hues,
tunics of yellow, red or blue,
endorse one colour and enthuse
      about its virtues.
O always heaven's precious news
      must come in courteous

monolingual monochrome.
For God when He is at home
and writing drama, prose, or poem
      has a one-hued ribbon.
He is imperialist as Rome
      was before Gibbon.

One only colour and décor
is what God loves. That is His gloire.
Flags constitute his long histoire
    and they are ours.
Let spring burst richly by the Loire
    with *single* flowers.

Flags wave above the random stones,
are winding sheets above men's bones:
because of them we hear the moans
    of dying flesh,
while knifing geriatric crones
    bitterly slash.

Over the ground in green and red
above the pale anonymous dead
from whom their riotous blood has bled
    the flags make sail.
Whereto, we ask. To lively trade
    or credal jail?

Ideas clash as soldiers toil
in naïve energy to foil
their enemies' imperial style
    backed by the critics.
There is a vicious bloody boil
    of different ethics.

Naïve soldier, you may be just
fighting your own interest
and the flag you capture with hot wrist
    may be your own,
and the knife that twists inside your breast
    made of your bone.

from THE LEAF AND THE MARBLE

(1998)

1   *The Green Leaf*

My doughty one,
when I think of you
I think of light leaves in Rome
above the marble-
green leaves, green leaves!

As Michelangelo
on his shaky ladder
so I also admire
courageous fire
fiercely blossoming.

My love,
you believe
that luck will feed us
as meagre saints
hold out their gifts
from empty cupboards.

Not the statues,
no, not the statues,
those imperial riders –
no, but the green leaves
of early April.

Out of the darkness
I rise once more
putting on my blossoms,
and you are there,
a loyal candle.

In the hecatombs of Rome
and at Monte Cassino
so many of the dead,
the young, the ancient,
the crazed, the innocent,
whom the stone imprisons.

In the old damp walls
the martyred Christians.

But the spring prevails
over the marble –
this shadow of the leaf,
this heartbreak green.

No, not the caparison
of majestic Caesar's
power-stricken hauteur.

But your frail moon,
wavering, shy,
over the dark Tiber.

The young wolves fed
at their lean dam

and I at times
have rested my rhymes
at your hopeful hostelry.

Courage, I am sure,
is the first of virtues

as among the libraries
of arid Ephesus
I saw the poppies
glowing among stones

or at Pompeii
among the ashes
a stubborn lion.

None shall be saved
who doesn't have courage.

As I am your judge
you have that power
which is beyond literature
and our screens of stories.

I come back again
to that bright green leaf
which is stronger than marble.

Rome may die,
as the slavering tribes
ache for its larder.
But that is all foam
if as the sun goes down
the emperor does not burn
in the light of love.

Let him recline
among spurious manuscripts,
how can he survive
in that acid air
of poisonous violins
without the passionate, clear,
gift of a companion.

So many statues,
heavy and firm.
So many riders
fixed in that stone
of determined time.

And the bridges tremble
among the daffodils.

Nevertheless
what without courage,
unwavering candle,
can be accomplished

as the dark Tiber
with its wolf-grey waves
is steadily flowing.

The leaf, the leaf!
April is here
with its constant shuttle.

And love is your
loyal imperative,
as hand in hand
we stroll through this grand

repertoire of scenes,

these pagan oracles
and pipe-playing fountains.

You pull me
out of
the deepest grave
with your bubbling music.
You do not let the antique
overwhelm you
or the helmets
of the dour legions

over whose shaded
and mortal faces
the green leaves play.

Play me my orchestra
of divine feeling
for April is here
and the grave is opened
and I see you there

my dear green leaf
which beyond art
is the gift of life.

O yes, O yes,
my hungry eyes
see this synthesis

though I do not despise
this weighty stone
from Carrara's shrine.

This leaf still plays
in front of the vast
marble arrays.

2

Seize it, seize it.
O it will not stay
and that is the mystery
just as imperious
as helmets and spears
among the roses
and the machine-made legion
among the judas
with its flowering sprays.

Slim as a faun
in the heaviness of Rome
I see you running
and you are piping

your quotidian pipe
and water is turning
over and over
among these frozen
forces of power.

Even were the lions,
composed of gaunt flame,
coppery imperium,
to enter the Colosseum
the green leaf will play
about the orchestra
of cruel desire.

And the green leaf will climb
the majestic marble.

Courage remains
the finest virtue
as out of Avernus
we repeatedly climb
into the daylight
where the green leaf plays
and the poet strums
his stony lyre

as he ascends
to the Colosseum
where the coppery lions
rasp their fierce tongues

slavering, furious.
As also Mucius

burned his own hand

and Horatius stood
on the shaking bridge
or the legions turned
at a crumbling wall.

Courage, I say,
my precious one
as the laurel grows
among the shades

like the common thistle.
I see you stand
in the strumming wind.
Rome is built

day after day,
stony, foursquare.
Persephone sways

among the daffodils.
Insoluble,
like Etruscan script
our serious days.

My love, I say
all is equal
among the *res*
mundi
          I've seen you take

a beggar in
from the wild sad road.
Praise O praise
generosity

and also courage,
the leaf that plays
untheatrically
among the operas

and difficult dramas
of our days.
Praise O praise
the local shires

we etch from the blaze
of blue and green.
In ruinous Rome
the poppies nosed

the arid stone.
Or at Pompeii
the fresco shows
cupids and fauns,

a bird on a vase,
a Bacchante nude,
an oven and mill
before the lethal

acid poured down
to fix us in
our contorted poses.
O like the roses

let us brightly wave.
I see you stroll
with your pleated skirt
as if made of marble

in this shuttling April.

Cave canem
I hear them say
of the thorny days.

But I see you put
in your jewellery box
the virtue of courage.
O beware of the dog

who guards the huge
weight of the dark.
If we face it straight

then the laurel waves.

In the fractured *res*
Orpheus strays

then rises again,

Puella, you are
the bright fresh leaf
of acid green
becoming later

the mulier,
the wife and mother.
Than talent dearer
than Roman coin

heavy and grave
is the leaf of courage,
a lunar portion,
or as Apollo

the sunny bow.
At Pompeii

out of the ashes
the poppies blow.

3

The Pompeii
of frozen ideas
let us now leave:
the slumped bodies

under the ash.
O dear was the life
common and clear
that these townsmen lived

as the chariot-wheels
carved their routine
on the daily roads
over which walked

in flowing togas
the magisters,
tribunes and plebs.
Dear those rays,

the smell of bread,
the sparse green olives,

the amoretti
plump and winged

and on this day
the stingless butterfly,

that tiny cloud.

4

Dear Lares,
protect our larders,
our loved pictures

hung on the walls.
Protect our wardrobes
with their loose blouses

and flowery dresses.
Protect our libraries
with their fine books.
Let no axe

flourish over us
with frosty blade.
Protect the desk
at which I weave

my arabesques.
Let only be published
the best, the best.

Protect the chairs,
the tables and blue
lips of blue rugs.

And do not let
the darkness cripple
in its ominous ripple

our sunny windows
and colourful gardens
where the azaleas
in mild nooks bloom.

5   *The Roads of Rome*

Courage, I say,
is the finest virtue.
For we all shake
more than the marble
which stares about us
from rigorous profiles.

Undeviating roads
the will propels
through marsh and moorland
where among boscage
the wet birds sing.

Through heat and cold
through dry and wet
the road proceeds,
stony, remorseless.

But it does not show
the power of the dark.

These many profiles
with their eyeless gaze
as if blinded by light
do not reveal
the shaking mysterious
deepening haze.

Across Britannia
and wooded Gaul
the roads are driven,
stone by stone.
The local gods
are shaken away
from branch and twig,
from their secret heaven.

And the will drives on.

Birds are scattered
out of their nests.
Their naked eggs
are now uncovered.
Through oozing mud
in rain and frost's
imperious crown
the emperor drives
his ruthless chariot.

The demons die
in a hiss of rain.

Bones are unturfed.
Into the air
there's a whirr of wings
of scaly fire.

And the road drives on.
Past Hades itself
at the foggy roadside
that giant cave
with its arrogant shades

of Aeneas and Dido
and huge Achilles.
The road drives on
scattering protean
feathers and leaves.

In the white dust
I see the helmets
of the legions flashing.
Bottomless quarries
are white as ghosts.

And the will drives on.

But courage, I tell you,
it does not speak
of the shaking dark
and the major lyric
that rises and falls.

It does not tell
how the world shakes
how the scenes flicker,
how on both sides
of the road there is heard
a secret snicker,
how on both sides
there is untamed nature,

and quaking bogs
re-form and pucker.

And the road drives on.
But Hades remains –
its bluish veins
and its changing videos.

Hold the green leaf
in front of you
just like a torch
as forward you go
lit by its glow
among the voices,
the sibilant noises,
the snakelike hisses,
the mosses, neuroses,
in a place without glass.

And the road drives on.

And frightened you hear
the sounds of water
ghostly yet clear

And in their hauteur

the ghosts are standing,
changing and bending,
always beyond
the adamant will.

6

And this is Hades, the maze of catacombs, the cupboards of the
                                                    dead. And
here also is a picture of a bird pecking at a bowl of fruit. Here is the
hiss of snakes, the fathomless wolf-coloured twilight, the shifting
panoramas of the heroes without substance.
This is Hades for which courage is needed, where the collars of
                                                    bone are stored.
Do not be lost in the labyrinth, find your way back.
Let the light of the ordinary day pour down on you,
let the hisses and the noises be erased.
Enter the shadowless video.

7   *In the Garden*

In the garden I see you
beside the azaleas,
beside the clematis,
among the daisies.

Heal us, dear blaze,
from the seething black.

Our colourful days!

Daffodil, primrose,
tulip, crocus,
no hocus pocus
from these magicians.

How Hades fuels
those innocent fires,
those swaying comely
sinuous flowers.

Hades propels
these impermanent petals.
From infernal cells
they hesitate upward.

No light without dark,
no god without devil,
no good without evil.
The technicians know
that we need the dark.

The leaf, the marble,
the mortal, immortal,
transient, eternal.

So you bend to the earth
with your gardening gloves
protecting your hands
from the rose thorns.

And on the stone
butterflies settle.
There's grass on the spade's
luminous metal.

Under the glamour
is poisonous Hades
with its swarms of worms.

Under the face
astoundingly cruel
sunny and pure
the storms of ambition,
limitless power,
imperial venom.

Under the bouquet
the exploding flame.

The muscular roots
develop in darkness,
though we can show
Michelangelo
dusty and white
rise to his quarry.

As art and ourselves
are haunted by wolves
snapping at flesh
bloody and vicious.

The wolves sit
at our picnic tables.
They face us and they
snap at the plates.

And Rome must suckle
even from these
tribes of wild beasts
as music too towers
from the inharmonious
and as the flowers
shine from the dark.

The wolf's green eyes
are scouring our days
and the red rose sways
out of the dark

and Cerberus barks
sharply, all ways.

8

When everything trembles, only love holds it together.
Rome is an act of the will, but the leaf protects us.
Day after day, year after year, Rome with its stony walls and statues is
built above a cage of wolves.
But love is not an act of the will.
No legions can defend or destroy love.
When the walls fly apart, when the horizons shimmer, only love can
save us.
Day by day it towers over us, with its forum, its atria, its columns.
We are inside its massive shadow.
And when Rome falls only the leaf can save us, the leaf of pathos, of
love, of the quotidian.
Its lightness is serious, its play is real.
Iron will not be our breastplate when the horizon shimmers.
Go into the catacomb bearing your wavering leaf.

9

The leaves are stronger than the gods, stronger than stone.
The fresh light leaves of love in the Campagna, under a blue sky.
O to be in Rome now that spring is here, now that April is a shadowy
play, is a drama playing over walls, over helmets, over statues, the
theatre
of the green leaves.
My love, this is our frail horoscope,
in spite of the drumming funereal Tiber,
in spite of the river which has drowned so many in its poisonous green.
My love, this is our April.
And surely I hear the chaffinch and the cuckoo.
I see the leaf twinkling, the fresh green lively leaf.

10 *Dido and Aeneas*

Rome stood up like a wall
and pulled you
from her.

The dark significant profile,
cave of lightning,
that magnificent circle,

Queen of the night.
City of the day,
male and soldierly.

And the god commanded,
This is your task,
not that wayward music,

wavering, indulgent.
Not that effulgent
moon, but Apollo,

bristly and rayed.
You must proceed
towards your fate

and wrap yourself in
the shade of
Rome,

that colossal imperium.
The will, the will,
it must not tremble

like the fresh green leaf,
it must be marble,
imperative.

The sails tremble
over the sea's
blue heat haze,

the fire trembles
just like Apollo's
commanding blaze.

My love, my love,
far from the armour,
imperative,

the quivering sail
in the sea's ring,
passionate beat

of the pulsing waves,
sparkling graves
of a lost love.

For the will must raise
its adamant walls.

Rome is our cost,
our official brute
masonical labyrinth,

bureaucratic mound
against the hyacinth's
vulnerable haze.

The dear *lacrimae*
tremble and play
but the great idea

enchants our days.
And the fire of love
burns the horizon.

The fragile sail
is a butterfly
quickly vanishing,

facing towards
the shelter of Rome,
the dark imperium

of power and hate
away from Troy
that also burned,

to Hannibal's face
set in the blaze
of avenging rage.

O all the light
is perpetual blaze
round the fleeing sails.

Where is the leaf?
The leaves of the waves
make an azure book,

a marvellous tale,
a historic story,
transitory

tale that is told.
Rome is thick-walled
and he hides behind

its massive idea.

To you the power
to outface the proud,

though you are proud.
And she is proud,
tall and unbowed,

bouquet of fire,
leaf on leaf
of miraculous life

and creative story.
Passionate, fiery,
she watched the sail's

perfidious journey,
luminous, finite,
minute, scintillant,

from her black threshold
where with a cold
imperious gaze

haughty and Roman
she never will smile
among the asphodel

though she wears like a scarf
her brilliant leaf.

The green leaf plays
on the victim's hard
and absolute sword.
He'll not outstare
that haughty profile,
he who hid in the haze

and tangled betrayal
of Rome's strict cage
of fire and light

and ponderous walls,
murders and coils
of wolf-like circles,

twilight of deaths,
suicides, myths,
homicides, wreaths.

And Scipio rears
on his smoky horse.
Carthage, he says,

'*delenda est.*'
All is a vast
circle of fire,

of poisonous power.
And you, my dear,
are watching the sail's

winking withdrawal
over the sea's
luminous plain.

But your heart is broken.
The leaf, the leaf
is suddenly shaken

but it still remains
in its frail pathos
against the marble's

memento mori.
Gaiety, sorrow,
delicate, various.

Rome's stone will not
show us the groves
of creative growth

of spontaneous leaves.
Its roads are the will's
dispassionate travels

over wayward belief.
Against the grave
marble, the leaf

in its delicate pathos.
The variorum
of wavering April

transcending the will.
She burns as the sail
burns,
   sacrificial sizzle

And the sail draws away
into permanent exile.
Among the marble

she's a star, a moon,
my nocturnal scene
of leaf and of moon-
struck nightingale.
My Dido, my love,
my dearest profile

invented leaf
of marvellous story,
pathetic, transitory
queen over all.

11

The story is vul-
nerable, mobile.

The wayward tale
winds through the
minatory

imperial wall.
The leaves will play
in shadowy April.
These will sustain
us, essential bread.

Out of the dead
ideas of Rome,
of Pompeii

the fresh leaf trembles.
Its brilliant twinkles
keep us alive

in our hazy days.
By the side of the road's
imperious brute

impulsion onward
the leaf's a quick
and powerful ray,

delicate story,
not mandatory,
this trembling tale

more than the marble
on which is inscribed
a deep-fixed script.

As among stone
I saw the poppy's
bright-red wine

foliate sign.
And though Rome may rise
huge and imperious

and spread its shade
over local shrine
and parochial ruin

it will not win
for the heart has days
when the *lacrimae re-*
rum mist the high walls
and rise like a crucial
haze on our souls

that no animals
in brutal displays
will solve, will solve.

And the haunting profile
of Dido slants
over the tenements

and bridges of Rome,
a moon, a leaf,
a sign of this life
that will not fail

our cowardly sail.

12

Who would descend
into that dark
from the wayward day

voluntarily,
his slender lyric
his only protection

against that Rome
of fiendish roads
and viperish lanes.

Who would not wear
that leaf-coloured sail,
a becalmed angel

in all that weight
of grief and dark,
that world of devil-

ry and pain,
and crooked Pluto
among his hoard

of gold and lead.

And who would not
when that time is past

rise like a leaf
emerald-fresh
into the light

where there are no ghosts,
only the nests
of vernal birds

with their sky-blue eggs,
the springlike garden
which was the Eden

of Adam and Eve
before they're expelled
in a storm of leaves

but now are fresh
among the various
blazes of rose,

daisy, azalea,
and all the marvellous
and airy blooms.

from THE LEAF AND THE MARBLE (1998)   459

Who would not hold
the breezy leaf
in his darkened hand

as on a lost
wind the imperium
of traditional Rome
disperses like smoke.

13

Out of Avernus
I steadily climb
bearing a leaf

so tremulous
in a flood of light
and here I greet

you in your fresh
leaf-coloured shirt
or about the house

your flowery blouse.
The tenderness
of this wavering breeze

how ever express,
or behind our reason
that Rome of dark,

vast and compressed,
as towards you now
I bear this leaf,

my joy and my grief.
Out of the grave
of flickering Hades

I joyfully rise
after these scenes
that hurt my eyes,

and terrified me,
the running wolves,
the emptying graves.

And now I bear

my quivering leaf
as an angel might
on the new found earth

or the gift of a rose.
So out of the gross
dark of Avernus

I freely bear
my gift of a leaf

from my renaissance
this light bright leaf.

Love, let you rise
as Venus might
from her leaf-shaped shell

in a storm of roses.
O primavera
out of the darkness,

clear mild spring
of the vernal goddess
all in a ring

of blooms and posies.
Or in modest grave
and serious dress

suitable to
a Presbyterian
(not Mediterranean)

severe land

Still
let the wind
be sweet and various

a million-scented
inventive breeze
of eternal days

fresh and hilarious
with a secret laughter
like a pulsing haze.

I put you in
my leaf-ringed diary
so large and airy

and these dark tombs
with their maze of worms
suddenly vanish

against this fresh
untarnished leaf
as out of darkness

I quickly step
into the chain
and the design

inwoven thus
of emerald *Amor
Vincit Omnia*

O not a trinket
but against insomnia
a holy cure

And so I bear
my renaissance leaf
away from mediaeval

theology
away from the bony
catacombs

and skeletons

into a sky
of airy blue

not Presbyterian
but Mediterranean

and pagan venue.

14

And so I have traced,
yes, I have traced
the secret at last

it is Rome that is
the Presbyterian
uncreative place,

it is Rome that has
the massive ponderous
unlifelike gaze

with its deaths and spies,
its historical bones,
its skeletons

of cobwebbed skulls.
It is Rome that dulls
bright nature's smile

with its heavy marble
and stony designs.
It is Rome that has

that fixed ingrained
Presbyterian gaze,
that marmoreal

visage of guile
that bends over all
unlike the tall

gaze of great Dido,
changing, spectral.

It's the leaf that is

what I now sniff
on a fine day
which is eternal

because it strays
about the nostril
and sensitive profile.

The leaf, the sail!

And you in your
domestic dress
and self-possessed

and clear Dutch light
are my desire.

And on your blouse
are flowers and light.

Rome, farewell,
from this airy place
that I have found,

this pagan heaven
and airy garden
far from your dull

and ponderous smile.

O pagan days
to you I rise
out of Avernus'

hinged skeletons
and caches of bones,
Presbyterian,

O I'll atone
for the will's design
by the wayward shrine

that I make for you
in that storm of roses,
that pretty shell,

so vulnerable.
And so I tell
that this is the best,

the vulnerable.
And all the rest
heavy and still,

made of hard marble.

But the wayward flesh
though not eternal
is the delicate bell
that freshly rings.

O the terrestrial
is the eternal.
That is what clings

to my soaring lyric
like patient grass.
We rise from gross

considerings

like the rose-lit spray
of Botticelli.

We're our own May
if we so wish.

And this I say

though Rome fall down
with its Colosseum
and brutal games

and the lion holds
us in its mouth
in its yellow folds

we always escape.

Your quotidian pipe
enchants me still,

veritas amoris

Out of stone quarries

the dear green earth's

amazing rays.

The Old Man

The old man does not think of himself as old
even when he sees children playing around the rowan tree

and around the garden well which has little water in it
though skin flakes from his stony head which he imagines as Roman

especially when he visits Italy and the peninsula of Sirmio.
Nevertheless, the old man has nightmares

of the friends he betrayed and who are now in Hades
at a smoky cocktail party vigorously talking.

He dreams of his clumsiness and inabilities
as he stands trembling before a spectral teacher

and a blackboard scribbled with incomprehensible words.
The dead extend their hands from hospital beds.

Who are these people racing towards him in his dream
passing milestone after milestone in their white dresses,

and who is driving calmly towards his destiny?
The old man without faith scratches his head

and hopes to let the bathwater cleanse him
and be perfumed by talc, shaving cream and soap.

But he knows that he is an arrangement of bones
and of flaking skin which hangs about him like a tent.

He remembers with anguish his adolescent over-confidence
and his cruelty to those who could not answer.

He remembers the moon shining over a loved city
and his boots echoing over its cobbles.

He remembers the drifters and motor boats he drew on rainy days
and the leaking toilets of his primary school.

He remembers his own invincible egotism
clearer to him than anything he reads

or the buzzard on the fence post or the trembling mouse.
All these he remembers, the old man who wishes to be loved,

whose stone head hangs out among temporary washing
and who watches his own nocturnal plays without denouement.

Those Who Talk to the Wind

Those who talk to the wind
in their jesters' tunics
what shall be said of them?

Those who have grown tired
of the ambiguities,
the ironies, the hypocrisies.
the double colours,
what shall be said of them?

Let them go to islands
and speak to the stones
which do not change
and also to the wind
which is severe with daffodils.

I see them,
yes, I see them,
in the many-coloured
jesters' tunics.
They are asking the wind
to cleanse them
and to blow through them
and through the mixter-maxter ideas
that protect them from the earth.

They are asking
to stand up like bridegrooms
with a new ring on their finger
and new music
to ruffle the bride's dress.

A new wind
a new rhythm
blowing over the moor
towards the old cottage
with the scarred door.

A new wind
a new rhythm
a new jester
dancing on the black hearse
with his new colours
and his intent white face
which is a mask for his joy.

Autumn

Autumn reminds one
of heavy wardrobes,
large and mahogany,
and of coalsheds
with frosty locks on them.

It reminds one
of tenements
with broken windows
and dogs running through puddles
to windy appointments.

It reminds one
of postmen
humping their bags
over fences and ditches
towards a spectral house.

It reminds one
of charity shops
with suits and shirts,
blouses and skirts,
and books from dimmed authors.

It reminds one
of those who have left
to seek new countries
and who gaze into glasses
thinking of the old one.

In autumn
children play with a coloured ball
beside the sea
where the sand rises behind them
in a fragile statue.

Names

In the cemetery at Aignish
the first name I see is Christina Campbell,
the name of my own mother
though she is not buried here.

And the names of many youths
lost at sea
on ships like the *Rawalpindi*
or the *Iolaire*.

The sea before me is glittering
and ducks flying over
a white avenue of light.

This is a township by the sea
where the villagers gather together
in eternal harmony
and the waves of green earth
are everlastingly fixed.

Look, an astonishing sight.
Here is a 'Charles Dickens'
surely an incomer
among the Macleods.

Dear novelist I read you intensely
when I was a sick child
your orphan Oliver
holding out his bare plate.

And here is your namesake
lying in Aignish
and his tall marble page
standing solidly against the wind.

Ashes

I scatter my brother's ashes on the sand.

The tide is breathing gently in and out.

I remember you in short trousers
climbing the pier's iron stairs
while the bees hummed furiously in the grass.

Now you have died in Australia,
with its incomprehensible deserts.
You set off with such youthful hope.

So we come down to a handful of ash
by the brine nosing like a dog
and that is all there is of those years.

Your suit (instead of shorts in Australia)
steadily burning like a last sunset,
a final fire among the local crofts.

Old Lady

I salute this gallant old lady
as I might a Roman heroine.

Protected by her Shakespeare
and her lovely classics
and her memories of a girls' school
she faces age with style.

She switches on the light
in a lonely house.
Daily through the window
she watches the leaves fall.

And she has a quotation from Shakespeare
with which to encounter death.

She will wear her quotations like a cloak
when he knocks on the door
and stands on the threshold
with, behind him, the moon.

A cup of coffee, she asks him
in her cool controlled voice,
you must be quite cold.

Is it as you like it?
she says remembering the wind
which blows through the leaves
of that Shakespearean play.

And she shivers a little
but retains her dignity
to the very end,

sitting quite upright
as the scythe-shaped moon
shines over the pale wood.

On a Photograph by Dan Morrison

Seven women in deep black
walk to the church service in Lewis

Lined up together
they look like heavy-set Russians
from an isolated valley

Does God prefer black
to the colour of the poetic rainbows
which are bridges over the moors
and the scarred peat banks?

Does he prefer light to be sunk
in these cheap furs and coats,
in this sturdy Politburo
arranged in a black row.

O let there be colour in your church
such as a stained glass window
hung up in the daylight
above the wind-driven grass.

Shorts

HIGHLAND HOTEL
Huge room in the hotel – O how dire
Tremendous portraits, juke-box – but no fire.

RANNOCH MOOR
Rannoch Moor where Eliot starves for the rifle,
how they tower up these tall post-modernist deer.

MAN OF ACTION
Where is the poet who would not prefer
to be a pilot playing in blue air?

ICONS
Once they're icons they do nothing wrong
Even their idiocies, subjects for good song.

ART
When I was young the humming telephone wires
were targets for stones and no 'bare ruined choirs'.

IF
If I could cry
I don't think I would stop
forever.

CHILDREN
The children are walking eternally
towards ceaselessly unfolding graves.

AS AN ATHEIST
As an atheist
I would invite red boiling hell
for the murderers
of the green children.

CHILDREN
Children, you are willing to learn
everything we teach you.

On your obedient spectacles
falls a diseased Fascist light.

BOOKS
The books pile up in front of my window
so that I can hardly see out.

Old Folks' Party

They all wear paper crowns
at the Old Folks' Do,
these proper kings and queens
(and nobler than them too).

Some have wounds sharp and deep
and will switch the cold light on
to silent living rooms
with their unringing phones.

But at the moment they
boisterously sing
songs of an earlier day
in their late evening

though above the cakes and tea
you'll sometimes see a face
stare unprotectedly
as into widowing space.

In Winter

The two doves
eat from the frozen plate.
Always together,
their constant faithfulness
is a grey dress
which outlasts the enamel reds
and blues of pheasants.

Neighbour

Build me a bridge over the stream
to my neighbour's house
where he is standing in dungarees
in the fresh morning.

O ring of snowdrops
spread wherever you want
and you also blackbird
sing across the fences.

My neighbour, if the rain falls on you,
let it fall on me also
from the same black cloud
that does not recognise gates.

MacDiarmid

After the excitement in your head subsided
and you settled down in a landscape of grass and stone
you read your green Penguin detective stories.

The portrait of your flame-haired wife blazed above you
and dogs barked on the edge of the horizon
and planets shone in their aristocratic colours,

and the ghosts disappeared from thorn and thistle
and chimney smoke climbed straight into the air
and you lay on your white bed far from red Lenin.

All Day

All day I have been reading.
I have lived inside books while the snow falls
very gently on the fields.
The mouse's small head is whitened
and the birds have a new weight on their wings.
I cannot stay inside this world forever.
Yesterday I saw an old man bowed in a chair
his face white with tedium and fear.
He was not able to read.
This was in a hospital
whose doors swung open and shut
faster than the pages of books.

The Old Men

On the dew on the faces of the young
and their hopefulness
the old men must not cast shadows.

For they remember how they would race
with a football along the wet grass
as if they were winged

and how spring leaves would touch the trams
as they set off in the morning
past devout cemeteries.

On the dew on the faces of the young
and their eyes which drink objects
and skies of early red mirrors

let the old men not cast shadows
or the knowledge of the depravities
which keep them at midnight awake.

Interviewer

To ask me of my history,
to strip me of my mystery,

to talk about salt exile
or the hard Protestant will

or my attitude towards Nature
(who has never seen a vulture

a tiger or a lion
but a mauled rabbit dying)

or in your young tones
question me of tombstones

of my common ancestry
and whatever sky

they lived their lives beneath,
and my stories about Death

comically reeling
or potato peeling

in grey or scarlet coat.

O if only when you quote

you knew the real sweat
the real dust and debt

the real gale and ache
how you might forsake

a nervous shaking face
confronted by blank grass.

Time to Stop

It is time to stop writing about the Highland Clearances etc.

'O welcome to you, blue cuckoo, with your melodious sweet song.'

The cuckoo does not know the Highland Clearances
nor does the lark.

Yet they live here and perch on the gravestones and sing.

It is time to stop writing about the Highland Clearances.

The scythe-beaked golden eagle catches the sun
and does not see watery portraits in the lochs.

The Old Woman

It took me a while to push her down,
the old woman dressed in black, into the graveyard
and listen to the music of the wind.

And learn to love the ripe corn and stubble
and the voice of the young man who sang all day
and the horizon which cut the sky like a knife.

And the rainbow too I learned to love,
that lovely bridge which arches our fences
and the scholarly owl perched among trees.

And avenues of trees, greenly shaded,
and stones, wood, leaves, all these I learned to love
and to hate the honey colour of coffins.

And old women telling black stories
as they swayed in their unconditional dreams.

Island, rise up and put on a fresh music.

Put on your comic, not your mournful song
about horses with heads like varnished fiddles
and the Callanish Stones swathed in pink and blue.

Parkhead

How is it that these splendid stadiums
are planted among grimy streets
where the shop windows are boarded
and black graffiti sign sad clouds?

How is it that these buoyant players
weave their patterns on a ground
which is surrounded by dark houses
which sniffle with a dampish wind?

These roars as of a lion
emit the repression of seven days:
and rage at inherited injustice
pours downwards towards the fresh grass.

And scarves are stretched taut by supporters
at the beginning of the game:
'We are with you, our dear champions,
though ourselves we cannot save.'

Then you walk from that arena
towards your crouched houses again
and the closes with misspelt slogans
and the roofs which let in the rain

jaunty after victory
or desperate because of loss
you with the most intense passions
hanging on the destiny of a cross

happy-go-lucky fanatics
who thirst for a magical move
in the midst of deceits and ruins
and wages which run away, like love.

For A.J. Macleod

d. May 1998

In the time of the winking leaves you died
who were as a brother to me through all seasons.
In winter you were armoured in endurance,
and in autumn you were not melancholy.
In spring you were hopeful and cheerful,
and now in summer you have declined to the earth,
ornate colourful and temporary.
At all times you were charitable.
The breeze blows your ashes where it will.
Of the good it can be said they left a fragrant name
which surrounds your perishable shape forever.

For Edwin Morgan

To swim out
into the impassioned light
and glint of the new,

as it seeks language
vulnerable, strange-spined,
blink-eyed

is for you mandatory.
Let the blue sky
bend over oddity

or even the monstrous —
The taste of poetry
is for you, this,

to substitute for the rose
in abandoned windows
the happy orphans.

Old Woman

I see the old woman behind the flowering broom.
I have followed her from poem to poem

and her grey coat is almost hidden by that yellow and red
on a May day with white clouds overhead

billowing with pillows. Yes, she carries her bag
home from the village shop.
                              And behind her a stag

in my imagination rears its magnificent head
out of the stones and flowers and small hills of the dead.

Leaves

O you come towards me
you mirror-like twinklings of the leaves
you multiplicities

you numerousness, you shining millions,
you ample magniloquence
you solar riches

bouncing of your leaves like crystals
like marbles, like ballets,

like whatever is improvident

extravagant hilarious
the constant laughter of dew.

Not a Day for Dante

This is not a day for Dante to visit me
and come in at the yellow gate.
The sky is overcast as it is not in Italy,
the rain smoulders on the hills.
I do not think he will like the cold
and this village is much smaller than Florence.
I suppose he could pull his cloak about him
as he mutters his three-lined verses.
There is no one here to be consigned to hell
and its mountains of flame
there is none here to be stirred about with a trident.
No the sky is too lowering.
But if you want to read a book I have plenty
and certainly I would refer to you
as to the greatest of masters.

Page after Page

We turn over page after page of the days.
Is it a tragedy or a comedy?
It is not, I think, either.
These colours simply dye the land.
These leaves twinkle and twinkle.
People pass on the road
and are finally swallowed by distance.

He Spoke

He spoke as if from the other side of death
quite clearly and quite impressively.

I think from your side it is tragedy
but from my side here it's really comedy
dry, not furious but temperate.

The tables spread with goodies for the guest
in blazing uniform looks aslant at best

and so does the orator with his spurious crown.
Young, the slightest shame is tragedy,

Old, it is comedy and cause for laughter
in a pure red weather in the evening.

from MY CANADIAN UNCLE

(2000)

1

Canada feels large and transient.
We leave Vancouver in a glittering sun,
heading for White Rock, my uncle's own
and carefully built house. We let the breeze
stream past us freshly through the open windows.
The traffic lights ahead of us hang down
at the road's centre, and we bullet on.
At eighty-five he's driving. He goes home
to Lewis every year, but all are dead
whom he once knew, all under white and red
flowers in the windy cemetery. He sits
crag-faced and tanned, short-sleeved, and beats the lights
with mischievous relish.

                              Canada extends
from Vancouver northwards: to where once he saw
black bears chew berries on a calm cool day.
'Old son,' they told him at the station, 'You
may drive the month your visitors are here.
But after that …'

                        I'll tell you' (in the clear
air, he says), 'You can exceed the limit
by a mile or so.' We tremble in our seats.
Impossible Canada so vast and mild.
You're not a Lewisman, you're Canada's child.
He fires his long white Plymouth at the gate,
puts on his glasses, backs out of the light
into the garage, as if he steered a boat,
gets out and says, 'Well then this is it.'
The wooden house, the garden, and the snake
basking in sunlight on his own White Rock.

2

'A "cattle ship" it was, on which we sailed
in 1912, and in the Irish Sea
a storm blew up. The Hungarians were sick,
not used to oceans. (They grew up on land.)
Even the captain and crew were sick.
He came to us and said, 'You know the sea.
You could rig a rope that would support their steps,
I mean the Europeans.' So we did.
None of us Lewis boys, you see, was sick.
So we rigged a rope up and they walked by it,
those who could stand: the rest were in their berths.
And the captain told us, "Have some extra food
and nips of whisky" … So we said we would.

'Leaving the cookhouse then one night Hugh saw
a big white cake that stood on a wooden shelf.
"The First Class passengers, they cannot eat,
they're far too ill," he told us. And he smiled.
"We'll take it," and we did. We ate it all.
Though I didn't like the theft, I never said.
(Hugh is dead in Flanders years ago,
a merry fellow full of jokes and jests.)
The second night we saw a turkey. Hugh
hid it in his jacket and we threw
the bones to starboard in the pitch-black night.
"Where is my cake, my turkey?" said the cook.
"We never saw them," innocent Hugh replied.
I told him later he was just a crook,
and not to steal again. Neither he did.
The ship plunged on and the sky became raw red.
We were the only ones could drink or eat.
"You must have stomachs hard as iron plate,"
said the steward, born in Skye.

                    There was a blacksmith
who'd sold his business, and sailed with us,
a muscular fellow who was always sick.

from MY CANADIAN UNCLE (2000)   487

"The ship is sinking," Hugh called one day
and the blacksmith left his bunk and rushed on deck
to find it was another merry trick.
"I'll kill you," he stormed at Hugh. "Just you wait."
And Hugh laughed. Sure, I can see him yet
with his moustache in the cold greenish light.
And there was another man who lay in bed
clutching his Bible. We would bring him food,
he said he was so ill he couldn't move.
Then one fine morning, icy cold it was,
when our hands were burning if they touched cold steel,
someone shouted, "It is land at last."
(And there it was, Nova Scotia, like a ghost.)
And that man threw the Bible from him, rushed
up the companionway, he who'd been so ill.
He had mastered even Hugh with his wiles.
And Canada lay before us. We were young.
The First Class passengers climbed up on deck,
and the Hungarians and Germans too.
They stared astonished past that blinding blue
at Nova Scotia ghostly under snow.

'And so I remember John and James and Hugh
long dead in Flanders under poppies. The
ship was a cattle boat. But quite proudly we
landed in Canada in our salt-stained suits,
among that flurry of Canadian lights.
The streets were paved with gold, so it was said.
We rocked a little on that foreign tide
and then walked up the gangway to our lives.
Some to prosperity and some to graves.'

3

A woman was preaching in the church. He says:
In my young days it would not be possible.
She says: There is the credit and the loss,
the one written in black, the one in red.

She is pencil-thin, black skirted. Says, We'll sing
this hymn because I like it. And he smiles,
thinking of home and of the minister
who flared through hell, with bullock shoulders, with
a bullock chest and red infuriate eyes.
At the back of the church are information packs
on alcohol and grass. ('Grass,' he says,
thinking of meadows and of cemeteries.)
A woman preacher? How should she know the truth,
moon-tugged and pagan? Bearded fathers sat
in Lewis with their Bibles in their hands.
The sea that ran between us, feminine!

The masts pierce the black clouds. We enter the
uniform brilliance of Canada,
temporary, sparkling, superficial.
'God is a businessman. The black, the red.
Our lives are trades conducted in blind salt.'

4

Sitting in his garden in the sun
in my green Canadian jockey cap I dozed
below the cherries, colour of red wine.
The crows had pecked them to a rotten brown.
He had a wire strung out from the kitchen
which he would pull, to a clamour of loud cans,
which then would dance and dance and dance and dance.
A Stetson hat hung high above the garden.
He knew by sight each individual crow
so sleek and black, a devilish Free Church hue.
'Whatever we would get we would have to pay
for later. I once told a man –
from Paisley, I think he was, he was making fun
of Highlanders – I said to him one day,
"We had the best of food when I was young,
crowdie and salmon, oatcakes and fresh fish.
We lived like princes in so-called barren Lewis."'

I peered beneath the visor of my cap.
He stood beside the red and velvety rose
he'd planted for his wife. The shiny crows
were hovering round us. 'We never once
quarrelled, Mary and myself. And I composed
poems since she died. I said, No drugs.
I held her hand at the end. Here the graves
are flat, not upright. I will take you there.
Vandals steal the flowers.'

                                       Later he said
'I'll bring some girls I know along for tea.'
They were seventy years old and both had sticks.

We sat in the cherry garden in the fine
monotonous sunlight. The two ladies' hands
trembled among tea cups.

                                          With a hose
he carefully watered the red Empire rose.

5

More than twenty channels on TV.
One day we watched a Nature programme.
A dog had met a porcupine on the road,
was trying to eat it, while each upright pin
needled his nose and eyes.

                                      You see that dog,
he'll not give up. But the porcupine will jag
him all day, if need be.'

                                  Whose side did he take?
The porcupine's, the dog's? The sharp pins raked
the dog's fierce questing forehead.

                              Some had died
in Canada, in Flanders, for the road
was a hard dog's slog from Lewis to the snow.
(Such Douglas firs we saw! The world was stars
sparkling and brilliant as if at Christmas.)
The stray dog burrowed but the porcupine
defended stubbornly. The trenches spun
with flashes of bright fire.

                              It turned away
dejected, haggard, tail between its legs.
'That'll teach you,' said my uncle. '*Nemo me
impune lacessit*,' sang the Scottish flag.
The Germans ghosted towards him in grey
with their thistly helmets, foggy, spiked, and rayed.
Icicles jagged moustached and stubborn Haig.

Crofter's Wife

She walks through the village
carrying her messages from the Co-op;
the mice are burrowing through the walls,
the rats gnaw the potatoes

which her heart-stricken husband has gathered
in the haze of autumn,
sweat in beads on his forehead
black dirt on his hands.

Prices are going up
year after year,
soon even the harmless daffodil
will be valued in gold.

Her husband has a head like a turnip
with the dirt adhering to it,
the ground bubbles with the costs
that the furrow must pay.

The bag grows heavier and heavier.
The girls are rotating
anonymously behind the counter
like fresh unnameable stars.

From the Train

As the train is almost entering Glasgow Station
it stops a while and I see on the stone wall
chalked in big white letters gangland slogans
the Weasel, Jaz, Rosko, and Animal,
and think before we enter the black tunnel
how these names by pure vanity might have been
Shakespeare, Milton, Wordsworth, Dante, Homer,
except that this is a far different scene
of rubbish without meaning, beer cans, bottles,
cardboard boxes, papers, rusty nails.
Of these they are the kings: these are their titles,
Weasel, Jaz and Rosko and much else
scrawled in the chalk that their teachers once would use
in the chaotic classrooms they have smashed
only to wear their self created crowns
among this littered acreage of grey ash.

Art

Art is decided by those
who are not creative.

Religion is decided by those
who are not loving.

Health is decided by those
who are not healthy.

I think that a nightingale doesn't
know why it's singing,

nor does the rock consider
the sharpness of eaves.

Those who don't know what they do
embroider most brightly

the constant invisible churches
where the music's most sweet.

The Lesson

Such bores they are – his operation, her
partial blindness. They go on and on
about the surgeon, hospital and the doctor.

My head is aching: surely it is a sin
to be a martyr to these illnesses?
Why, being hypocrite, did I ask them in?

Should we pay to pity such inflated prices?
How simple to be Darwin, see them changed,
the unhealthy races into more healthy species.
Active and animate, and yet quite estranged!

O listen carefully to the individual
though time should last forever. You may hear
from obsessive talk a word to make you whole,
less blind, more healthy, being transformed to some
merciful species, not triumphant, tame,
compassionate sport of a less greedy range.

Shylock

Shylock, on you in the house of grey ledgers,
interest, red ink, offices, the moon shines down
a balloon of circuses, without gravity.

The students in long cloaks sing among nightingales.
Rings are exchanged, the constancy of hands,
Italy is a night of a million stars.

There is no justice for the knotted heart.
Law becomes feminine, engagements of night streams,
night is when lovers kiss among wise owls.

Your author is unjust to you, Shylock.
On your Jewish bible of iron there flicker green leaves.
Laughter rebounds from your locked and beaten chest.

Imagination is against you, and your daughter
enters the coach at midnight. Let you stand
in your convict clothes striped with a pitiless prose,
watching her ride into an exile of Gentiles,
into the exile of youth. The moon shines down.
What shall you say of its coin fruitfully changing?

Lear

The holy fool snaps at the heels of Lear,
a mouse in jester's clothes out in the storm.
Greed opens its maw. It has a seagull's head.
Are the stones just or unjust in the raging moon?
The journey takes you through branches in the dark
to the eerie gothic cave of questions and answers,
the interrogation of phantom chairs.

Kingdoms shrivel away in an hour of nagging.
The only power is the wind and the heart of man.
Slowly the wind calms down. With a flower in his teeth
the king in his ruined sails runs through the meadow
heavy with summer. Heaven is the haunt of the mad
where a face bends down lightly touching his beard.
The messenger's always late and the hangman is dressed
in his Sunday best not knowing that the soul is at stake,
the question of law that sleeps through the heartbreaking tune.

The Forest of Arden

Forest of Arden, you outlast everything,
the poisoned crowns, the sweating beds, the ropes
that haul the innocent apart in dungeons.

You outlast everything, so green and fresh,
your dew is the dew of youths and bachelors,
of rings that shepherds crave and do not crave.

O your foliage hums like music,
violins inhabit you and no ravens,
you are the space of origins and of intervals,

before the hearse travels through power's lightning,
a black snail with the horns of tragedy,
bearing the knifed bodies towards flowers.

Wood of Arden, let us cherish you.
Women that still play games are sharp and witty
before the rendezvous at the red gates.

On an Icy Day

We walk on mirrors today just like Hamlet.
The state is as slippery as this, and just as subtle.
What contortions we must make to keep our balance!

With rosettes on our shoes we almost dance as we go.
What is the yellow bird perched on glass, is it Osric
in his folds of transparent gullery, extravagantly winged?

And what is that face in the mirror? Is it Claudius
blowing his drunken trumpet, power at the source?

The ordinary folk are sliding hither and thither.
They never look in the mirror but straight ahead of them
towards the shrunken branches, baskets clutched in their hands.

On Seeing a Russian Version of Richard III
at the Edinburgh Festival

Power is amazing theatre
    even in another language.

The blindfold is placed on the eyes,
    the queen is swaying.

The coffin contains her husband whom now she betrays.
Someone is squeezed to death between rippling muscles.

Death with her black wings walks from the back:
    in their shelter the queen trembles.

The king's face is contorted, he chews the crown with his teeth:
    it is bread of the spirit.

The princes in white walk past over and over,
    replayed by his mind, the agony of his limbs.

Their candles held high are ghostly daggers of flesh.

On a cloth map of Britain the king and new king clank swords.
The wary Tudor climbs the infected ladder.

The cabaret music plays. The clown with the blood-red cheeks
grins and dances and grins.

Van Gogh and the Visitors

You who visit me how can you know me?
You are, I am sure, thinking of yourselves.
You wear jeans, you are often American.
You're the innocent heaven I might have known.
The cornfield boils towards the horizon,
I'm fastened to my vision. There is no way
I can unlock myself from this wheel.

Poor innocent dewy-lipped Americans
you come from Ohio, places of fine water,
ordinary cornfields, I suppose,
ordinary pure unslanted churches.

The heat in my head is killing me, bejeaned
watery girls who live among the stones
in such an airy atmosphere. My one ear
I hold towards you to hear you talk.

I hadn't believed such children existed,
inured to innocence and photographs.
For myself, my beard is like the corn.
I look in the mirror. I am honed down
to a grizzled autumn and to trampishness.
Go out into those fields which aren't art.
I'll never see them as they once were.

See, I have them inscribed on my brain.
You don't understand, poor innocent ones,
how much I envy you, despise you too.

Go into the water, innocent ones in jeans
perfect as summer. I'm the stone you meet
warm underneath you, and pure solid art.
You aren't worth my painting after all.

Flow away like water, pale scholars,
your speech is random... but, your perfect jeans...

In Paisley Library

If there should come
                        even here
even in Paisley Library
brown among traffic
  if there should come
a breeze from Alexandria
  across the centuries
redolent of leaves and of Latin
of legions and squares
  if there should come
out of the blue Mediterranean
Venus scaling the waters
  if there should travel
through the Dark Ages, its windows,
  the sound of traffic
from Paisley
  Alexandria
              Greece
if there should voyage
Homer bowed in his house
Virgil working in marble
Dante assigning to hell

his crans of souls
if there should come a style
Lucretius travelling
in ice through a sky alone…
Outside the window
all the red buses.

Return to Aberdeen

Returning to you once again
I feel as if returning to my youth,
irresponsible days in university,
the granite that glittered brightly by the sea,
students in cloaks about the Upper Kirkgate,
naïve actors who may not be acting now.
Books are what we fed on in those days
of libraries, pubs, and cheap cafés,
from which we saw the statues of the dead.
Hazlehead was where the girls strolled
on Sunday evenings with their cracked handbags,
or walked down Union Street in cruising pairs.
Debates and dances… As the train pulls out
from the sodden platform of Queen Street,
later to run alongside the North Sea,
I know that this is not a real return –
too much has happened in the interim,
battering the student's helmet, opening doors
on stiff responsibility and horrors.
The voices in the train have the old brogue,
the people are different. When I shall unboard,
it will I hope be to a real stone,
though ghosts will flit around me. It is hard
to forget happiness, to forget you, town,
the busy Market, Marischal College, the
careless Sundays spent in Duthie Park,
while the sun shines hotly down on the *Aeneid*.

Hard to forget that, and yet one must,
as the train pulls out from Glasgow's dirty grey
October rain, through whose wet yellow sheen
I'll look in vain for that early Aberdeen.

The Old Lady

Autumn, and the nights are darkening.
The old lady tells us of her past once more.
She muses on the days she spent nursing

at ten shillings a month. 'And what exams!
I could understand anything in those days.
What summers we had then, what lovely autumns.'

And so I imagine her cycling to her work
among the golden leaves, down avenues,
to hospitals which were disciplined and stark

with hard-faced matrons, doctors jovial
with an authority that was never quizzed,
while grizzled Death suckled at his phial,

and autumn glowed and died, outside the ward,
and girlishly she saw it fade in red
in sky and sheet, and evening was barred
with strange sweet clouds that hung above the bed.

Predestination

The tram ran on rails.
My predestined stories.
We sat on the top
trailing our fingers through the leaves.

Theology
had put out its blossoms.
The end was in sight.
But along the pathway was flowers.

The Red Horse

'Art costs everything,' I said.
'Think of the red
horse in the field
abandoned by everyone but itself.

Even the generals leave the dead
bones shimmering quietly in the heat
and would love to ride
the magnificent red steed.

So, she is weeping quietly at the sink
submissive as a horse that has been tamed.
The plum tree in the garden points north,
to where the lean priest in yellow weather
studies the waterfall.

The clouds move towards him. He rides away
on his red horse towards a sound of battle.
Grey is her hair, obedient like the rushes.
No messenger comes ever to her door.
The sound of war is distant.'

I Remember I Remember

I remember I remember the house where I was born,
there were roses made of light and a laburnum tree.

It must have been in a different country, black lady,
who sit in the chair rocking and stare at me.

I swung through the blue air towards you,
merciless Muse, with the black watch on your wrist.

The air, the air... Throw the big windows wide.
The boy is playing his violin among the stones.

My Brother

My brother, today the rain is falling,
I haven't heard from you for twenty years.
When you left first you were so confident,
riding your new horse from coast to coast.
Then after a while you stopped writing.
My letters never reached you for you changed addresses.
Were you ashamed that your new horse never lasted?
Sailors from the old country have seen you in bars
but you don't speak to them.
Success is demanded of the exile.
Today as the rain falls it occurred to me
that I do not know where you are.
How the world comes between even two brothers!
All I can see is the horse you wrote of
standing in a cage of rain somewhere
with the burrs of twenty years on its skin.

Old Characters

Where are all the 'characters'
who had stubby pipes in their mouths
and stood by ruined walls
as if they were captains.
Their faces were brick red,
they had stocky bodies,
draughtproof, rainproof, snowproof.
Into some hollow
as into a ring of tides
they have vanished forever
leaving a scent of tobacco, a smell of tar,
at the edge of the grave
a grey sough of moustaches.

Martha

Martha, you are the necessary one
you wash the dishes in a thunderstorm
you clean the treacherous glass

When earthquakes skittle our bubbles
you are to be seen with your Hoover
sucking the fire and soot,

and when the dead so pale and luminous
lie on the shelves, you comb their stricken hair
and calm its ruined grass.

Where sorrows are everywhere looking at us
as on the touchline of a cindery park
you hang your washing out

in winds that travel at large blustery speeds
ballooning shirts which have no smell of sweat
or of mortal brine

but are the wings of hope, eternal angels
wrestling with the temporary, in a gale
that makes your cheeks dawn red.

The Unemployed

Yes, I have seen you in the railway station
with your VP bottles. In a witches ring
you suck the morning's wine,

the unemployed, and useless vacant ones,
for whom the day's a weight that will not lighten,
of darkening fumes and clouds

and fags that cling to lips. I hear you singing
late in the evening in the loo,
shoulders festooned with arms.

Companionship! The last companionship!
And then the quarrels under the wandering moon,
round gravestones in the sky.
'I'll get you yet, bald bastard.' All that hate
seething and boiling, and each coat
held tightly by a stringy belt.

The trains set off in their white gouts of steam
bouquets of transience on directed rails
towards new work and hope

but around you your bottles squat and burn,
covens of morning, and of an afternoon
that hangs its marble cloak,

Autumn

Let me read again the autumn newspapers.
There are no accidents, no disasters,
only a natural failure of the green.

No individual sorrows, only general
losing their imperium and their crowns,
an emptying of a house towards the sun.

Window on window slowly closing,
hedges perpetuated in frost,
the wires that trill with a remembered tune.

The animals are seeking temporary graves
that later burst in foliage, in the tears
that spring will fashion from the art of frost.

Reminder

Today, receiving a letter from a friend
who was once a schoolmate, now in Canada,
I am returned to what seemingly I was.

'I remember talking to you about Graham Greene
for two hours together on a freezing day
in bleak November in the "Royal" doorway.

Another time, our cases soaked with salt
from a stormy crossing, all that worried you
was whether all your poems were still dry.'

I can remember nothing. Was I like that?
The anthology of memories of the other
is a book I hadn't reckoned on. My fear

or rather hope is that I am put back
further and further in that clutch of tales
till I am lost forever to time's fables,

O false and lying and yet perhaps true.
I would be barer with no foliage round me,
without a title, a great blank behind me,

and only a real future ahead,
myself with a caseful of impersonal poems
unsalted, bare, and floating out of my arms.

For Peter, Leaving for the RAF

Standing on the platform as you leave
we are so nervous and solicitous.
The train breeds blossoms of a uniform grey.
I remember, as I wait, the pitiless army
of long ago, the square, the barrack's hive
busy but not sweet, and rigorous.

Each of us falls back on what we are
in the world's terrors, when the sergeant raves,
when the boots clang on stone, and buttons shine,
and about the camp drifts the aimless rain,
or in the evening on homeless graves
the bugle calls, a bronze and fading star.

Your smile is pale. Triumph or loss is still
vivid rose or wound, the world a judge
more merciless than we in age confess.
Trembling, you trudge as through a wilderness.
Have you the weapons made of stainless steel
to defend yourself, honed to unyielding edge?

Or is your smile a flag above the void?
About the train there blows a greyish steam.
It stutters first and stops and then glides on.
You wave, we wave. We've sent you out alone
and now we must withdraw as from a dream
when the day stands up with its raw unbroken sword.

The curve makes you invisible, and we turn
from your quick vanishing. The gap remains,
questioning, enigmatic, cruelly bare.
From elsewhere now, there gathers care on care,
those saving graces of fresh imminence
which hide you from us, in your creaking iron.

The Tape Runs

The tape runs
bearing its weight of poems
conversations
echoes of past rhymes.

Sometime I think that time
is odder
than any order
for to gain one future
is to lose another

Calmly the tape runs
The fruit of dead voices
composes
itself on the brown wheels.

They return to us
over and over
in this calm weather
of continuous hum

Dear dead voices
dear dignified ones
I see your bones
in this green focus

narrowing widening
the grass of your burying
small set green window
pulsing with a whole life.

Sometimes When I Am Alone

Sometimes when I'm alone I think of you
like a picture in a glass of vodka

as clear as
fish in the water,
breasting the river,

sensing the first salt,
the first onset of ocean,
the first taste of brine, breeder of ships.

On National Service

Our mess tins soggy with stew
we sat around the campfire
in the October woods.
The unmilitary owls hooted
and the trees
learned the embrace of ice

Such millions of stars shining.
Such a brown
ending to autumn
and our khaki
imitating a season
that would surely die.

Soldiers of the queen.
The trees were abdicating
laying aside their crowns
and rustling finery
in that court intense
with a smoky burning

tang of autumn leaves.
How like the legions
late in the late woods
of a decaying Empire
we ringed the pale campfire
with our rusty badges.

Young so young.
Hard to remember
that bewildered boyhood
holding that cold tin
fork knife and spoon
among the acorns

among the autumn woods
all sentimental
lying on coats later
while down our white throats
the radiant moon poured
its white powder.

Hallowe'en

Hunting for apples
through the brown autumn
in your gross faces
with the long noses
and the crooked eyes.

Children
I offer you love.
I offer you
the round apple of sin.

I offer you
the charred face
of the posthumous
demented one

I offer you
children
for your fresh faces
your apple cheeks
your faked hunched backs

memories of the fire
the sickening stench
the pale witch floating
under the red moon
of a crooked evening.

The long body
the thin pointed nose
the head shaking.
In a deserted house
an armchair rocking.

Top of the Pops

This is the time of the body not the mind
You sway in time. Your eyes are closed and glowing.
The scholarly helmets in the armchairs turn
to Dionysus in his wheel of hair
and Greece thuds hollowly to the ordered legions

crewcut and lotioned. Let the dance begin
which brings hypnosis to the stoa and
the loose and amateur stars into the hall.
The philosophers are halfway here and there
half satyrs and half Saturns in their minds.

Let the dance begin. The music of the spheres
distorted by the stormy Goths is heard
only in private rooms whose walls are shaken.
O in a trance of dancing see them share
their bodies with the spaces of the light

though still Narcissi in their secret moons
lilies and schoolgirls virgins of their joy
hysteric against matronhood. They move
as riotous stalks might move and writhe and sway
mindless of mind whose needles pierce and sew.

By the Sea in Autumn

The mussels clamp their miniature helmets to
the salty rocks. The sea comes pouring down.

It is the war they shelter from, my fathers,
it is the war these summers long ago
the blossoms of the hedges and of bone,
the horses and the seagulls in the blue

You in your yellow dress peering about
your shells and fool's gold in your sprayed glasses
are a permission of that resonance
that sucks the mussels from their parapets.

The large continuous ghosts come pouring down.
By these sieged heads you bend your luminous dress.

The Autumn of Experience

This is the autumn of experience.
The drooping leaves are like the hair of one
loved long ago and in another land.

There was a summer when we tiptoed over
a floor of green linoleum till we came
to a clock that ticked above us in the hall.

Hansel and Gretel. Scandinavian woods.
The Ugly Duckling that became the Swan.
The red plump dolls in all the picturebooks.

Now its the autumn of experience
The frost is calm and white. We walk together
arm in arm along the slippery roads

at midnight with glass shoes. While all the stars
shine quite clearly and the whole of heaven
is incomprehensible and garrulous.

And every star is just as precious
as every other star and like a glass
in which the beggars become princesses.

Mirror mirror. In the autumn wood
the witch in pointed cap among the leaves
becomes a Snowwhite gazing in the pond

and all the faces are of equal worth
sparkling in fact and pallor, lined with time
but constant in the heaven of our gaze.

'She goes off to be a missionary'

She goes off to be a missionary
with her long coat
and her tidy hair.

Her cheeks have not known powder
nor her lips lipstick
Her vanities are elsewhere

She imagines savages
to whom she firmly rides
on a tall saddle

with the Word in her hand
blazing like arrows
a quiverful of God

She imagines greenness
and a cosy church
surrounded by roses

and the savages bringing
their darkness to be scoured
like pans or dishes

to be cleaned whitened
all their gods brushed
onto tiny shovels

of shiny yellow brass
into a dustbin
in the middle of Africa

where the white stars look down
so gentle and approving
like the little mother
that she herself once was.

Fairy Story

Snow. Much snow. Ice. A cottage.
The small gnomes were digging underground
their tiny spades shining in the lamplight.
The world of fairy stories. And I turned

another page. The whole alphabet
was lovely icicles, needles. You were there
whitely lying on a white bed.
There was a crown of blossom on your hair

syringes rings, blue Icelandic nurses.
The small crystal radios were hung
among reindeer, birches, bearish furs.
The cottage crumples slowly. It is going

down to a white plate like blancmange.
The gnomes are digging busily. I see
their neon spades flickering, their hands
are small and yellow. In reality

I turn another page, crackling like ice.
Oh love how long ago it all was.
The white earth is pleading with black heaven
demanding justice, demanding more than justice.

Morality Play in Cambridge in the Open Air

We hear the devils hiss among the trees,
as Death, long-stilted, in his tall black dress

sways among the apples: and we hear the bell
toll from the college: the late chilly soul

drifts among skulls, the always leaving flesh:
from church to inn it wanders, a debauch

of spirit after spirit: while the cross
nails it between the sky and the hard gloss

of the inflamed roses: not the mind
can save us even here, in this refined

blandest of cities, when the scaly wings
rustle about us in our blossomings

and second-hand reflections. Among trees
the devils blow their cinders to a blaze

and in the college grounds Death in black cloak
walks tall above us, smiling at our books.

At Ely Cathedral

Shaved grass beneath my hand
I sit on the green lawn
in front of Ely Cathedral
where the knights sleep in marble
their helmets laid on their breasts
like large and marbly eggs:
birds painted on their shields
and the eternal roses

of England's threshing fields:
where saints stand in each niche
in their humble offering pose:
and angels plunge from the ceiling,
wings radiantly unfurled:
and I think of that lost world
massive, incredibly detailed,
foliate, cut and scrolled.
Ship that sailed on the Fens
where stilted they used to walk
among the marshland birds
and a maze of secret paths:
I feel so small and still
in this vast stony shade
though once I would have sat
with the whole weight of my soul
as solid as the marble
in which this knight is cased
with the painted birds on his breast
his helmet and long sword
so obvious in his world
his slightly eroded head
pointing towards the east.

Incident

As we sit in the theatre a tall cloaked man
wings his way past us to his velvet seat
in a flurry of Gothic drama, like a great
actor in this life which seems so mean.

And sitting just in front of us a grey
humpbacked fellow sits with his aged mother
to whom he tells Brecht's plot. O who would rather
be which good hero of the human play?

Those

Those who are given early retirement and the radiant handshake
shuffle after their wives in crowded rooms;

following them like dogs as they used to follow ideas
over horizons which were once fresh and blue.

They come to rest in fields on which once rainbows
rested like bridges among summer flowers

but now the end is in sight, the box is open
with its sweet poisons of the merciless days

and the sought fragrances which never really appear.
The Hoover bites at the legs, as at great windows

they look out at the sea where boats with names
like Dayspring and Diligence rock on their rusty chains.

'The Tiger' by Franz Marc

The tiger curls among cubes
with its savage friendly head.

The tiger's made of cubes
and planes of yellow and red.

But its eye is not weary
nor its blunt brutal head.

Art is a way of placing
a tiger among cubes,

a tiger made of cubes,
cubes which are tiger-like.

'Don Quixote' by Daumier

On a ghostly roan
corrugated as a melodeon
Don Quixote rides on
with a red blob of a head
and a long thin body
his lance raised absent-mindedly
into the stunning blue.

Detail from 'The Triumph of Death' by Breughel

I

A skeleton horse droops forward. On it sits
sideways a skeleton with a lantern. It's

a brutal parody of a lady's pose.
On a cart of skulls a seated skeleton plays

the hurdy-gurdy while, in front, there's dragged
a dying cardinal by a skeleton rigged

maliciously in his hat of velvet red.
A king in armour sags, right leg outspread

and gold mace in his hand. A skeleton, funny
and wicked with his power, fumbles the money

in two brown casks. And at the very back
a skeleton broods by water, hand on cheek,

philosopher of bones. From a slab of stone
three skulls peer out. And lastly there is seen

a skeleton with a net by the pale water
behind this wicked busy skeleton laughter.

II

On the table with white table cloth there lies
a dish with a small skull in it, a spilt glass,

and the remains of food. Before it stands
a soldier with sword drawn against the swarms

of skeletons like locusts. One pours wine
out of blue jugs, another with a smile,

infinitely mocking, bears a tray
towards a table with a skull as menu.

One embraces a lady from behind
with his long bony arms and, beyond,

an army of skeletons hungers to get in.

In the right hand corner playing a mandoline

or some such instrument, a lover turns
towards his sweetheart, while the party churns

in a disorder of overtoppled chairs,
and in a corner fleeing revellers.

Scales upon scales are everywhere, death infests
the desperate music while the witty locusts

seek flesh to feed on, and the mandoline
mourns in one corner the outpouring wine.

Goya

The doll-like royal family looks out
from one picture, propped up by paint,

and in another, at an opera,
Death in a black cloak leans over to say

some words to a girl in jewels. In another
men without faces are preparing to fire

muskets at their victims. And in one
a gigantic presence overshadows Spain

eating the people up. To paint like this,
Goya, you couldn't live in lovely Venice,

to paint like this, Goya, you had to have claws –
not Don Quixote wandering on his horse,

the stunned professor, but a deeper madness
which stains the world and darkens each warm dawn.

Botticelli's 'Primavera'

The Graces with brown curly hair
dance round and round,
hands loosely intertwined,
in spring, the time of rings,
in their flowing drapery,
half showing and half screening
long white legs and bums,
bare-footed and serene
in a flowery wood
somewhere where such women
complete within themselves
dream through the glorious flesh.

The Cry of the Woman

No, I do not wish my hair to go grey,
I wish it to remain brown.
Why should I be a ghost too early?

There is a style of illusion
that we all have to learn
to make the evenings bearable.

A white helmet I will not have,
before the mornings of the snow
in the theatre of the rainbow.

Sprightly, I shall run
among the toilets, among the rooms
of my schooldays again.

The Poet

I have outdistanced the music
I am travelling in silence
through the shadow of posthumous metres.

What my metres will be
will be what I shall become –

I am the skin-made drum

which the wind will fill.

'If in this summer'

If in this summer
the dead should return
they would be happily dancing

holding out their arms
on which the flowers bloomed
in a haze of purple

singing with the underground water
that is deeper than Hades
that is intertwined with daffodils.

If the dead should come
they would not be dressed in white
like nurses or doctors.

No, they would know the way through the old woods,
and they would teach us
how salmons climb thresholds.

INDEX OF TITLES

INDEX OF FIRST LINES